SWING YOUR SWORD

SWING YOUR SWORD

LEADING THE CHARGE IN FOOTBALL AND LIFE

MIKE LEACH
BRUCE FELDMAN

DIVERSION
BOOKS

Diversion Books
A Division of Diversion Publishing Corp.
443 Park Avenue South, Suite 1004
New York, New York 10016

www.diversionbooks.com

First Diversion Books edition July 2011
First Diversion Books paperback edition August 2012

Edited by Bruce Feldman and Sean Mahoney
Copyedited by Lisa Grzan
Cover design by David Ardito
Cover image © 2007 L. Scott Mann/Picture Mann

ISBN: 978-1-938120-12-1

11

This book is printed on acid-free paper.

Foreword

The Importance of Peeing on the Dog

A few years ago, on a hunch, I flew to Lubbock Texas to write a long article about the Texas Tech football coach, Mike Leach. At the time Texas Tech was beating teams with whom it had no business being on the same field. Its players, as a rule, were kids who hadn't been offered scholarships to the region's big time football schools: Oklahoma, Texas, Nebraska. Even Texas A&M had more ability to attract high school recruits than Texas Tech. And yet, under Leach, when Texas Tech went up against Texas A&M, or even Nebraska, they were not only often the favorite, but a threat to run up the score.

From a distance it was hard to see how Leach was doing what he was doing, but it was clear that he and his players were ignoring a lot of football's conventional wisdom. Leach spread his linemen across the field instead of bunching them all up in the middle, for instance, and didn't fully distinguish between the running game and the passing game. Fourth down deep in one's own territory wasn't a problem but an opportunity to go for it. Being ahead by forty points wasn't an excuse to mail it in but a chance for the second team to score a lot of points. On the sidelines during the game Leach didn't hide behind one of those giant laminated play charts so favored by coaches these days. All he had was a scrap of paper with some plays scrawled on it. It turned out that the scrap of paper was the closest thing Leach had to a playbook.

And yet somehow every quarterback he touched turned to gold. The kid who hadn't been recruited by Texas A&M, once inserted into Mike Leach's offense, became the guy who broke NCAA passing records. How did that happen?

In the financial markets there is always and everywhere a desire to be seen as a little different from the next guy. Professional investors love to present themselves as "contrarians," people who think originally about the world. No one ever says "invest your money with me because I'm an ordinary guy who knows how to follow the herd," even though that is a fair description of most professional investors. Sports has a different value system; in sports there is a bias against being different, or breaking with convention. To do anything differently is taken as a kind of insult to all the great men who came before you, and did things the same old way. When a person does something different in sports they expose themselves to ridicule and ostracism. Innovation in sports requires a special bravery.

This bravery turned out to be something like Mike Leach's central character trait. When I went to Lubbock to write about him I thought I was writing a piece mainly about football. Pretty quickly it became clear that I was writing a piece mainly about an endlessly innovative and original character, who happened to coach football. There were so many stories that confirmed this that I was spoiled for choice. For instance, the Texas Tech strength coach, Bennie Wylie, told me the story of his first encounter with Leach off the field. One night not long after Leach's arrival in Lubbock he, Wylie, was driving fast down Lubbock's busiest two lane road. Cars whizzed past at speed; up ahead Wylie spotted, rollerblading down the middle of the highway, what he took to be a lunatic. He drew closer and thought, "that looks like Coach."

Then . . . *that is Coach!*" Leach, it turned out, was perfectly sober. He'd thought it all through. He was learning to rollerblade, he explained, and the middle of this highway was the flattest, truest surface in all of Lubbock.

If you want to think originally, it helps to actually be original, and Leach was. At some level he knew it, too, and knew that it was a tactical advantage. So did his players—who adored him. They adored him because he helped them to win, but they adored him also because they knew at bottom he was acting in their best interests—and making their lives more interesting in the bargain.

It borders on a sin that Mike Leach is writing books instead of coaching football right now. But he'll be back, and he'll be as successfully interesting, and as interestingly successful, as ever. In the meantime we have this book to remind us that he simply isn't like other football coaches, or other people. Few other coaches in big time college football, or anyone else, would respond to an aggressive dog that insists on peeing on his possessions by peeing on the dog. No other big time football coach would ever see the lesson in it. But if you want to address your problems, and live your life the way it needs to be lived, peeing on the dog is sometimes just what you have to do. The trick is to think of it.

—Michael Lewis

Acknowledgments

The first person I want to thank for not only supporting me in my career, but in everything I do, is my wife Sharon. She is the best thing that has ever happened to me. I am also grateful for our four children, Janeen, Kimberly, Cody, and Kiersten, as well as my parents and siblings. They have all been great influences on me as have many of my teachers, professors, and friends over the years.

In addition, I have relished the opportunity to coach so many great and dedicated players over my near 25-year coaching career. The experiences we have shared and the things we were able to accomplish together, I will never forget. I also want to thank my fellow coaches. This includes those whom I have worked for and with, as well as those I have participated in clinics with or visited. It's always been a pleasure to be in the company of individuals who are so passionate about the great sport of football. You have all had a significant impact on me and I've enjoyed my time around you. I take great pride in the profession I am in, and in the relationships that I have built.

Mike Leach
June 3, 2011
Key West, Florida

CONTENTS

SWING YOUR SWORD

GROWING UP

The Early Years

I probably don't go two days without somebody asking me about how my mind works. My answer is that everyone is a product of their environment.

I was born in Susanville, California, near Reno. We moved around a lot because my dad was a forester. When I was three we left for Fall River Mills, California. Then we moved on to Alexandria, Virginia, then to Saratoga, Wyoming, then to Ft. Collins, Colorado, on to Golden, Colorado, over to Sheridan, Wyoming, and finally to Cody, Wyoming. That was all before I turned 12.

All of that moving teaches you to become pretty adaptable to whatever comes your way. No kid realizes that while it's happening, because it seems like you're just constantly fighting to get out of your shell. I always hated to move because just as soon as I'd feel like I had things figured out, I had to start all over again. There were definitely times when it was painful growing up, though looking back, those uncomfortable moments have proven immensely beneficial to the man I've become.

My low point came in Sheridan, Wyoming. We'd just moved there from Golden, Colorado. In Golden, I was comfortable. I really liked our house. We had a great basement. My friends loved hanging out down there. I knew all the neighborhood kids. Then when I was between the third and fourth grades we moved to Sheridan, which was a much more cliquey place than where I'd been before. That type of environment can be tricky for the new kid to navigate. You're trying to fit in, but you're being told—in pretty blunt terms as only kids can tell other kids—that you don't. For me, it became one of those deals where four of the guys are on a roll messing with the new kid in town. Attacking my psyche became part of their routine. That was tough. I had to work through it because I didn't want to be seen as soft. It's the sort of situation where you can't complain to your parents and you know you can't whip all four of them.

One day our teacher told the principal what was going on, and he called all of us kids into his office. He read the four of them something out of a book about how hazing is wrong and violates the law. I didn't know what hazing meant till he read to us how if you engage in hazing someone, you can go to jail. I got a dirty look from each of 'em.

"I was pregnant that year. Mike mentioned something to me about those kids. I talked to the principal about it. And he talked to Mike and the kids. It did seem to get better after that. Mike even became pretty good friends with one of them. Mike was kinda quiet back then. He was a bit shy. I don't think he really knew how to handle some of these kids because he hadn't been around too many people who were mean."

—Sandra Leach, Mike's mom

The biggest factor that contributed to settling things down was always time. I'd hang in there long enough till they got used to me. Because I always started as the outsider I could watch it all from a distance, and I came to realize just how different one person is from the next. I began to analyze people: How does this person fit in? Does he want to be liked, or respected? Does he want to be seen as a leader or a follower?

You learn what's accepted and what's not accepted. You also realize that if you want to get along with someone, you find what you have in common with them. You think: "What's important to them? What are they like? What would appeal to them?"

I learned and developed my ability to communicate mostly from my mom. She was a great communicator. She was very patient. I could talk with her for hours.

I could literally ask my mom anything. One day I came home from school in the second grade and asked her, "Hey Mom, what does fuck mean?"

She didn't flinch or run for cover. She said, "That's a bad word," and then she started to give me the background. She wasn't graphic about it but she laid it out there. "When a man and his wife love each other . . . " And she called it making love.

I was confused.

I said, "Dean says that it means when a guy sticks his wiener in a girl's you-know."

She paused.

She kinda had a startled look on her face.

I said, "Well, there's no way that could be true, right?"

Mom?

Mom?

To me, that sounded like the most illogical form of behavior possible. As a second grader, I couldn't fathom who would ever even think of doing such a thing. She proceeded to explain where babies come from.

Honestly, the only thing she ever lied to me about was the Santa Claus issue. She lives in St. George, Utah, now and she's not really a phone person. I miss being able to talk to her like I used to and I've missed it for decades. Any subject with her was fair game. I could have her point of view on nearly anything. It may not have been the same as mine, but she was always honest and straightforward. She opened my mind to so many new ideas, and for that I'll always be grateful.

This probably isn't a shock, but I've always had a big imagination and would become obsessed over a variety of subjects. I'd talk to some of my friends about things till I wore them out. We were into Tarzan, Daniel Boone, and Geronimo. I'd try to find out everything I could about those heroes of mine, and I really do mean everything. I was determined to discover all the places Daniel Boone had trekked, what he'd pack to get there, and the challenges he faced along the way. I also loved the New York Yankees and Lombardi's Packers. My parents were independent thinkers and they were very well read, and following their lead I read everything I could about my obsessions. I was curious about everything.

Growing up in Wyoming perpetuated that curiosity. We were so isolated, there was nothing to do but dream big and fill in the gaps with whatever facts you could find. It also fostered that western frontier mentality, which I believe encourages a spirit of perseverance and optimism. On top of it all, I was the oldest child of six. Being the oldest is hard. In most cases your folks are starting their careers and don't have the same amount of time for you as they might for your younger siblings.

I have no doubt in my mind that the combination of these factors helped me become pretty good at finding solutions to my own problems. Although my mom probably wouldn't agree that the following "Pepe the Dog" story is the best example of that . . .

When I was growing up, there were basically two types of kids—Daniel Boone kids and Batman kids, because that's what was on TV when you got home from school. To me, Batman was too cartoonish, too inanimate. I always watched Daniel Boone and I read books about him. I loved Daniel Boone. He was a real character, yet larger than life. He went places before other people went there. A lot of what he did was solo and introverted. He'd just go on these walks and stay gone forever. He was courageous, fearless.

One particular weekend, a friend and I were going to have a big Daniel Boone night. We had toy Daniel Boone guns. We had frontier-style clothes. We set up a tent in my backyard with our sleeping bags inside. I remember thinking this was going to be the greatest night ever. We were fearless hunters. But there was one big problem: Pepe.

In my neighborhood there was a malicious Golden Lab named Pepe. Those words together—malicious and Golden Lab—scream oxymoron, but he literally terrorized me as a child. Pepe would take my baseball glove that I'd left sitting on our porch and just bolt. He was too fast, and I could never catch him. He'd snatch my glove and run with it three houses down and just stare back at me. I'd give chase, running the way little kids run, arms swinging up past my ears and back. Before I could get there, Pepe would chomp down onto the glove in his mouth, snatch it up again, and take off running for another house. Then, he'd drop the glove there and taunt me with a look I still remember, as if he was saying, "What are you gonna do? You can't catch me."

Eventually, Pepe would get bored after running what seemed like a couple of miles and I'd find the glove left on some stranger's lawn all gnawed up and covered in spit. I'd be so furious, but there was nothing I could do to control him and I was nowhere near as fast as him.

On the night of the campout, after setting up most everything and heading back inside for more supplies, I came back out to find that Pepe had peed all over the side of the tent.

I was crushed.

My mom gave me some stuff to clean it all up so our tent wouldn't smell like dog urine. I did the best I could and then brought the cleaning supplies all back inside. When I returned to our campsite, I discovered that Pepe had gone inside the tent and peed on my sleeping bag. And there was Pepe, sitting on the edge of our yard staring at me, taunting me, watching my reaction. I was so humiliated.

I did what most kids would've done at that age. I broke down. I bawled. My mom placed her arm around me. She explained, "It's not Pepe's fault. Pepe can't help it. He's just a dog. That's what dogs do. They pee to mark their territory. They pee so other dogs will know that this is their home."

"Pepe doesn't know your yard from anyone else's. He just thinks this whole area is his home."

Well, I was listening to her but I was not too sure of this "can't help it" stuff. To me, an awful lot of this "territory-marking" is on temporary things: my glove, my sleeping bag, my toys. I'm not so sure this wasn't malicious.

She helped me clean off the sleeping bag and tent. Eventually we got the tent back in order.

I realized then that I needed to go back into the house to get my toy gun. But I was afraid to leave the tent even for a minute. I figured if I ran inside and rushed right back out, I'd be back before Pepe could mess with my stuff.

I looked around to make sure the coast was clear, then I ran to the house, hurried to get my gun and came back out. This time Pepe had peed inside of the tent, and actually had pulled my sleeping bag out into the yard and peed all over it again.

I was completely enraged, broken down, and desperate. I had hit rock bottom. Perhaps, because I was out of options, my mind began to clear. I realized Pepe was attacking me close to home and where I was most vulnerable. Pepe's strengths were his speed and his athleticism. I was neither fast nor athletic. All of my weaknesses were being exploited. I kept thinking about what my mom had just said.

The thing that stuck out in my mind was the "mark-your-territory" part. I had cried like most kids do, and that didn't do any good. I thought of ways to kill Pepe: Maybe I could run him over in a car . . . Nah, that won't work, because I can't drive and my parents would never go for it.

I became calm and had another idea.

I went to the refrigerator and found some meat scraps. I went back outside, looking for Pepe.

"Here, Pepe. Good dog, Pepe," I called him in as calm and friendly a voice as I could. "Come here, Pepe."

And sure enough, eventually, he came over towards my hand and began eating the meat scraps. Then I grabbed Pepe's collar with my other hand and dragged him over to a vacant lot next door where no one could see me. Holding Pepe's collar with one hand, I unzipped my pants with the other hand. Still running through my head was this business of marking your territory.

I proceeded to pee all over his head and face. I aimed for eyeballs, nostrils and mouth. Any orifice I could find, I wanted to soak. I drenched his whole face. Pepe struggled frantically until he broke free and ran off.

He never messed with me or my stuff ever again. After that day, whenever I'd come out of my house, Pepe would see me and turn and run in the other direction. I'm not sure if this says more about animal behavior or my own, but it was an amazing turn of events.

Daniel Boone was my first childhood hero, but around the time I turned 11, Bart Starr took over the top spot.

At a ridiculously early age I read Jerry Kramer's book *Instant Replay*, a bestseller written by the Green Bay Packers' offensive lineman about the team's 1967 season. That was the season the Packers won the NFL championship by beating Dallas in the famed "Ice Bowl" game, where Starr followed Kramer for the game-winning touchdown on a quarterback sneak.

Starr had an underdog quality, a Clark Kent persona. He was quiet and dignified off the field. The Packers selected him in the 17th round of the draft (the NFL hasn't had a 17th round for decades). He was smart, disciplined and tough as nails. He would play injured. He was a leader of men. He was the kind of football player, the kind of man, I, as an 11-year-old, wanted to be. His name even sounded like a hero's name should sound.

Bart.

Starr.

It was like part Old West Cowboy, part superhero. I wanted to be Bart Starr.

Starr and Vince Lombardi were like the perfect storm. Green Bay had only won one game in 1958, the season before Lombardi was hired to take over the team. After that, the Green Bay Packers seemed invincible.

In school, you could order books out of these pamphlets the teachers handed out every month or two. I ordered any book that was related to Bart Starr, the Packers, or football. I'd read those books two and three times over. I loved how Lombardi valued toughness and that nothing replaced the fundamentals. With him, execution was paramount: "We know what we're gonna do and you know what we're gonna do, but you know that we know that you know and you still can't stop it." There is something inherently powerful in that.

The one thing with the Packers, whether they were the best or not, you knew they were the tougher team.

I was in the fifth grade when I wrote a letter to Bart Starr telling him of my admiration for him and the Green Bay Packers. He was the first famous person I ever reached out to. A few weeks later, a big manila envelope showed up at our house. The postmark was Green Bay, Wisconsin. The envelope was addressed to me. Inside was a glossy 8 x 10 black and white photo of Bart Starr. The odd part of it was that the photo was of him punting the ball at Lambeau Field, not playing quarterback. No matter. I hung the picture over my bed in my room. And, because Bart Starr had responded to me, I was empowered. I wrote letters to other football players too. I wrote Paul Hornung, Jim Taylor, Fran Tarkenton, Chris Hanburger, and John Riggins. Some replied with pictures. Some didn't reply at all.

I was always very self-motivated. I worked hard but I didn't really like school, which may sound surprising considering I did well in my classes and earned a law degree. I saw doing well in school not so much as a way to appease my parents, but as something that was good for me, no matter how much I disliked certain parts of it. It was going to push me forward in life.

But I was also free-spirited and mischievous. I was the type of kid that wanted to see reactions. If there was a frog in the middle of the road, I'd get a stick and poke him in the ass just to see how far he'd jump. I wasn't trying to hurt anybody. I just wanted to see what they did and how they'd respond.

In retrospect, I was an early student of human nature. Not consciously of course, I wasn't thinking, "Hey, this will be great if I can learn about all different kinds of people because someday it will help me relate and motivate various personality types in my far-off coaching career." I've just always been curious about how things work. Being curious and inquisitive, you provide yourself with a lot of opportunity to study folks, to see what makes them tick. Maybe most importantly, you wonder what makes yourself tick.

I never liked math, but I did pretty well in it. Though I didn't have the warmest relationship with one of my math teachers in seventh grade.

The teacher would stand outside in the hall before class. I would strut past him into his room. "Well, another day, another A." I'd been popping off to him for weeks. His tests were worth 100 points, plus you could get 15 points extra credit. I'd been getting 115 on everything.

One day, about two-thirds of the way through the school year, he was sitting on his desk at the end of class after handing back the results of the latest test. A few other students were hovering around him when I walked over. "Well," I say, "Another day, another A."

He didn't acknowledge me initially.

Then, a few seconds later, "Wham!" He kicked me right in the thigh. It felt like getting hit with a baseball. It hurt like crazy. He did it right in front of a couple other kids. A girl standing beside his desk gasped. The kick was so sudden. It was pretty violent. I didn't realize he was so thin-skinned. It was the second class I'd had with him and up until that point I had liked him. I didn't get that my comment had bugged him to that magnitude.

I didn't say anything, I just limped off. I didn't want to show weakness. I wasn't going to rub it or touch my thigh to give him the satisfaction. But I left pretty quickly because it hurt so much.

As bizarre as this may sound, getting hit by a teacher wasn't that uncommon, especially in the '70s in Wyoming. Teachers would routinely swat you with a board, sometimes it was even a flattened baseball bat. They'd whittle it down so it was skinny and they'd whack the shit out of you. However, the threat of those swats wouldn't stop everything. If you had a good caper going, it wouldn't deter you. But if it was something minor like spitwads or gum, you'd weigh whether it was worth taking a couple of swats.

I backed off making any comments to that math teacher after getting kicked. Then final grade time at the end of the school year came. He gave me a C for the class . . . A C?! I had not missed one day of class. I'd gotten not just a 100 on every test, but a 115. Every test, I earned a 115. How can I have a C? I went to his office. We argued for an hour and a half. He told me how there was one test that he couldn't find and that he had to give me a 0 for it.

I was fuming. Here he is trying to give me a grade that I didn't get, and on top of that he, a grown man, had kicked me right in the thigh and I hadn't ever said anything about it.

I remember thinking, "OK, I didn't say anything about you kicking me in the leg. I limped off. I got on your nerves. I didn't even know I was getting on your nerves. You never gave me any warning, but that's fine. OK, what you did is probably illegal but that's fine. We're even. But you're not going to cheat me out of my grade. I worked for that. I earned that A. If you had pulled me aside, I would've quit mouthing off."

Finally, I said, "We're going to the principal on this because I didn't get a C. I know I was here every day." I was polite. I didn't raise my voice. I got more than an A actually. As soon as I started talking about going to the principal, the teacher caved.

"Whoa, hold on. Well, uh, maybe, uh, I can add up all of the other tests and I'll divide it by one less. If it equals a C, I'll give you a C. If it equals, a B, you get a B."

It ended up equaling an A.

The situation with that math teacher was the first time in my life I ever experienced how adults, just like kids, could be immature and petty. I learned that they can screw you over if they feel like it. Or if you find yourself sideways to their agenda, right and wrong may not play into the equation.

I went from idolizing Daniel Boone to Bart Starr, and when I was 15, my new hero was from a different sport. He was a leader too, but he carried himself much differently than Bart Starr did. Billy Martin, then the manager of the New York Yankees, had a personality that was a lot more aggressive. I tried to read everything about Billy Martin that I could find. He was passionate and driven, but didn't have a lot of natural athletic ability, at least in comparison to other major leaguers. He was an overachiever.

I loved Billy Martin. Still do. He was determined to make others work harder. He was always looking for an edge. He wasn't an "old-school" guy, he was innovative. He came up under an old-school guy in Casey Stengel, but Martin was a creative, find-a-better-way guy. He was an incredible student of the game. The fundamentals of baseball were sacred to him. He lived the game of baseball and studied it from every angle.

He got results everywhere he worked. He won a division title in his only season managing the Minnesota Twins. He led the Detroit Tigers to a division title, too. When he took over the Texas Rangers the team had never had any success, but he turned them from a last-place franchise into one that came in second in the division. The Rangers lost 100 games in the two seasons before Martin arrived. Then in he steps and they finished eight games over .500. He was hired by George Steinbrenner after that, and led the New York Yankees to their first World Series in a dozen years. Did Billy Martin piss some people off along the way? No doubt about it. If he thought he was right, he stood up for it. I loved all the energy he brought to his teams.

"I coached Little League baseball. I never was a good coach. I was in real estate and your demands get screwy. Mike became my assistant when he was 15 and took over two years later. He was pretty autonomous. I was really a figurehead. He was a good coach and the reason why he was such a good coach was because of his spirit of optimism. He didn't feel like any lead was insurmountable. When he was 17, our team from Cody played this great team from Cheyenne in the state tournament, which was a double-elimination tournament. They had to beat Cheyenne twice. Everybody expected the championship game to be between Cheyenne and Casper, which are places that are about 10 times the size of Cody. We were the upstarts. Nobody expected us to be there.

"Mike was doing all of these strategy things that were really irritating to the Cheyenne team. He'd call time so he could talk to his batter right when the pitcher was about to go into his motion. He'd be out there doing his Billy Martin thing complete with his Billy Martin-looking sunglasses. Mike always loved Billy Martin. He and I used to argue about

*that. I thought Billy Martin was a bush leaguer.
I saw Martin play second base for the Oakland
Acorns 15 years before Mike was born.
Anyhow. Some of the crap that Billy Martin
did, I didn't admire at all. Kicking the dirt all
over the umpires? But Mike really loved it. He
saw the other side of it. He thought all of that
was part of the game. Of course, Billy Martin
won games with mediocre players. But I didn't
like the idea of Billy Martin. Anyhow, Mike
was a master at irritating the other team. His
team beat Cheyenne and there's not a way in
the world that our team should've been on the
same field with them. We lost the following day
to them in the championship game, though."*
                                        —Frank Leach, Mike's father

My dad and I always argued about Billy Martin. My dad would
get pissed about Billy. My dad was all about the by-the-book, Joe
Paterno- and Tom Landry-types. Even then, I was more interested
in coaches than I was of a particular team. I was fascinated by how
all the parts came together. What did the guy do and how did he
do it?

Back then when I was managing that baseball team, we would
take pride in trying to blow up the other team's pitcher. I was
always big on getting people on base—walks, hit-by-pitch, anyway
you could. It burned me up if a guy swung at a bad pitch. Anyway,
we'd do whatever we could to rattle their pitcher. That season
they even legislated a rule against us because we'd have our guys
grab the fence in front of our dugout, shake it, and scream just as
the guy was about to pitch. We were also really aggressive on the
bases. We took huge leads on the bases, and I'd talk to my guy
leading off first base really loud, just so the pitcher could hear it:

"One more step!

"C'mon, one more step.

"C'mon!

"Don't worry about HIM!

"Back!

"Bаск!

"BACK!"

I'd want him to lead off a body length plus one step. "He can't get you anyway!" I'd shout it loud enough to get the pitcher's attention.

That state tournament was unbelievable. Cody was a town of about 6,000 people, while Casper had a team drawn from a town of 60,000, and we still beat them 2–1. Cheyenne was like 50,000 and they had a military base there so you had all of these kids from military families. They were really great. The rules at that level of baseball are to end a game if your team fell 10 runs behind. Cheyenne 10-runned everybody they faced. Our team looked like a bunch of 12 and 13-year-olds. They looked like high school seniors. Some of them even had facial hair. Their pitcher was about 6-foot-3. They had some cocky managers. They expected the whole tournament to be some sort of coronation ceremony.

The first time we played Cheyenne we were determined to keep them off balance. We almost beat them, but we lost, 6–4. We wanted another shot at them, but we had to fight our way through the losers' bracket in order to face them again.

The Cheyenne team didn't intimidate us at all. In fact, we liked that the pressure was on them. We were going to milk that by cranking up the tension as much as we could. I sent in five or six pitchers over seven innings that day. Some of the pitchers threw twice, maybe in the second inning and then I'd go back to that pitcher in the fourth. I'd have my shortstop come in and pitch to a few batters. Then I'd move him back to shortstop and bring the rightfielder in to pitch to a few batters. Then I rolled another guy in. I'd rotate from a slow junkballer to a harder thrower. It had nothing to do with putting a lefthander against a left-hand hitter. I wanted their guys off balance. Anything we could do to disrupt them. They hated me changing pitchers all of the time. They had these big, overpowering guys and home plate would've been a launching pad if we didn't break the pace. There was no way I was going to let them feel like it was batting practice.

When we were up, we'd bunt. We'd fake a lot. I'd call timeouts a lot. As their pitcher would begin his motion, I would have our kids step out of the box. It was psychological warfare—anything to mentally break their pitcher. And we did. We beat them to get into the championship game.

The umpires lost control. In the championship game, they tried not to let me call timeouts because Cheyenne had complained so much. In the third inning, I said I was protesting the game.

"Why? Does the rulebook say I don't get timeouts?" I argued.

The umpire tried telling me I couldn't replace the pitcher. I responded that I could replace whoever I wanted. I knew the rule allowed me to move pitchers around as long as they didn't leave the game. It was just crazy.

We ended up losing the championship, but it was close.

Coaching baseball taught me a lot about the value of commitment and what guys can accomplish if they stick together as a team. I also realized how vital it is to maintain your poise and stay focused. The other major lesson I learned is that you may need to use different tactics to reach—and motivate—different people. I would contemplate ways to get each of my players to flourish.

Early on, there was a kid that I felt I made a difference with named Kevin Showell. He was an introverted kid, but for whatever reason, he responded to me. Showell had been hitting eighth in the batting order, but I moved him up to second. I had wanted to show that I believed in him, but I didn't want to move him into the lead-off spot where he'd have the pressure of batting first. Kevin went from being probably a .300 hitter to a .400 guy.

Sometimes, the responses weren't as good. Todd Frost was this really athletic kid, but my intensity didn't work for him. I unsettled him, made him nervous. He was talented and a big kid for his age, so my assumption was that he could handle my intensity. I should've tried to relax him. He was a laid-back guy. My inclination was to fire him up a little bit. That just wasn't his style and not what he responded to best. I became part of the problem, not part of the solution. But by the time I realized it, two-thirds of the season was over and the toothpaste was already out of the tube.

One of my proudest moments as a coach at any level involved a kid named Joe Cronk. He was undersized, like I was when I was his age. He was an oldest child, like me. He had this buzzcut. He had always been stuck out in right field, where coaches usually stick their worst player in youth baseball. His parents weren't into sports. He was one of the younger guys on the team. He also batted cross-handed, which I spent some time working with him to correct.

Late in the season we were playing the other top team in our league. It was the last inning of the game. We were down two runs. There were two outs. We had runners on first and second. Their stud pitcher, Sean Tidball, was on the mound. Every little league has its Kelly Leak, ace pitcher for the Bad News Bears. Tidball was our Kelly Leak. You could hear the catcher's mitt pop on every pitch Tidball threw. Then he'd go off and strut in a circle around the mound. Tidball had a presence to him. He actually had muscles. He also always had a bunch of adolescent girls parading around him. He was immensely confident, and I would've been too if I were him.

Then comes Joe Cronk walking up to home plate, with a determined look on his face. I could tell he was scared. Never in my life had I wanted to replace a guy as badly as I wanted to replace Joe Cronk in that at-bat. But I just couldn't do that to him. This moment meant the world to him. I wanted to call time out. I wandered back and forth between the coaches' box and the dugout thinking about taking him out of the game. He was our weakest player, but it would just crush him emotionally if I pulled him. So I went up to him before he stepped into the batters box.

I said simply, "Watch the ball carefully. Make sure you swing at a strike."

And with that, off he went to the plate. I was hoping maybe little Joe would crowd the plate and Tidball would walk him or hit him with a pitch.

Tidball reared back and fired. Strike one. Joe swung the same moment as the ball crashed into the catcher's mitt. I looked at Joe's face. He looked determined. The next pitch whizzed past him again. Strike two.

Joe didn't budge on Tidball's third pitch. It sailed just a bit outside. Ball one. Then, on Tidball's fourth pitch, something amazing happened. Joe whipped the bat around. CRACK! The ball sliced down the right field line into the corner. Both runners on base scored. Joe Cronk had tripled home the tying runs. My brother Tim ended up driving him home. We won the game.

Joe Cronk is why I love athletics. He is the reason why I coach.

BYU

When I was 17 I earned an academic scholarship to the University of Wyoming. I turned it down to attend Brigham Young University in Utah instead. I was raised a Mormon, and though that was a factor in choosing BYU, it was not a big factor. Your religion is your religion no matter where you go.

I wanted a change of scenery. BYU literally had students from everywhere. They have one of the biggest international programs in the world. I liked that the school had such a strong academic reputation. I also liked the fact that it was 10 hours away from home. I figured if I took the academic scholarship to Wyoming, it would've been an environment similar to what I already knew from high school.

When I left home for BYU I wanted to reinvent myself. In high school, people tend to get rutted into little cliques. I did. Maybe it's instinctive that people fall into the same patterns over time. Everybody gets a little bit rutted by their routine, by what's comfortable. Problem is, if you're doing the same old thing that everybody else is doing, that's who you become—everybody else. What's more, you start to become the person you think everybody expects you to be, good or bad. Those expectations seem to weigh especially heavily on kids. They may never fully blossom, and years later, they cringe when they think back on what could have been, and end up resenting the people around them.

When you're young, your instincts tell you to conform to surroundings or to roll with the expectations. It's the path of least resistance. Even if you don't like who you are—or who others have perceived you to be—that's how you manage to find acceptance. It's easy for you to exist that way, rather than to shake things up. But it can be suffocating, or at the very least, stifling.

I have always encouraged my kids to go away for college because I valued my own experiences away from my home turf. It allowed me to carve out my own deal, to reinvent, or more specifically, to develop myself.

If you go away for a fresh start, people have no expectations— they don't know you, so you're not bound by your past. You can build on your best qualities without being pigeonholed by the expectations of people who may have known you your whole life. Even though I went to one of the more conservative schools in the country, because I struck out on my own, I found college to be amazingly liberating.

In college, I wanted to meet, know, and grow to understand a wide variety of people. I'd ask all sorts of questions to strangers on the street just to see their reactions. It was like a cross between an interview and an interrogation. I'd ask them questions, which may have included what kind of music they liked, what their favorite food was, what their love life was like. I've never viewed any question to be too personal.

My freshman year, I wrote a folklore paper on prank phone calls. I got so into it that I wrote up about 60 prank calls.

I would also dial up random numbers. I wouldn't say anything really offensive. I'd start talking: "So what are you doing? What's going on?"

They'd ask, "Do I know you?"

"No. I doubt it. I just randomly dialed this number and I

figured I'd introduce myself and talk to you."

Some would get nasty or just hang up. I wanted to see how long I could keep them on the phone. Usually, I'd end up chatting with them for a while. I had this one lady who was in her late 20s on the phone for two hours. She'd gone to BYU. Her husband was working on some graduate degree. She started telling me which teachers to take in which courses. She told me all about her husband, and we just went on and on. I'd never met her in person. I'd never even talked to her before that conversation, nor have I since. It was a fishing expedition to see what I could catch, born more out of curiosity than boredom. I really wanted to broaden my horizons as much as possible.

When I returned to Cody in the summer, I felt like I came back a different person. I was more independent. I realized that any problem I was faced with—whether it was money-related, academic-related, or anything else—only one person is gonna have the solution, and that was me. It was then that I realized that your choices come down to either ducking your head and running, or stepping up and attacking your obstacles aggressively.

My parents weren't paying for my schooling. I was determined to pay for college so my summers were packed. I was getting about $600 a semester in scholarship money. I had jobs painting and working at a hotel. Plus, I was coaching baseball, which I really loved.

"When Mike played football for me, he was probably 145, 150 pounds. He wasn't a great athlete. He was a back-up, a good team guy. But when he was 18, he actually coached my boy's baseball team. We had a 14-year-old all-star team and we were hosting this regional all-star Babe Ruth tournament. We weren't very good. He ran this shadow infield or some ghost deal to warm them up. It was the

craziest thing I've ever seen. He'd be up there at home plate, like he was hitting a grounder to shortstop and he'd have them turn a double play on it, only there was no ball. They'd fake it all. Anyhow, my son was a centerfielder and in the first inning, he had a ball hit way over his head and took off on a dead run and he made a catch. Might've been the only catch he made in his life. It was amazing. Course the roof fell in a couple innings later, but he made it fun for them."

—**John McDougall, football coach, Cody High**

I always wondered what Coach McDougall thought of that whole ghost infield deal. He was one of the most intimidating people in the entire world. He was like 5-foot-10, 230 pounds, and had the face of vicious intensity. His dad was a sheriff named Pee Wee McDougall. That ghost infield deal certainly wasn't his style.

This was the summer after my freshman year at BYU. The team I was coaching was my little brother Tim's Babe Ruth All-Star team, who was hosting a regional baseball tournament in Cody. There were teams from Washington, Montana, Idaho, and Oregon. We were not very good. To be honest, we stunk. We were in so far over our heads. The boys were totally down and I don't think anyone besides me wanted to coach. Every other state had a higher population than Wyoming's, and to be fair, we hadn't even earned the right to play in the tournament (in Babe Ruth baseball if you host the tournament, you automatically qualify). We didn't have to beat anyone to get into it: We didn't play in a district tournament, we didn't play in the state tournament, but we're in this regional tournament playing against tested state champions.

My friend Mike Clayton, who played baseball at BYU, told me about doing this ghost infield once, and thinking about it I figured there was no sense in showing how bad we were during warm-ups. Plus, I wanted to get our kids really pumped up to play.

I would stand up there with the bat and toss the invisible "ball" up in the air, glance at it and then swat at the "ball" like I was hitting a grounder to third. The kid playing third base would uncoil from his stance, take a few quick steps to his left, scrunch down like he was fielding the ball, then pop up and throw it over to first. And so we went around the whole infield like that, faking it. Then the team really got into it. Instead of making the routine plays, they're making all of these super baseball highlight plays. They're going deep into the hole and diving for balls and laying out. Everybody on the team, in the dugout, even in the stands loved it. They're laughing and getting all fired up. We ended up winning a game before we got eliminated from that tournament.

I liked BYU. Everything was clean. The place is like Disneyland, only without the rides and merchandising. If you dropped something, someone immediately raced over to pick it up. I also really like that BYU has people from all over the world there. The negative would be all of the rules. For example, one time I went to a bowling alley and some random guy thought my hair wasn't short enough. He turned me in to the honor police. It was like that all the time. I had to deal with a certain amount of uptight judgment at BYU.

> *"We were in college during the Jim McMahon days at Brigham Young University. There was a little bit of McMahon in Mike. Of course, BYU is this very traditional, strict, conservative university that requires every student to sign the Honor Code. I had this professor who said, 'What this school needs is a few East Coast Jews to shake this school up a bit.' Mike was kinda one of those I guess. He would get*

*called in by the Honor Code patrol because
his hair was flopping onto his collar. [The BYU
Honor Code says that locks be 'trimmed above
the collar, leaving the ear uncovered.'] So Mike
goes in to the hearing and brings the student
newspaper. In it, there's a photo of one of the
professors with equally long hair. Mike says,
'Why does he get to have his hair like this and I
can't?' I think they finally got tired of listening
to him, because they let him go. But he kept
getting brought in and they'd keep letting him
go."*

—Mike Clayton, college friend from BYU

It's just the way my head is formulated. I mean the shape, not
necessarily what's inside. I had the same haircut since I was eight
years old. The whole deal about haircuts and hair length at BYU
was foolish. It was an overreaction to the '60s.

The first time I was called in by the honor police, I noticed a
copy of the student newspaper around campus that had a story on
this professor, Omar Kader, who was born to Palestinian immigrant
parents in Provo, Utah. The story was about some award he'd
won. Accompanying the article was a picture of him. His hair was
as long as mine. When I got my notice from the honor police that
said I had to come in, I mailed the note back to them with a copy
of the picture of Omar Kader from our newspaper. I said, "Here
we have a professor we should all be proud of, and his hair looks
great, and mine looks like his. This should take care of it."

I still had to go to see them. The Honor Code Police just
stared at me with this mortified look on their faces, like I'd started
trimming my toenails in front of them. I even referred to the statue
of Brigham Young in the quad that I walked by every day. "I look
at that statue with admiration, and I've noticed [Brigham Young's]
flowing hair also. I'm not asking that mine be that long, but why

are we fussing about this?" They weren't buying it. I couldn't help but think, "Why worry about rat turds when there are elephant turds flying around everywhere?"

They responded with something about how one gnat can sink the whole boat. They insisted that my hair had to be styled above my ear and collar.

"Well fine, I'll style it and jam it above my ear. How about if I get hair spray and stick it up like Bozo the Clown or get some bobby pins?"

When I was gone they called Omar Kader. I heard they gave him a lecture about how he set a bad example that led me astray.

I called him to explain. The next semester I took one of his classes. He was a good professor. I liked him a lot. It was by no fault of his that I was called in about the Honor Code. I was called in four times and I never changed my hair once.

For as much as I liked the place, I do think the rules being so tight at BYU can inhibit creativity. I was certainly never a fan of the hair thing. I had my periods of civil disobedience, but I can admit that I was more focused there than I may have been if I'd gone anywhere else. I've always been regarded as an independent guy, but beneath it all there is structure. BYU was very much a part of building that side of me. I don't think all of that would've come together without it. Not to mention I ended up meeting and marrying a great lady named Sharon, who had been living in the next building over from my apartment, just a few hundred feet from me.

Law School

The setting at Pepperdine looks like an episode of Baywatch. We had beautiful facilities, friendly people, and an amazing view of the Pacific Ocean. However, once you got inside your classroom, the vibe was the same as any other law school full of stressed-out people—tense.

Law school helped me in ways I could never have imagined as I was making the transition from law to coaching football. During my first orientation at Pepperdine, one of the professors said that as a law student, you won't be getting a degree in case memorization or rule memorization. Instead, you learn how to take a variety of facts and a certain amount of precedent, and apply them to the problem at hand. You are actually getting a degree in problem solving. Well, football certainly supplies a lot of problems to solve.

As a football coach you begin every week with a fairly sizeable problem: how to beat the next opponent. You have a ton of material at your disposal—statistical breakdowns, game film, scouting reports, and you have to prioritize what you're going to delve into, because there's not nearly enough time to cover everything. You choose what to worry about, what to set aside, and what to feature. Then, ready or not, the game comes, and it's off you go. In the thick of it you have to think on your feet, adapt, and be ready for surprises.

Besides the big picture challenges, being a head football coach means having around 50 staff members and 125 players all depending on your problem-solving skills to help them through the week. You're always working on what they need to perform at their best. Law helped me manage the details, but any time you try to keep that many people moving in the same direction, it's going to be quite an effort. On top of that, you don't want to disrupt people's creativity. There are so many variables at every level of coaching that it's important to encourage the creative process rather than try and impose some sort of one-way, my-way-or-the-highway, assembly-line tactic. I've found that keeping the door to creativity open helps problems get solved better and faster. At the same time, everyone needs to understand that decisions need to be made quickly and definitively, because a bunch of people second-guessing their way around a solution is not doing anyone any good.

As a coach or as anyone leading a group of people will understand, people are fickle, and you have to be ready for just about anything. You're always thinking about how you can reach someone to get the most out of him because conditions are bound to shift. Always do. A guy who was up is going to be down. Another guy who was down is going to be up. Somebody thinks they're getting screwed. Somebody's really coming along, but you're just not sure if he's ready. You haven't seen him get enough reps, so do you start him ahead of the other guy? He's more talented and explosive but you're wondering, can he do the job consistently?

Law school provided the kind of training to make these decisions, because just like the Big 12, it was incredibly competitive. I dealt with people who were smart, ruthless, idealistic, noble, and morally deficient. All were very capable students and no one was willing to be denied a high status in an academic environment. The talent in a law school becomes apparent and it can be intimidating if you aren't careful. The classes added to the intimidation and could sometimes feel overwhelming. You would be bulldozed by a pile of information, much more than you could master.

Even the application process for law school taught me lessons that apply to football. We select the best and the brightest athletes to award our football scholarships, and once we have the student-athletes in our program, we test their limits and see how badly they really want to be there. That's how law school is too. Both view it vital to select the best, then battle-harden the charges before turning them out into the world. In law, if you are going to advocate for someone during the most trying times in their life, then you need to be the kind of person who has the toughness to act fully on another's behalf. In football, we recruit only the best high school and junior college athletes, and test them in our program to see if they can hold up under the physical and mental demands of college football.

From a mental and emotional standpoint, law is certainly a great way to prepare for this level of cutthroat preparation. It forces you to think on your feet, just like you have to when you run a college football program. Law professors make you stand up in the middle of over 100 people. They try to hammer you as they make you recite your cases in front of your classmates.

"OK, Mr. Leach . . ." I kinda got a kick out of that because you'd get to banter back and forth with the professors.

"Tell us about the case of so and so," and you'd try and state the facts. A favorite trick of the professors was to constantly interrupt you. Some of them would do anything to rattle you. You'd be there giving the facts: "Blah-Blah-Blah, and then the plaintiff accidentally cut off the defendant's leg with a chainsaw and . . ."

Then they'd interrupt you, "Whose chainsaw was it? Since it wasn't his chainsaw . . ."

I didn't mind having those little debates, and I learned a lot from watching my other classmates get frazzled. People would literally quit law school over having to stand up and battle. It helped me realize that it wasn't just what you said or what they said. It was about preparing myself mentally for what they could say. I approached those debates thinking, "OK, he knows more about the facts than I do, but he doesn't know more about my own opinion than I do."

One of my first cases in law school was in Willard Pedrick's torts class. Pedrick was a renowned professor and leading light in the field of torts. He'd been the dean of the law school at Arizona State and was a visiting professor at Pepperdine. He was like Malibu's version of Mr. Hand, only more of an intellectual, which made me Spicoli, at least by law school standards.

Pedrick called on me for a right-to-privacy case involving a genius kid who spoke eight languages by the time he was eight years old and earned a degree from Harvard at 16. The kid, William Sidis, had been featured on the front page of the *New York Times*, but 20 years later *The New Yorker* wrote another article about how he'd turned into a lonely recluse and he sued. My position was that he had a right to his privacy.

Pedrick is going at me, "Well, Mr. Leach, Sidis had unique abilities. He spoke eight languages and . . . "

Pedrick is bringing up music and what I thought were other unrelated points, saying, "How can you deprive the world of this, and furthermore, there was already an article about him. Mr. Leach, doesn't the public have a right to know?"

"No, the public doesn't have a right to know," I said.

"Mr. Leach, are you questioning the wisdom of the Justices since they ruled against him?"

"Yes, I am," I said. "You asked me what I think. Not what they think. This guy is like the Elephant Man. He didn't ask for any of this. That poor guy was tortured because of his uniqueness. They were passing him around at a carnival, whereas this other guy happened to be a genius. Happened to be a genius. So everybody poked him and prodded him like they want him to do some tricks. People used to pay money to go see this masked individual who had been deformed from birth, and for a certain amount of money, you got to look underneath the mask. It's essentially the same thing. Only the genius's mask you may be looking under may seem a bit more positive. However, I did not think it was right then, and I do not think it is right in the case of Sidis. If the Elephant Man wanted people to look under his mask, that should have been his business. And if the genius wanted somebody to look into his life, that should be his business too. Why is it their prerogative when it should be his prerogative?"

I mostly winged it. I knew the framework of the case. I knew my opinion on it and after that, I described it. I've always felt my opinions were as good as the next guy's. In these cases, there's a lot of devil's advocate in there because the professor is going to just attack all of your arguments from as many directions as possible and see if he can blow them up. My particular position was different from the holding of the case, meaning I was saying the Justices were wrong. Well, I didn't have any problem saying that. Then, much to my delight, a few cases down the road, they had overturned it. I just think it comes down to trusting yourself. I wasn't always prepared for the cases they might throw at me, but I trusted my instincts and my ability to focus on sorting out the details for a solution.

> **"When I teach, I kinda roam around in the rows. My corporations class is a large class, usually it has over 100 students and I'm walking around. So I look down and I see Mike's mapping out football plays. I asked if he'd come by after class. I said 'Mike, what are you doing?' He said, 'Well, I love football and I got all these plays in my head.' I said 'OK, but you do realize you're in law school, right?' And then after that, we talked about that passion.**
>
> **"I really think he would've been a great lawyer. Why I say great is because he does have an**

outstanding analytical mind, the ability to make connections between diverse things and be able to pull everything together. I think if you can do that, you can be a great lawyer, but I believe that's what also makes him such a great football coach. He can think analytically, connect things that seem to be diverse, and yet make things understandable to his players and inspire people."

—Professor Janet Kerr, Pepperdine Law School

During law school I started acting. I found an agent by the name of Joe Kolkowitz. He had a stable of athletes he used for commercials. At one time he represented O.J. Simpson and he had also gotten Howie Long into acting. He even had Long's picture over his desk. He told me where to go to get my head shot and he liked that I played rugby in college, assuring me that I was his rugby player if the role ever came across his desk. It never did. "No, I got nothing for a rugby player right now," he'd say whenever I could get him on the phone. I was at the bottom of his list and he made sure that I knew it.

Acting was a hobby for me. At the time I was still doing other jobs, clerking or being a swimming instructor, but I still landed some auditions. I got into two movies, though neither is exactly a classic. One was *Grunt! The Wrestling Movie*, where I played a security guard. The other was *J. Edgar Hoover*, a TV mini-series starring Treat Williams. I played an FBI agent in this big meeting taking place in the '60s about how they were going to handle all of the demonstrations over the Vietnam War. I didn't have a speaking part. I just tried to look like an FBI agent.

For the FBI part, they cut and styled my hair to reflect the times. I didn't want my hair that short, but my wife, Sharon, liked the way it looked so much that she wanted me to keep it that way. In the movie, I'm one of the G-men sitting at this massive table with J. Edgar Hoover at its head. I've never actually seen *Hoover*, so as far as I know my part could be on the cutting room floor.

"I represented that guy?! Holy smokes! That's wild.

"I had O.J., Howie Long, Todd Christensen, Roberto Duran. I represented a lot of wrestlers, Superstar Billy Graham, Adrian Adonis. I got Andre the Giant into *The Princess Bride*. I absolutely remember *Grunt!* I put some people in that movie."

–Joe Kolkowitz, agent

In my second year of law school I took an acting workshop with a casting director. She taught us to draw from our own experiences to create a character, and how to interact with other people while staying in character. I'd always been a people watcher, but those classes made you focus on it even more. I was only able to go to the class six times. When I went on auditions, I just tried to do what they told me. I really didn't have enough time to get into the acting thing, though. Between law school and coaching, my time was mostly spoken for.

I didn't realize until way later how much you draw on the same skills in coaching, acting, or making a legal case. At the heart, what you're doing is making a presentation in one form or another. You're trying to connect with people. The best actors are the ones who best connect with the audience. The best lawyers are the ones who best connect with the jury. The best coaches are the ones who best connect with their players.

When I was in law school, there was a lawyer who fascinated me, Melvin Belli. He was a trial attorney from San Francisco and known as the King of Torts. I studied his trials. I read all of his books. Everything about him was flamboyant. Belli had represented everyone from Errol Flynn to Mae West to Lenny Bruce to Muhammad Ali. He appeared on talk shows and even on an episode of Star Trek. He used to try cases for free at San Quentin just to practice his skills. Whenever Belli won a court case, he would raise a Jolly Roger flag over his building and fire off a cannon he had mounted on the roof. I once saw Belli try a case in Santa Barbara. He was in his '80s at the time. He brought his yacht down from San Francisco to Santa Barbara for the trial. He did legal research in his law library on his yacht. He didn't win but he helped build the file to what eventually led to liability against the tobacco companies.

One of Belli's most famous victories was in the early 1940s when he represented a young mother whose leg was severed by a San Francisco trolley. A jury awarded $65,000 to her, but lawyers for the trolley company appealed because they argued that the amount she received was too much. Melvin Belli came to court with this L-shaped box wrapped in butcher paper with a white string tied around it. It sat on his table throughout the trial. He never introduced it as evidence. For the first few days of the trial, everyone—the judge, the opposing lawyers, and the jurors—kept staring at that box. You know they're all thinking, "Did Melvin Belli really bring the amputated leg into the courtroom?"

The attorney for the railway argued that the woman could be fitted with an artificial leg that would be just as good as her old flesh one. Then Belli began to pull at the strings of the knot on the mysterious package. The jury was petrified. Finally, Belli ripped open the box, turned to face the jury. He held up an artificial leg that had been wrapped in butcher's paper.

"Ladies and gentleman of the jury," Belli announced, "this is what my young client will wear for the rest of her life."

He approached the jury and promptly dropped the mannequin's leg into the lap of a juror.

"Take it!" Belli told him. "Feel the warmth of life in the soft tissues of its flesh. Feel the pulse of the blood as it flows through the veins, feel the marvelous smooth articulation at the new joint and touch the rippling muscles of the calf."

The jury deliberated for less than a half an hour. They awarded Belli's client $100,000, 10 times the going rate for the loss of a limb back then.

Belli said that a lawyer's performance in the courtroom is responsible for about 25 percent of the outcome; the remaining 75 percent depends on the facts. He knew all about presentation and impact. This was demonstrative evidence. Coaches are in the presentation business too. We're right in the thick of it, and the better we present, the better they learn.

The nature of law school breeds combative personalities as much as it attracts them. There are ultra-competitive people who are surrounded by the law all the time, and it gets to a point where it's all they can think about. There is a kind of mental wrestling match going on constantly as you get your mind around the concepts and learn to best express yourself verbally and in writing.

Shortly into the first year you learn to scream and yell at each other, then happily go to lunch together. After a couple of months of this sort of badgering, you start to assume that people from all walks of life act the same way. It doesn't take too long before you realize this is not the case. The rest of society is not prepared to be challenged from every angle, engage in heated arguments, and then go off and be friends afterwards.

One evening after I got married, we were eating at my in-laws' house. My father-in-law was a college professor who taught public relations. He liked to think he enjoyed vigorous discussions at the dinner table. Being in the middle of my first year of law school it was impossible for me or any other first-year student to avoid any level of debate or discussion. My father-in-law enjoyed playing devil's advocate, especially when engaged in conversation with my mother-in-law, my wife, and my wife's four sisters.

The topic of conversation at this particular meal was the

superiority of Japanese culture over American culture. My father-in-law cited several examples for his argument: their cars were better, their employees exercised at work, they had a tremendous level of enthusiasm, and, though they made less money, they were far more efficient due to the fact they were able to live on less. After pointing out several factors I thought were valid, such as high suicide rates in Japan, the fact that my father-in-law hated exercise, and that they only led the U.S. in small car manufacturing, he began to get a little upset. Like a lot of first-year students, I didn't know when to stop. After the discussion was already winding down, I suggested that if Japan was so superior and he liked Japan so much better, that he was welcome to pack up and move to Japan, where I felt he would be much happier. He didn't appear too thrilled. Maybe a dubious move for a new son-in-law.

These debates are healthy—despite what my father-in-law might have thought afterwards. They often elicit more reasoned ideas and solutions. Your points become more focused, often because the fat has been trimmed away. I've always thought that whenever someone challenges my opinions, I end up learning new things and I become even more focused in my thought process.

Not everybody, though, likes to be challenged. That's unfortunate. I suspect many people shy away from challenges because of their own insecurities. But being open enough to engage in sometimes difficult discussions is a great thing. It prompts some level of the unexpected, and anything that provokes a response provides you the opportunity to generate ideas, which is hugely beneficial.

As much as I loved debating and all of the mental contortions that come with being a lawyer, I just wasn't convinced it was the right career for me. I reached out to Gerry Spence, the famed trial attorney who epitomized what I hoped to achieve by going to law school. I'd wanted to be a tort attorney, to fight for the little man against corporations and insurance companies. Make a difference. I wanted to impact society in a positive way because of principle, not just money.

Gerry Spence was what I'd hoped to become as an attorney. He was the most famous attorney in the country. He was the lead counsel in the Silkwood case, where he won his client over $10 million. There was a major motion picture made about the case. He defended Imelda Marcos and got her acquitted. He went after a guy who blew up a judge's house. He won $18 million from *Penthouse* magazine. He had the ability to work both sides.

I was an idealist then, and pretty much always have been. Gerry seemed like the same sort of guy. He was from Wyoming, same as me. We had even lived in some of the same towns. I felt like we had a shared background and I was hoping to achieve some of the things he personified.

One day, I wrote him a letter:

Dear Mr. Spence,

You are at the top of your field in law and have accomplished what I would like to achieve. You are doing what I am going to school for.

Was it worth it? Do you love law? Do you hate law? If you had it to do over again would you? Are there any changes you would have made in regard to pursuing law?

A few weeks later, I received a letter back from him.

Yes I love law. Yes I hate law. But, most importantly, I am consumed by law. I think about it all the time, and yes, I would do the same thing again because it is fulfilling to do something you are consumed with. If you are consumed by law, go be an attorney. If you are not, find something else.

Reading his words was not an earth-shattering moment for me, but he made a good point. He suggested that I carefully consider what exactly consumed me. What did I think about when no one else was around? What did I think about going from the sofa to the refrigerator? What did I think about when filling up my car at the gas station?

Gerry Spence's opinion reinforced what I'd thought for a long time. The words he used resonated: *being consumed*. Most people will say you should love what you do or enjoy what you do. Enjoy what you do, though, is an oversimplification. If you're ever really good at anything, you don't enjoy it all of the time because there's a chase and a challenge to it that goes beyond enjoyment. There is a certain pain that goes into having truly great success. You will have to overcome a lot of obstacles. He encapsulated all of that.

I thought about law some, but I thought about sports, football in particular, a lot.

Yes—YES!—I should go out and try to become a football coach!

And if he had written back encouraging me to practice the law? I probably would've looked for someone else to tell me what I wanted to hear.

Then again, I could see why some people wouldn't think this was the smartest career choice. At that point, I was married with a child and was flat broke. I owed $45,000 in student loans, so the notion of going to Europe to "find myself" for a year was eliminated. Instead, I did what many professional students do: I decided to get another degree. I attended the United States Sports Academy in Alabama, took out another student loan and earned a master's degree in sports science.

I didn't want to look back on my life and regret never having tried coaching. So I went for it. I loved coaching from the time I was a 15-year-old little league baseball coach. At best, I figured I'd end up coaching college football for a couple of years, then I would go back to law.

One year after I graduated from the Sports Academy, I talked my way into a part-time assistant job at Cal Poly-San Luis Obispo. I called my wife and told her about the salary.

She said $3,000 a month sounds like good money.

"No," I told her, "it's $3,000, total."
But it was a good start.

> *"I receive letters from students often. I am humbled and frightened that what I write or say has such an impact on young people. One must be very careful about what one says or writes. We are taught to respect our elders and to believe them wise when most of us are not. I never learned anything worthwhile from a guru. I have learned more from the honesty of my dogs and kids than from my supposed wise elders.*
>
> *"The greatest gift we can give our youth is to confirm that they are unique and worthy, that they are special in this world since there is no other like them, nor has there ever been. They should be encouraged to follow their passions. I take it that Mike followed his into coaching. His gift to himself became a gift to many others."*
>
> —Gerry Spence

FINDING MY WAY

Why Not Me?

I went to see Michael Jordan play for the Chicago Bulls a few times, but I didn't become a big Jordan fan until I heard that, at the age of 31, he was trading in his high-tops for baseball spikes.

That announcement created quite a commotion. All of a sudden, you had all of these commentators criticizing him for trying to play baseball. I thought that was one of the stupidest reactions I'd ever seen. This guy had accomplished a tremendous amount as a basketball player, led his team to championships, won MVP awards, and now he wanted to check out something else. He wanted to go slay another dragon. I thought he should be admired, not ridiculed. Keep in mind that this guy had been told flat out that he couldn't play basketball after he failed to make his high school team.

But Michael Jordan wasn't picking up a baseball bat for the cynics. He left to play baseball because he wanted to see if he could play baseball.

We have too many "non-tryers" these days. They're afraid of how things may look. Rather than experiencing the journey, they're worried about how they'll be perceived. It's really unfortunate.

Come the spring of 1994 there was a daily Michael Jordan watch from the media. He had a lot of 0-for-4s at the plate. He batted around .200 in Class AA ball, but he did steal 30 bases. The press boys got in their digs and called him "Err Jordan." *Sports Illustrated* put him on their cover. Next to a picture of him breathlessly flailing at a pitch, the headline read: "Bag it, Michael! Jordan and the White Sox are embarrassing baseball." It seemed like people were enjoying watching him struggle. They wanted him to admit that he was overmatched. They wanted him to fail. They loved to report that he didn't do particularly well. The thing about it is, particularly well, compared to whom?

First of all, he got on the team. Most people couldn't even dream of making a team at the professional level. He was athletic enough to compete in not one, but two sports. Everybody wants to gauge Jordan's baseball success by whether he became a major leaguer, hit .300, or played in a World Series. In my eyes, he was an incredible success in baseball. He had the opportunity to try something he was interested in. He had the opportunity to test his abilities in a different field and to see where starting from scratch would take him. You had the greatest athlete in his sport at that time riding busses between dusty little Southern towns playing minor league baseball. In that alone there is something noble. This was a guy that craved experience, wanted to test himself and see what else he could accomplish. Yet all of these people giddily point out that he didn't make it to the major leagues. So he wasn't successful? That's crazy. Just having the desire to be more, to do more, well, that's a big part of the reason why he is Michael Jordan, and that's why I think his baseball experiment was an incredible success.

You never know who you really are until you get out of your comfort zone. Some of the media's take on him was just cowardly. The stories were probably written by some short-sighted guys afraid of independent thought. How dare Michael Jordan step out of his box? He's testing the norms? It's like telling that reporter at *Sports Illustrated* that he should never try to write the Great American

Novel because he'll never be more than a sports journalist, and then ridiculing him if he makes the effort.

Jordan's mindset was a great inspiration for us. When I was at Kentucky our strength coach, Rob Oviatt, had a Jordan quote from his time playing with the "Dream Team" hanging in the weight room:

> *"I saw some Dream Teamers dog it in practice before the Olympics. I looked at them and I knew that was what separated me from them."*

That Jordan quote is more meaningful than ever, since the "Show-Me-The-Money" attitude has been embraced by so many athletes. He could tell from that one practice that it was the difference in his preparation, in his work ethic, that made him the best of the best. It was rooted in his focus, his mindset. That's why "Be Like Mike" can be a powerful message.

I've always believed that you will succeed if you have an unobstructed mentality, as opposed to having some Barney Fife-type frightened reaction to adversity. Don't let fear of failure cause you to hesitate. Hesitation is just like busting a play. It's the same with calling a play or giving direction. When you tell the guys what you want them to run, you have to let them know that you 100 percent believe in what you're calling. Otherwise you diminish your chances of success.

Trying to jump into the football coaching world without having played college ball may seem risky, especially after going through all of the effort and expense of completing law school. I never saw it that way.

When it comes to taking chances and sizing up risk, there are certainly some wrong decisions that get made, but they happen less often than you'd think. What affects an outcome more than anything else is effort and attitude.

About 10 years into my coaching career I was the offensive

coordinator at the University of Kentucky. We'd go for it on fourth down about 40 times a year. That's nearly double the amount of everyone else in the SEC. Statistically, the times we picked up that first down led to touchdowns between two and three times more often than our opponent's touchdown rate if they took the ball over on downs.

The aggressive attitude that you're stoking within your players is key, especially if you're coaching at a program where most of the recruits have repeatedly heard how they're not as talented as their opponents. When we're going for it, we're making a statement: You have to stop us. The team philosophy becomes, "We're going for it." The guys take a lot of pride in that spirit. They also know that if they're unsuccessful too many times you're not going to keep giving them the chance. Almost every player wants to go for it. They don't want the privilege taken away from them. In their minds they know that if they don't make it, they're responsible. They're determined to find a way to make it work.

Certainly any decision needs to be evaluated, but just because "conventional wisdom" suggests something is too risky doesn't make it so. You think it through, and if you believe the benefit outweighs the risk, then you need to do it. Life is a series of risks, and it's about how well you manage them.

Every great thing that has ever happened in my life is the result of taking a risk. Ask yourself, "Why not me?" I would not have married my wife if I wasn't willing to take that shot. We were neighbors in our junior year at BYU and had some mutual friends. I could've sat there and overanalyzed it, thinking, "Uh, well, she's too pretty to go out with me."

"He'd go out on other dates and then after he'd drop them off, he'd stop by my apartment. 'Hey, what's going on?' And he'd just keep talking or he'd come over to watch TV for another hour. I'd have the channel on M.A.S.H. and he'd turn it to watch some Gunsmoke re-run. This

one time, it's like 11 o'clock and he says, 'I'm hungry. Maybe we ought to go to A&W to get something to eat.' That was basically our first date. After that, most of our dates were to fast food restaurants or places where he had two-for-one coupons. Pretty soon, we kept going out and then we both stopped seeing anyone else and we had become best friends."

—Sharon Leach, Mike's wife

Was that really taking a risk? Much of it is rooted in your mindset. If you convince yourself that something is risky, then it is. People assumed that when I walked away from a law career to pursue football coaching, it was a major leap. I didn't see it that way. You have to be disciplined enough to do the routine day-to-day stuff, but also not be afraid to take a shot, especially when the potential payoff is bigger than the risk.

Any time you take a risk you try to make sure that it's well calculated and that there's good value in it. The decision to walk away from the law wasn't a huge risk because I knew I could go back to it, and that knowledge was empowering. Whether it's going for it on fourth down or leaving the law, you just want good value. Do the best you can, and once you make the decision, live with it and go forward because if you have regrets or second-guesses, you're going to hurt yourself.

The year I began coaching college football was the year they limited the number of graduate assistants each team could have at Division I schools. They were cutting quality young coaches. It was impossible to become a graduate assistant at a Division I team because I had no connections. I hadn't been a player, and hadn't had any prior opportunity to build relationships with any coaches. They weren't going to take some slap-dick out of the Sports Academy. The high schools didn't want me either, because I didn't have teaching credentials.

I sent out nearly a hundred résumés, including the one to Cal Poly in San Luis Obispo, California. Lyle Setencich had just been named the new coach there, and his offensive line coach Bill MacDermott called me up. Over the phone I told him about my desire to coach, about how hard I'd worked in college and through law school, but that I wanted to try coaching.

MacDermott was a great O-line coach who at one point had coached Bill Belichick in college. He was intrigued by the law degree and asked why a lawyer wanted to be a football coach? It wasn't really that tough to sell them on the idea of giving me a shot. I was basically free help.

I told them I was committed to learning and was willing to make a lot of sacrifices. They told me they'd pay me $3,000 a year to help coach at Cal Poly, which at the time was a Division II school.

I guess Lyle said to Coach Mac, if the guy shows up, fine, let him work. If it doesn't work out, let him hit the road. So I packed Sharon, my baby daughter Janeen, and what little belongings we had into this big, white '79 Cadillac. We made it from Alabama to California in two days.

We were really excited by the opportunity—I had a foot in the door—though for most of those two days on the road, I kept thinking, "I have no idea how we're going to live on $3,000 a year."

I was a substitute teacher in the off-season to make ends meet. My wife worked at various jobs so we could support ourselves. The three of us ended up living in Mustang Village, the school's off-campus dorm. We slept on mattresses on the floor.

"I'll never forget the day. I was a player and I'm in Coach Mac's office at Cal Poly. This skinny guy, looking like a surfer dude, with his t-shirt hanging out and cut-off jeans comes to the doorway. He goes, 'Hi, uh, I wanna help coach some football.' Coach Mac says, 'Sure, come on

in.' They talked. I just listened. He said he had a law degree. I'm thinking, 'Is this guy for real?' The next thing you know we're out at practice and this guy's out there, every day. Everyone liked him. He was so personable. He assisted Coach Mac for the season and after the year ended, I got hired to be a graduate assistant. Coach Mac says to me, 'That guy right there is going to be a big-time head coach someday. You watch.' I said, 'You're crazy. There's no way. This guy? He doesn't know football. He doesn't look real tough.'

"But when I GAed with him, I figured out pretty quick that Leach was out of my league when it came to intelligence. He has this insight and can see things that other people just can't. I guess it's because he analyzes things so well and asks a lot of questions. He always wanted more knowledge. He analyzes everything. Nothing is cut and dry with him. He thinks above and beyond. He understands movements. In our world, Cover-2 is Cover-2, where you have two half-safeties and two rolled-up corners, but in his eyes, I don't think he sees it that way. He sees more than that. What that is I don't know, but it's on a different level."

—Jim Mastro, assistant coach, UCLA

Throughout my career people have called me asking, "How do you get in? What should I do? Can I do this?" In many cases, I think they're just looking for reassurance, for someone to tell them to ignore their reservations and don't hold back. Or maybe they're waiting for one person to say they're about the make the biggest mistake of their life.

I get a lot of letters, some from law students. I tell the whole Gerry Spence story and tell them you have to be consumed by your passion. I also tell them what I went through to become a coach, and a lot of times I end with the old Bear Bryant Quote: "Don't coach unless you can't conceive of doing anything else."

If they ask me about following their dreams of a coaching career, I tell them they should be prepared to do it for free. The best time to go for it is when you're just out of college, because if you wait until you have two kids, a boat, and a house payment, then it's really hard to change. It's much easier to have nothing and continue to have nothing. There's no better point in your life to be a vagabond for a couple of years.

I did it, and I know how tough it is. I have a lot of admiration for people who take this path. When I got into coaching, I thought I would try to hire guys who had made sacrifices. Of course, more than that even, I wanted to hire the best man for the job.

"I went to the University of Texas for four years, then worked on the Hill for a year under Senator (Joe) Lieberman and went to the Kennedy School to get my Masters at Harvard before going to Harvard Law. My last time playing football was as a senior at Mt. Pleasant High School in Mt. Pleasant, Texas, in 1996. I wasn't good enough to play at UT. So while I was in law school working on a paper for a seminar, I had come up with the idea of writing about coaches with law degrees. I wanted to see if there was any carryover between legal

training and football coaching. My search generated a few names: Derek Dooley, Rick Neuheisel and Mike Leach.

"I tried to contact Neuheisel. I tried to contact Dooley, and it was to no avail. Leach was the most prominent. Two minutes after I called Leach, he called me back. Our first conversation on the phone lasted about two hours. Fifteen minutes was about football, the rest of the time was about everything but. We talked about everything from the Arab-Israeli conflict to the courses I'd taken in my first year of law school to North Korea to quantum physics. He seemed genuinely interested in my experiences. It turned out well for me because he allowed me to sit in his world for a couple of weeks. I was really surprised that he would spend that kind of time with me. He was the antithesis of what you'd think of a football coach in Lubbock. He was a renaissance man. He was as well-read as anyone I encountered at Harvard Law School. The intellectual side of Leach reminded me of the people that I sat in classes with, but there was a daredevil approach to life that was missing from my classmates.

"My talks with Leach probably laid the groundwork for me to make my decision to transition over to coaching. I left Lubbock thinking that there's no better training I could get for football coaching than law school.

Everything that he told me and all the advice that he gave me for ways to break into the profession were all at the forefront of my mind when I was writing my letters to college and NFL teams for jobs.

"After talking to him later, I felt like it wasn't such a great leap. All of my classmates at Harvard were like 'Did you play at Texas? No. Have you worked with anyone closely in the coaching profession? No.' The fact that I wasn't the son of a coach or hadn't played college football didn't cross my mind as much because I had talked to Mike Leach. He worked his way up. I thought to myself I can get in and put the sweat equity in and show that I am willing to work. Whenever someone would say to me, 'You didn't play,' I'd always bring up Mike Leach. He is the precedent. I am pointing back to him. And the other point was that legal issues aren't going anywhere. I could still do that. He helped me with all of the naysayers.

"My guiding philosophy is 'Why not me?' The fact that I had graduated Harvard Law School meant that any decision that I made regarding my career was a low-risk proposition. In my mind, Leach really flipped the risk model."

—Daron Roberts, Detroit Lions secondary coach

Most people aren't going to believe this, but opportunity trumps money. It's true, and I'll say that until I'm blue in the face. Obviously, money is a factor, especially when you're trying to figure out if the powers that be are actually dedicated to you and your program. If they're not going to pay a competitive rate, then it may not be that great an opportunity, unless there are a lot of outside factors that you're considering too.

Several times in my career I've taken less money for what I considered a better opportunity. I even applied for a job coaching high school football down in Key West. That didn't work out. Maybe they didn't think I would leave Valdosta State, where I was making about $48,000, to come coach at Key West High School for considerably less. But a big part of my thinking was about my family.

Imagine how good my kids would be at swimming and fishing right now if I'd been the head coach at Key West High School and raised them down there? Well, I wanted that job very badly. I went down to Key West on my own dime. I was 32, the youngest guy they interviewed, but with the most experience. The guy they ended up hiring had supposedly coached semi-pro football up north somewhere. I think the folks doing the hiring might've gotten caught up on the word "pro," but semi-pro may just be a beer league. I guess they thought he had more "professional" experience. Well, I played in a league they called "a semi-professional baseball league," and didn't get a dime. It was pretty much city baseball for adults. I tried hard to get that job, and it remains the only high school job that I have ever applied for.

As for college programs, I've probably applied for almost every college football coaching job that exists. NFL jobs too. I sent résumés out for years. I filled two boxes full of rejection letters sent back to me on team letterhead. I have them from dozens of famous coaches. You name it. I even got a rejection letter from Charlie Sadler when he was the head coach at Northern Illinois. He later became my defensive line coach at Tech.

Gene Stallings called me from Alabama when I was at Valdosta

State. He told me, "Don't you be afraid to do that. You need to build your career as a young coach, so you shouldn't be afraid to call or write anybody and everybody. Now, I've already got a guy in mind, so I'm not going to hire you, but I hope I meet you somewhere down the road." It was really nice of him.

I received a lot more responses when I was offensive coordinator at Kentucky than when I was at Valdosta State. After the 1997 season at UK, I tried to get the head coaching job at Arkansas, but Houston Nutt got that job instead. I spoke to Frank Broyles about it. Frank told me that he liked me but that he had his eye on some other people first and if he couldn't get them, they'd bring me in.

There's something to the expression "ignorance is bliss." I might not have pursued a college coaching career after law school if I'd listened to most folks in the coaching world. I'm sure I wouldn't have even tried to do a lot of the things I've done in my life if I'd only listened to people who supposedly knew better. If you're not loaded down with reasons why something won't work, the reasons why it can work become much clearer.

One of the people who I have a lot of respect for is Kevin Plank, the former Maryland fullback who started his own company out of his grandmother's basement, and turned it into a billion-dollar business—you may have heard of it, it's called Under Armour. We've become good friends. He's a ridiculously grounded guy. He's still close to a lot of people that he knew before he made it big. He is also awake *all the time*. He hardly sleeps at all. He is one of the most active people I know. Kevin took that whole business on his back. He's told me, "If you're always trying stuff, something's going to work. It doesn't matter what field you're in."

He thinks anything can be done. He is aggressive, and not restricted by convention. He wasn't a Wharton Business School grad. He took the side door in. Heck, he invented his own door. He might've been redirected or set limits on himself if he wasn't broad-minded enough to see beyond the pitfalls that deter most entrepreneurs.

> "I have a saying: 'I was always smart enough to be naïve enough to not know what I couldn't accomplish.' When I started out in the business, I didn't think, 'Oh, crap, I can't compete with these guys with all of their resources.' Instead, it was, 'Screw it. Why not us?' My feeling is that anything I would've gotten into, I would've worked my ass off on. One part of our motto when a lot of people first got to know Under Armour was 'Protect this house.' The other part of that was 'I will.' And that is truly more like a mentality. I. Will. People ask me all the time 'What do I need to do to grow my business from doing one million dollars to 10 million dollars?' The answer is you have to will it to happen. You have to put your head down and find a way."
>
> —Kevin Plank, founder, Under Armour

Iowa Wesleyan

I was a 28-year-old coach when Hal Mumme hired me at Iowa Wesleyan College, an NAIA school with an enrollment of about 550, in Mount Pleasant, Iowa. In the previous three years, I'd been an assistant at Cal Poly, San Luis Obispo, and at College of the Desert in Palm Desert, California, and had coached a team in Pori, Finland, where half my players puffed cigarettes on the sidelines. Hal had just been hired to take over an Iowa Wesleyan program that went 0-10. I'd sent my résumé to him. We spoke on the phone. We both wanted to run a wide-open offense like BYU did.

Hal always tells this story about how when he got to Wesleyan he had 50 of those little yellow call-message notes waiting for him. He thought they were all from prospective assistant coaching candidates. Instead, all but two of them were athletic directors looking to schedule his new team at their homecoming game. The other two yellow notes were from guys looking for work. One was from some gang leader in Los Angeles who said he could bring a bunch of his guys as players to Iowa. The other was from me.

I liked Hal from the moment I met him. He has a natural

charisma and he seemed like a down-to-earth guy. He was smart, and the BYU guys were always really supportive of him. Over the years we made a lot of pilgrimages back to BYU to study their offense. Back then I felt like the best offensive combination was what BYU was running: the 3-step drop, like Dennis Erickson had going at Washington State and later at Miami, plus the Buffalo Bills' no-huddle attack from the Jim Kelly days. There was a lot of good run-n-shoot stuff out there too.

> **"Going down to BYU made my career. The best thing I did was that I kept going back there. You don't really see everything in one year. You might run a route and one year they're playing it with zone and then you come back the next year and they're trying to defend it with a whole bunch of man-coverages."**
>
> **—Hal Mumme**

I was fortunate to have had a great training ground of lower-division schools as I started my coaching career. At various points, I'd worked in Division II, junior college, NAIA, and the European Football League. I was with Hal in Georgia at Valdosta State University at the Division II level. Down there, coaches aren't scrutinized much, and because of that, they can literally run anything they want. There's also a greater disparity in talent between a team's best player (who is probably some Division I transfer that dropped down because he had some baggage) and their worst player (who probably didn't even start for his high school team) than there is in major college football. As a result, those smaller-school coaches try to feature and move guys around to find mismatches, and it all makes for some pretty elaborate formations and plays. Some of it is ingenious. Some of it is really stupid. That doesn't change the fact that you have to be prepared for it.

I saw way more scheme at Iowa Wesleyan than I've ever seen

at the 1-A level. I know I saw way more scheme there than I ever see watching the NFL on Sundays, where teams are often very similar to one another on both sides of the ball. The NFL doesn't possess a ton of independent thought. A lot of teams copy each other.

Before Hal and I got to Iowa Wesleyan, they ran the single-wing offense, an old-fashioned, run-oriented formation that dates back to the early 1900s. In the single wing everyone is lined up tight, the ball is snapped to the quarterback, and he runs like hell. It's as old-school as it gets. Our approach to the offense was a drastic change, and we caused a lot of attrition. We probably ended up having to bring in 50 new players.

What type of players were we seeking? Warm bodies to be honest. We recruited all over the country. We got a bunch from Texas, where Hal had been a really successful high school coach, and a bunch from Illinois and Missouri, in addition to some locals from Iowa. We had less speed than just about every other team on our schedule that first season, but Hal and I were convinced we were still going to win a lot of games.

In these sorts of situations, it's easy to fixate on how the other team has better resources than you do. But it's more important to concentrate on maximizing your own resources instead of worrying about things you can't control. It's a challenge, obviously, because the stronger and faster the other team is, the better they can minimize damage and the better their chances of popping open a big play. Regardless, you just can't spend a lot of time dwelling on what you don't have. Instead, you think about the areas you need to fortify and find your opponent's weaknesses so you can direct your attack. Of course, the better your opponent, the more the temptation there is to worry about them rather than focus on yourself.

I once saw something on the History Channel about the David vs. Goliath story. David evaluated the situation and said,

"Yeah, this guy is really big, but if I'm clear back here and I try to drill him in the head, he'd better be quick enough to duck." So he drills him between the eyes and, sure enough, Goliath goes down.

Could others have prevailed in that situation against Goliath? Maybe, but David was the only one that confronted and overcame his fears and went out there. Were there other people who could've drilled him in the head? Perhaps. Were there other people who could've outmaneuvered Goliath and then stabbed him in a British ships vs. the Spanish Armada kinda way? It's possible, but David controlled his fear, found his strength, and didn't worry about what Goliath could do. He focused on what he needed to do, which was use a slingshot really hard and really accurately from a greater distance than Goliath could target with his spear or lunge with his sword.

Overcoming your fears and whatever other nagging resistance you may have is always the first step to solving any problem. You have to defeat yourself before you defeat someone else.

Football is even tougher because it's a team sport. You need a lot of people to conquer their fears and only worry about their own capabilities. It's difficult to be successful as a team if you go out on the field with a third of the squad non-believers. So you gotta either convert them or get rid of them.

I do kinda wonder if the David vs. Goliath story doesn't get misinterpreted sometimes. What David did was impressive, but it doesn't just illustrate that the little guy went out and beat the big guy, and it was a miracle! It's more an illustration of how if you find a way to master the mental, physical, and spiritual aspects of your life, problems that previously seemed insurmountable suddenly don't seem all that big. Any problem is solvable if you allow yourself the clear-mindedness to find the solution.

Including Hal and myself, Iowa Wesleyan had five full-time coaches (half of what most college teams have) and a lot of volunteer coaches. Hal and I used to go drink coffee at Dickie's Prairie Home.

We'd sit there and talk X's and O's for hours, drawing up plays on napkins. We also went to the Iris Restaurant, which was the nicest place in Mount Pleasant. They once got mad at us because Hal drew up some plays on their cloth napkins.

We tweaked a lot of BYU plays, where we'd change a receiver's route on a given play because we believed it would be more effective. Hal and I would sit there for hours: "If they're in zone (coverage) and we do this, where's the space gonna be? . . . Are they gonna be more vulnerable here or here? . . . If we do this, what depth do we want the receiver to be at? Because the quarterback will read this and he'll need to be right around here."

We got ideas from almost every direction we turned. We ran a lot of crossing routes that were similar to what BYU was doing. Not many teams were using crossing routes. I really like them. It's not an incredibly long throw for the QB to make. More importantly, defenders can get lost in transition as they're chasing their receivers, making decisions difficult about which receiver is getting passed on to which defender. It's pretty disruptive. Give a defender cause for indecision and you just made him play slow. You can have the greatest technique, and all of the strength and speed in the world, but those things are negated if you hesitate. When a player hesitates, it can be as bad as busting a play. If you have a 4.5-forty guy who hesitates, then he's playing like a 4.9 guy. If another guy is a 4.7 guy but he reacts decisively at the snap of the ball, he's probably moving like a 4.5 guy.

We adapted one screen play from the University of Montana. We took another screen, something very close to what is now known as a "Tunnel Screen," from a now-defunct CFL team, the Sacramento Surge, so we called it a Surge Screen. We ran all of these screen passes to get those big defensive linemen to change direction and give chase, and we'd wear them out.

I'd always been surprised at how little most teams threw the ball and how even fewer offenses seemed committed to attacking the *entire* field. We did a lot of things that most other teams on our schedule wouldn't dream of trying. We ran a no-huddle offense.

We believed if you gave the defense less time in between plays to get refocused, they'd get frazzled. Plus, the pace would tire them out faster. The no-huddle would drain them as much mentally as it would physically.

The other programs we faced had their offensive linemen wedged together shoulder to shoulder. We wanted our guys to have wider splits with a three-foot gap between each man. It was an approach we'd seen BYU use successfully. If that was working, we'd widen out the gaps even more. Most people assumed those gaps left your quarterback more vulnerable. For us, it actually did the opposite. It forced the defensive line to stretch so that their defensive ends, who are their best pass rushers, would begin the play even further away from our QB than normal. The wider splits created running lanes and throwing lanes, reducing that glut of traffic you typically have in the middle of the line of scrimmage. And it made it harder for the defense to run stunts that would have otherwise lured our offensive linemen into picking up the wrong man once the ball was snapped.

We were changing the geometry of the game.

It's vital to make things more complicated for the opponent. There are two ways you can do that to a defense: One is to have a whole bunch of plays. But the trouble there is that your offense has to deal with as much complexity as their defense does. The other way is to have less plays, and run them out of lots of formations. That way you don't have to teach a player a new assignment every single time, just a new place to stand.

Simply put: If you wanna screw with the defense, screw with formations, not plays.

We also decided we were going to let our quarterback check to other plays at the line of scrimmage.

Play calling is important, but the more control we could give our quarterback at the line of scrimmage, the more flexible we could be. After all, he was the one in the middle of it. We knew that he could see the defense better than we could from where we were standing. He had information from ground zero.

You had to coach that guy up, but we were going to trust him. He could check to any play he wanted. We let him check from goal line to goal line. Through the course of watching film with us, correcting mistakes and misjudgments in practices and talking about what they saw, our quarterbacks got a firm grasp of what we wanted. We coached them over and over about what they needed to do, which is why we gave them more freedom to check at the line than most other teams did their quarterbacks.

One of the guys Hal brought with him from Texas was Dustin Dewald. He played for Hal at Copperas Cove High School before becoming our quarterback. Dustin set all kinds of national records during his career at Iowa Wesleyan. In one game, he completed 61 of 86 passes. In another three-game stretch, he threw 21 touchdown passes. He had a good understanding of the offense. He was mature. The team desperately needed stability—Dustin provided it.

Why don't more college coaches give their quarterbacks the same freedom? They don't trust them. To me, though, it just makes more sense to run your offense this way. The quarterback can adjust the play call right at the snap. I could guess what is going to work from the sidelines, but the QB has the quickest, most immediate ability to react to what the defense is doing. We relied on him, not so much to get us out of a bad play call, but to give us the opportunity to have a big play.

We didn't approach offense with some bunker mentality, "Oh, they're doing this, we have to protect ourselves!" Instead, it was about how we could best attack them: "OK, they're blitzing from our left side. Good, good. Then let's throw a slant right behind it."

We knew that would give our team the flexibility to attack instantly. There's a blitzkrieg quality to it.

After going winless and averaging less than a touchdown per game the year before we arrived, Iowa Wesleyan went 7-4 our first season. We lost our first two games, each by a field goal, because the players just didn't believe they had the ability to win at first. They knew they were getting better and the confidence started to rise. We finished the year scoring more points than the school had scored in the previous three years combined.

In the off-season after that first year, we pared down our offense. It was one of the best moves we made. We executed better at what we really wanted to run because we had more time to rep it at practice. Over the next two seasons we won 17 games, and in 1991 the Tigers earned a spot in the NAIA playoffs for the first time in their history.

Life at the NAIA level in Iowa was quite a bit different than it had been anyplace else we lived. After Sharon and I, along with our daughter, arrived, we lived in a hideous one-bedroom trailer. It was in a nasty trailer park and I'm pretty sure we had the worst trailer in the place. I had bad allergies and the grass was three feet high outside. There was mold and mildew everywhere.

That trailer was outright creepy. The bathtub leaked all over the bathroom floor. The bedroom looked like something out of a bizarre sexual bondage scene, with two-inch, deep-red shag carpet on the floors, walls, and low ceiling. Nothing is more unnerving than being in a room that is just bright, bright red. The room had a ceiling fan that only had one speed: too fast. Its blades hung down at just about five-and-a-half feet off of the floor. If I wasn't careful, it would hit me right below the nose. The room was so dark that if the lights were off you couldn't see the fan at all, and of course the only switch was on the other side of the room. I nearly got drilled in the face more than once with that thing. But the place was free through the school.

My salary was $12,000 a year, and after a few months in that trailer we rented the downstairs of a drafty old house behind an insurance office. The owner wrapped the exterior of the house every winter with plastic to keep the wind and cold from ripping through. Sharon, who was pregnant with our second daughter,

Kimberly, worked for Hal as his secretary.

I was the offensive line coach, the offensive coordinator, the recruiting coordinator, the equipment manager, the video coordinator, and the sports information director. I also taught two classes. As the sports information director, it was my job to try and get some publicity for our team. I helped get Iowa Wesleyan College written up in *USA Today* three times that year.

My role as the sports information director fell under the supervision of Iowa Wesleyan's director of public relations. She was very controlling and had more clout at the school than she probably deserved.

She didn't appreciate the national attention from *USA Today*. In her mind, the SID was supposed to write a press release about the game's outcome and then mail it to the papers around the state. Her system made no sense. This was before email, and the mail wouldn't go out till Monday, meaning the papers wouldn't receive it till Tuesday or Wednesday. By the time they got the score, statistics, and information on the game, it was no longer relevant. Since the information was so untimely, they wouldn't bother with writing a story.

I had a better idea.

I'd call the *Burlington Hawk Eye*, the *Des Moines Register*, and all of the other papers with our score from Saturday so that they— and through them our potential recruits—would know how we did. When you're a lower division school it's difficult enough to get the attention of recruits without hiding your results.

She wanted to be an autocrat. She didn't pay attention to football. She probably thought that the *Des Moines Register* and the *Burlington Hawk Eye* actually attended our games and hand wrote the play-by-play from the press box. That couldn't have been farther from the truth. I called them up and walked them through every game. I called pretty much any media outlet that would listen.

We were breaking all kinds of school records and led the nation in passing. I kept reaching out to *USA Today* and before long they began writing about us. Well, someone told her that her school was in *USA Today* and she got all flustered. She called me screaming, "How dare you contact *USA Today*?"

"Mike, I know you've been talking to other newspapers and that's bullshit. I told you that you have to write a press release and mail it out, so that it's fair for everyone. So everyone gets the information at the same time. It's not fair to the weekly newspapers. I know for a fact there was an article in *USA Today* about Iowa Wesleyan."

I explained a number of times how ridiculous it was for the papers to get the Iowa Wesleyan score on Wednesday. By then, they're supposed to be talking about who we were playing next, not who we played five days ago. It's called "news" after all.

She was incredulous. "That's bullshit," she said, going on about how it's not fair to those weekly papers in the state. "That's bullshit, Mike!"

I told her, "Iowa Wesleyan sports information has gotten Iowa Wesleyan into *USA Today* three times this year. Your office couldn't get Iowa Wesleyan into *USA Today* unless there was a mass murder on campus."

About an hour later, the president of the school came into the football office. His face is bright red. "You're banned," he shouted. "You're banned from the campus! You're banned from campus for three days!"

"I had a meeting with the president. I went in there loaded for bear. But the president was just laughing about the whole thing. He was a big, gregarious guy. He sat there puffing on his pipe and laughing about the vision of Leach having words with the public relations director over getting Iowa Wesleyan into *USA Today*. Getting into *USA Today* at Iowa Wesleyan is pretty hard to do.

"Mike is the most brutally honest person I've ever met. He's not going to back down on what he believes. If he believes that he is right, he will not back down. He's a highly principled guy. I admire that."

—Hal Mumme

It was during my time at Iowa Wesleyan that I became enamored with Key West. I'd drive all over the country with Hal for recruiting and coaching clinics. There was about a foot and a half of snow on the ground most of the winter, so we bought Jimmy Buffet's album *AIA* thinking that would warm things up a little in the car. I'd started listening to Buffet during law school in Los Angeles. Buffet definitely romanticized Key West and that lifestyle. Hal immediately liked it.

One year, Charlie Moot, our defensive coordinator, and I took a three-week recruiting trip through Missouri, Arkansas, Mississippi, Alabama, Texas, and all the way through Florida riding in his Dodge Dynasty. Charlie was a funny guy. He said he always wanted to be a Marine and a football coach, and he'd become both. He was in his early 40s, and was one of those guys who wasn't from Texas, but had become a Texan. He was actually from Ithaca, New York. That fact didn't seem to matter to him one bit.

There's a saying people outside of Texas have, along the lines of, "The only thing that's more annoying than a person from Texas is a person who grew up someplace else and moved to Texas, and wishes he were native Texan." Charlie was one of those, but I still enjoyed being around him. He was completely committed to the coaching and recruiting lifestyle. He knew everyone. Many of the best recruiters seem to.

Charlie loved to drive. There is a certain peacefulness you can get when you're riding all over this great country, just absorbing

Americana. Charlie was one of those guys who could drive forever. He'd be driving along and you'd look over and he would be peeing in a Big Gulp cup. We had a lot of laughs on that trip.

I was the younger coach and he was older. We'd head into town and split a hotel room. Then, I'd rent a car and we'd each go off in our own directions trolling for players.

Hal wanted me to make my way to Key West and find out more about it because Buffet had made the place sound so intriguing. Charlie and I reconnected in Miami for a bit. Then, I drove on my own further down to Key West. It was over the weekend when you couldn't recruit, and since Iowa Wesleyan didn't have the funds to fly me back for the weekend, I checked into a room at the Budget Inn by the IHOP in Key West. I had a blast down there. It was a lot like I thought it'd be: people from all walks of life, a great place to people-watch and just hang out.

Key West was about as different from Mount Pleasant as our offense was from the single wing. After that trip, I was convinced Key West was a place I wanted to live at some point in my life. I just didn't know how it would fit in with my coaching career.

Valdosta

Hal was hired as the new head coach at Valdosta State in Valdosta, Georgia in 1992. We'd spent three seasons at Iowa Wesleyan College together, transforming what had been a winless program into one that, in our final year, won 10 games and advanced to the NAIA playoffs for the first time in school history.

Hal asked me to come join him at Valdosta. I knew he was going to rise in the coaching world. He had enthusiasm, focus, and optimism. He was clearly a cutting-edge guy. We were on the brink of something big. I jumped at the chance to go with him.

Valdosta, which is located just north of the Florida border, was an NCAA Division II program. The area was known for its high school football. The coach at Valdosta High, Nick Hyder, had won seven state championships and three national titles. At the time we arrived in Valdosta, Hyder, who was a terrific man, had won six state titles in a 10-year stretch. You can feed off that kind of success.

Whenever people talk about how football is a religion in the South, Valdosta (pop. 43,000) is what they have in mind. Football links generations and connects all parts of their community. The *New York Times* wrote about how football helped usher the town through integration in the '60s. *Sports Illustrated* had done this big story on Valdosta High football a few years before we arrived. The town had nicknamed itself "Winnersville."

Still, what we were doing offensively was radically different from what the folks down there were used to. There was a mixed reaction about us bringing a more wide-open attack into the Gulf South Conference. Though some people were excited, many more were skeptical. The supporters were friendly enough, but they just weren't sure about us. The local newspaper didn't think our offense would work at all. Sometimes people would come up to me at the coffee shop and say, "I hope you guys do well, but you know, you're gonna have to run the ball up the middle here."

I'd say, "Well, we'll see how it goes." And I'd usually leave it at that, but if they got too aggressive with their skepticism, I'd point out, "That run-it-up-the-middle stuff had already been tried there and it hadn't worked. So let's see what happens when you try to attack all portions of the field and utilize all of your offensive players, not just the guys in the backfield." If they didn't buy that, I'd tell them the definition of insanity is doing the same thing over and over again and expecting different results.

It was fun chatting with them because we knew how much they were into it, and we had no doubt we were going to win big. Plus, the people were so warm and friendly. The first time we visited Valdosta, I was in a restaurant with my family and we were talking about where we might live. Someone overheard us. They said, "Hey, are you looking for a place?" And they gave us all of these suggestions. Right away, we were touched by how everyone in the town treated each other like family.

> **"Mike is the only reason I even applied for the Valdosta job. I was working on trying to get the University of South Dakota job. Mike comes to me, "You oughta go after this Valdosta State job. They have a swimming pool right next to the football offices!" I said they're provincial,**

Mike. They're not gonna hire anybody from Iowa, especially when they find out I'm from Texas. But if you really want to, you can send them my information.

"One month later, I get a call from this real estate person in Valdosta trying to sell me a house. I'd forgotten about the Valdosta thing. I didn't know I actually got the job till that person called.

"Then our first Christmas in Georgia, we're all at a party. The AD's wife tells me the reason I got the job was because of the video I had sent with my résumé. That was the first I'd heard of any video. Turns out, Mike had included this video of our highlights at Iowa Wesleyan that he had made and set to music to send out to all our alumni, to try and raise money to offset the costs of our flight to Morehead, Minnesota, for the NAIA playoffs. She tells me her husband would watch that video at night and go, 'I can sell this.'"

—Hal Mumme

Valdosta State usually hovered just above .500. They had really good players. A lot of what they did system-wise paralleled what they were doing at the University of Georgia, right down to their red-and-black color scheme. On offense they were a power running team, also similar to Georgia.

The quarterback was a 5-foot-10 guy named Chris Hatcher, who had just finished his freshman season as a starter. He was a very smart guy, real accurate too, but he was shorter than what most programs like for their quarterbacks to be. His best attribute was his leadership. He had the whole team behind him.

I learned a lesson that first year at Valdosta. We tried to do too much. We lost three of our first four games and finished 5-4-1 in 1992. Our players had good speed, were aggressive, and very committed to football. We made the mistake of assuming that since they were talented and passionate about football, they were sharp enough to retain as much information as we could throw at them. They could not. They didn't necessarily pick it up any faster than the guys at Iowa Wesleyan. Yeah, they could run faster and lift more weight than the players at Iowa Wesleyan, but they still needed time to let what we taught them sink in. We tried to install too much too quickly.

One of the biggest mistakes coaches make is over-tweaking the playbook. They mess themselves up by constantly tinkering and putting too much in, or by trying to run too many different plays, and they end up overlooking what they really need to do. It's not about tricks. It's about execution. You need to get sharper running the plays in your bag by focusing on technique:

Are our hips low? Are we getting our heads around? Are
our eyes in the right place? Where were our hands?

How can you be precise with all of the detail that's vital to making a play work properly if you're giving them dozens of different plays to digest? You can't. We need all of that detail stuff to become second nature, so the players can just react and do precisely what they did in practice.

Technique is more important than scheme. People wanna say, "scheme, scheme, scheme." No matter what plays you run, technique is always more important. You have a chance with whatever you run, if you have great technique. If you have a great scheme but you don't execute it well, you have no chance.

Coaches are their own worst enemies. We constantly draw

ourselves into the trap of doing too much with a play. It reminds me of watching TV as a kid. I'd be sitting there enjoying some show. Then my dad would come in and start monkeying with the picture. Pretty soon, nobody could watch anything.

When that first season ended we spent a day with Raymond Berry, one of the best receivers in the history of football. He said in his career he hardly ever lined up on the other side of the field. He viewed that as a big asset. He was able to really develop his skills by catching the same balls from the same positions.

> **"Raymond drew up the formation in the ground where he played, and where (Baltimore Colts wide receiver) Jimmy Orr played, and where (Colts tight end) John Mackey played, and he says, 'I caught all the passes in my career from this side. It'll work, coach. It'll be real good.' So we did it. Our quarterback Chris Hatcher went from completing in the mid 60s to being an over-71-percent passer in one year. A lot of it was just because the split end and the tight end caught the ball from the same side of the field and we had cut the reps in half for those routes. We've been doing it ever since.**
>
> **When we tell people that's how we do it and why, they have this paranoid look. Like somebody's gonna know what you're doing. I always go back to something I heard from Bill Walsh one day. He said you know it's not a rule in football that you have to have a symmetrical offense. Just 'cause you run a play to the right doesn't mean you have to run it also to the left. I always adhered to that."**
>
> **—Hal Mumme**

Raymond Berry didn't flop sides. Almost every fade route Raymond ever caught was on the left. He really developed his skills and got good at catching balls over that shoulder because he had twice as many repetitions to work on it.

The other thing we realized is that just because we had a play from the right side, it didn't mean we had to run the same play from the left side too. Lots of coaches think if you don't run the mirrored version of a play (like having a Student Body-Right to go with your Student Body-Left), the other team will be all over what you're doing. But our quest wasn't about trying to fool 'em. We wanted to out-execute them. You're better off having the play run from one side and giving your guys a lot more repetitions at it, so they learn to execute it better.

One significant advantage offense has over defense is that the offense runs their package more than any defense works on defending it. An offense can run the plays that they rep every day, providing they're not changing things all the time. A defense has to work against a variety of different offenses throughout the season. They can't work against the same offensive scheme every week because the teams vary. They simply don't have as much time to fine-tune their execution as the offense does.

It's not that you should feel above "tricking" them, but there's no long-term pay-off with that method. If the play works, it's usually a one-shot deal. However, if the play is based on technique and execution, you can run it many times in the course of a game. Changing formations and motioning players helps disguise the same play. It'll look much different to the defense, but there is very little change for the offense, leaving them to focus on their technique and execution.

That first season at Valdosta we averaged 25 points per game. In each of the next two seasons we averaged 41 points per game. In 1994, our third season at Valdosta, we advanced to the NCAA Division II playoffs for the first time in school history. Hatcher, our quarterback, won the Harlon Hill Award, which is the Heisman Trophy for Division II. We made it to the quarterfinals before losing to North Alabama in double overtime, and only after they blocked our field goal attempt that would've tied the game.

Word about what we were doing had started to spread in the football circles. They saw we were near the top of the national rankings in most offensive categories. Coaches from all over the country said they wanted to come in and watch film and talk football with us, or have us visit them to share ideas. We met with coaches from Auburn, Florida State, and Georgia, among others. We were pretty open about explaining what we were doing. After all, it's all on film, and for the most part college coaches are typically open about sharing this stuff. I suspect it's partially because they aspire to coach at other places and bigger schools, and they're eager to let others know how good they are. We were happy enough to talk because we loved what we did, plus, we figured we could learn from them, too.

Valdosta was a great place to coach. It's the one school that I've worked at where, when we lined up, we were usually physically better than the guys across from us. Everyone in town embraced our offense once they saw the results we were getting.

I'd tripled my salary from Iowa Wesleyan, going from $13,000 to the high 30s. But we had two kids to feed, daycare costs, and big, hungry student loans to pay back. In the off-season, I took classes so I could defer my student loan payments. I took Greek Philosophy, History of Cuba, History of the Caribbean, and Contemporary Art. I would've kept teaching, as I'd done at Iowa Wesleyan, but Valdosta State had a rule against football coaches in the classroom. I felt a lot of pressure because money was so tight. My salary had increased a little. Our expenses had increased a lot.

The nomadic existence for coaches at smaller schools can really rattle a family. I have the utmost respect for football wives and the sacrifices they make to hold everything together. Being a coach is not a 9 to 5 job. The hours are brutal. The recruiting travel is insane. Back at Iowa Wesleyan I'd be on the road three weeks at a time. It's easy to be completely consumed by the job. That's why coaching marriages have a higher divorce rate than the national average.

I can see why a lot of guys don't stay with college coaching. The money can be better and it is a lot more stable if you're working at a high school program rather than working your way up from a small college program. Even if you are fortunate enough to rise up the college ranks, your family is going to end up moving around a lot. With the exception of Joe Paterno, the question isn't if you're gonna move, it's when you're gonna move.

Did I ever thinking of walking away and going back to law? It crossed my mind, especially in Iowa, but I took comfort in the knowledge that I could always go back and practice law if all else failed. Initially, I'd figured I'd give coaching two or three years and then assess where I was. But we kept advancing. Our team was getting better. We were building and that was exciting. I kept getting sucked in more and more. Each year was either a better job or an improving team, and the promise of next year always seemed worth the chance.

At Valdosta my family was breaking even financially, but our student loans still hung over us. We'd get these threatening calls and letters from the lenders, but I always saw my coaching career as a process. I was blessed that Sharon stuck with me. She was always steady. Anytime I sounded like I was wavering, she was really supportive and totally solid. Knowing the sacrifices she was making brought us even closer.

Sharon worked as an administrative assistant. We shared one car—an old, white Cadillac Deville that I'd bought in Mobile, Alabama, for $1,500 before I even got into coaching. It had almost 200,000 miles on it, but I rarely drove it. I'd bike to work so Sharon could use it. We were really busy all the time and we were quickly outgrowing our little two-bedroom, two-bath apartment.

Valdosta, though, was a fun place to live. I loved that town. I loved the pride of the place; they were committed to everything they did, whether it was cooking, telling a story, or digging a hole. I loved how football was so important to their way of life.

The Deep South is a lot like the state of Wyoming, except in Wyoming we had worse weather and bigger mountains. In both places, everybody drives a pick-up truck. Everyone hunts and fishes. Everyone takes so much pride in what they do. They're tough, committed people.

It was also the time in my life when my kids were growing up. My son Cody was born there. My oldest daughter Janeen went to this predominantly black elementary school. I really liked that she was exposed to people who were different from her, and different from what she already knew. I didn't want to shelter my kids. It would help toughen her up, make her more self-reliant. She was young for her grade, the youngest one in all her classes. But she never batted an eye. She got along great with the other kids. Years later, Janeen told me that whenever she heard people talk about how there was racial tension in the Deep South, she would remember how when she lived in Valdosta she never felt any of it because everybody got along well there.

When I wasn't coaching, I'd work with her on softball. I'd come home from work at 9 or 10 at night and wake Janeen up. We'd walk over to this tennis court that had lights and practice for an hour or two every night. We'd work on throwing, catching and hitting. I'd play Add One/Subtract One with her, where she had to throw 25 good fastballs, 10 good change-ups, and 10 good drop-balls. If she threw a good pitch, it counted. If she threw a bad one, I'd subtract it from the running total. I told her, if you're going to do something, you're gonna be good at it. And she was. Even though she was often one of the smallest on her team, she was always among the best.

I thought it was important for her to do well in sports. I knew we were going to move around a lot because of my career, and if she was always the new kid in school, softball would help her adjust socially and find friends more quickly.

For all of the clubs that exist on a school's campus, none equal an athletic team insofar as working together. You develop a competitive attitude and learn to battle through adversity with your friends by your side. Those are great lessons to learn. At the same time, the blending of people from different backgrounds can make an impact on a person that extends far beyond sports. Athletics have done more to bring people together than any government or law. Nothing has done more for race relations than athletics. Nothing.

I started with Janeen when she was six and we practiced together all throughout our time in Valdosta. She later became all-district as a pitcher for four straight years and is now a doctor. Growing up in Valdosta was great for her. It was great for our entire family.

In 1996, we averaged 39 points per game. We broke the school record for rushing in a season with over 2,000 yards, and almost broke our own school record for passing again. Lance Funderburk, our quarterback after Chris Hatcher, was the runner-up for the Harlon Hill Award. But we lost in the quarterfinals of the playoffs to Carson-Newman. It would be our last game at Valdosta.

Three days after the loss to the Eagles, Hal was hired to be the head coach at the University of Kentucky. I heard through the channels that a lot of people were surprised that he landed that job. I wasn't. Hal always believed in us, and in himself. We were doing things in a big way.

I could've stayed in Valdosta and possibly become the next head coach. I was intrigued by the idea of doing it on my own, but experience-wise I knew I had to go to Kentucky. I still had things to learn, not to mention it was an opportunity to make inroads into Division I. After all, it's easier to maneuver in the pond you're already in.

We'd gone from NAIA in Iowa, to Division II in Georgia, to a team in the toughest college football conference in the country, the SEC. I was excited about the challenge, but it was bittersweet. I've lived in some great places. I've lived in some horrible places. Valdosta, Georgia, is the only place I've ever cried over leaving.

Kentucky

The skepticism over our new, more open offense at Valdosta was nothing compared to what people said when we entered the big, bad SEC. Folks would call up the radio station or write to the newspaper claiming we weren't bringing anything but a bag full of gimmicks. They didn't know what they were talking about. Our system was fundamentally sound. An offense doesn't just accidentally work.

C.M. Newton got it. He was the Kentucky athletic director that hired Hal. The most important thing that Hal had going for him in making the transition from a Division II program right into the SEC was that C.M. had done essentially the same thing in his own career. Bear Bryant hired C.M. right from Transylvania College in Kentucky, an NAIA school, to be the head basketball coach at Alabama in 1968.

C.M. knew that the big barrier to the Division I level was complete B.S. Through his basketball background he understood the principles of space and tempo, and the effect both could have on a game. Heck, his first move as Kentucky's A.D. was hiring Rick Pitino as the Wildcats basketball coach after the program got hit with an NCAA probation. C.M. had a lot of stroke there.

Other administrators would've been scared. Other guys might've thought, "Well, we have to go with a 'three-yards-and-a-cloud-of-dust' offense since this is the SEC." I saw them doing the same thing for years, and thought it just made it all the more stupid.

We'd hear all about how rough and tough and physical SEC offenses had to be. These skeptics would cite examples of how so-and-so won SEC titles by running over teams. Well, if someone overpowers you and they just run it up the middle, that doesn't mean the offense is better, it just means the players were more talented.

If they asked, we'd tell them: "How do you get the most out of your offense? You utilize all of your people. You attack all parts of the field."

To me, there's nothing less relevant than moving up a level in coaching. After all, the rules are the same. Yeah, you're playing against better players, but it's relative. Your players are better too. Before our first game at Kentucky, I heard so much about how dominant the SEC defensive linemen were. Well, shouldn't our offensive linemen be pretty big and talented? It's ridiculous. "OK, great. Your corners are like Deion friggin' Sanders. Did it occur to you that my receivers might also be like Jerry friggin' Rice?" I didn't get it then and I don't get it now.

The fact that someone coaches in the SEC doesn't mean that he's any smarter than someone who coaches at a small college or in high school. Yeah he might be smarter, but then again he might not be. If some sheer unadulterated moron gets hired in the SEC, that doesn't mean he's automatically a smarter coach, it just means whoever hired him made a big mistake.

Running our offense in the SEC was going to be a challenge, but we had no doubt the stuff we were bringing was going to work there.

When C.M. hired Hal, he said Hal was someone who would put the fun back in Kentucky football. The team had finished 4-7 and was ranked 109th in offense the year before we arrived. The Wildcats had not had a winning season in eight years.

We inherited some talented players. Tim Couch was a 6-foot-5 quarterback who'd been the top recruit in the country when he signed with Kentucky. Before Kentucky hired Hal, Couch thought about transferring. The previous staff apparently told him they were gonna throw it and they really didn't. He didn't want to run the option. Tim watched film from our offense at Valdosta and he loved it.

We loved him too. Tim was quiet but had this confident demeanor. He was a guy the entire team loved. He would hang out with anybody. His work ethic was off the charts. He was as hard a worker as I'd been around to that point. We were excited about him.

The guy who had been the starting quarterback, Billy Jack Haskins, was a really popular guy with the fans. Hal tried to talk him into being a slot receiver in our offense. Haskins then called a press conference to announce he was transferring. That only added to the skepticism over what we were doing.

About midway through the first half of our season opener, we gained a whole lot of true believers. Couch threw three first-quarter touchdown passes and ended up with a school-record 398 passing yards as we upset Louisville 38–24. The previous year they'd beaten Kentucky by 24 points.

Couch really fit our offense. He was the all-time leading passer in the history of high school football. He was big and athletic. He had these enormous hands, which is something you like to see in a quarterback. Those help because the ball doesn't get easily shaken loose in traffic and he had a better handle in bad conditions.

We tweaked the offense some. Hal hired Guy Morriss, the old All-Pro center for the Philadelphia Eagles, to be our O-line coach. He wanted tighter line splits. We found a happy medium. There wasn't as much pocket space, but Tim had such great pocket awareness and nimble feet, he could get off passes that most other quarterbacks couldn't.

About one month into the season we beat #20 Alabama 40–34 in overtime after Couch threw a touchdown pass to Craig Yeast. It was the first time that Kentucky had defeated the Crimson Tide since 1922. Fans stormed the field and tore down the goalposts. George Blanda, who was a football legend and had played at Kentucky, came into our locker room after the game, and so did Turner Gregg, the last Wildcat quarterback to beat Alabama. Turner was in his late 90s. He said he had two goals in life: the first was to see UK beat Alabama again and the second was to live to be 100.

They wheeled him into our locker room to present Couch with the game ball. As he's handing it over he pulled Tim in close by his jersey and whispered something in his ear. We later asked Couch what he said: "He chewed me out for not getting them out of the huddle fast enough."

The school really got behind us. Kentucky's marketing and the sports information staff really pushed the "Air Raid" handle for our offense. The stadium would even blow an air horn during games. There were Air Raid t-shirts and bumper stickers all over the state.

"The whole Air Raid thing was Mike's idea. He came up with it when we were at Iowa Wesleyan. I was never for labeling, but he saw how Steve Spurrier was calling his system when he was winning at Duke "Air Ball." Mike goes, 'We'll call ours 'Air Raid.' He tried to sell me on it. I didn't really care. Then, when we got to Valdosta the father of one of our receivers, Sean Pender, would stand at the top of the stadium and blow this air raid siren every time we scored. And we scored a lot there. The rival

coaches hated it. The Gulf South Conference passed a rule saying you couldn't have noise makers in the stadium. So they went across the street and put the air raid siren on top of the KA house."

—Hal Mumme

That kind of branding works well in sports. It can be a powerful rallying force if you get your fan base to identify with it. People love to be part of something bigger than themselves, and all that enthusiasm helps the coaches as much as it does the players. Hal was loved. The school created these Hal Mumme masks on popsicle sticks, which started popping up everywhere. I got the sense that Hal didn't like those masks. All the coaches had a Hal's Face-on-a-Stick mask in their offices. We'd hold 'em up to our faces and talk to each other. He was a good sport about it.

We improved from 109th in the country in offense to sixth, but we finished the season 5-6. We should've gone to a bowl that first year. We lost three games where we had a chance to win on the road: at Mississippi State, at South Carolina, and at Georgia. We also set the school record in attendance, averaging over 59,000 per game, up from 40,000.

Moving to Kentucky didn't just mean a bigger stage for our offense, but also, for the first time, Sharon and I could afford to buy a home. We bought a three-bedroom house with a big backyard. Sharon didn't have to work any more. She'd spent most of our marriage making more money than I did. It had been hard on her that she had to work and couldn't be home to watch the kids. We were all happier. Bouncing our older daughter, Janeen, around between daycare and babysitters until we got to Kentucky is the single biggest regret I have. Janeen weathered it pretty well. She always had the best grades in school, was really happy and had grown to be a good athlete. She was playing in two softball leagues around town—one an Under 14 league, the other an Under 18 league, even though she was only 13. My younger daughter, Kimberly, really took to Lexington too.

We had more and more coaches come visit UK to see what we were doing on offense. One of the coaches who came through in the off-season was a young receivers coach at Notre Dame, Urban Meyer. He wanted to see our drills, plays, all of it. He was such a big student of the game. He spent two days with us. It was a lot of fun to talk football with him. You could tell he was going to do big things in football. Urban has amazing focus and vision.

There was a buzz building around Couch and Kentucky. People were talking about him as a Heisman contender. We opened the 1998 season on the road at Louisville and beat them 68–34. Tim threw for 498 yards and seven touchdowns. We got off to a 4-2 start. We were averaging 40 points per game. Next up was 21st-ranked LSU on the road. Kentucky had not beaten a ranked team on the road since 1977.

My all-time favorite road trip was that visit to LSU. I have coached in a lot of fantastic atmospheres, but LSU is the greatest place to play.

The fun started when we left the hotel, which is only about a half-mile away from the stadium as the crow flies. Usually in the SEC, you're given a motorcycle police escort that whips through crowded highways at 80 mph. Some of these highway patrol guys are pulling off death-defying maneuvers as they run interference for the team bus. LSU is the total opposite. Their escort took us on a slow, circuitous route covering several miles, through a dilapidated, menacing neighborhood that looks like the opening scene from the movie *Blue Chips*.

There were rusted cars on blocks, old living room furniture in the front yards, and the streets were lined with people that you wouldn't want to meet in a dark alley. It's on the edge of the Bayou, and debris was scattered around from the last time they had high water—my guess was the day before.

As the bus rolled into the grounds of Tiger Stadium, it had to work its way through a huge crowd of people that got denser and denser as we went further into the heart of darkness. Most of them had been out there drinking for about a week. Soon enough the mass of people start pushing and rocking the sides of the bus and chanting, "TIGERBAIT! TIGERBAIT! TIGERBAIT!" There's everything from little old ladies to children, and they're all yelling "TIGERBAIT" and flipping you off: "Fuck you, Kentucky. You suck!"

We pulled up to park, and there's a big, fat, hairy guy right in front. Shirt off, gut hanging out, he went up to Hal's window and flips him off with both hands. "Fuck you, Hal Mumme. FUCK YOOOOOOOU, KENTUCKY!"

With a police officer standing right there, Big Fat Hairy Guy proceeds to drops his pants, bend over and show his ass to our bus for about 30 seconds. I just start laughing and so do most of the people on our bus. The excitement is huge and we haven't even gotten out of our seats yet.

Hal was chuckling. He loves the pageantry of college football.

As our team stepped off the bus, all of the LSU fans formed a gauntlet so we could only go by them in single file. The LSU fans don't pinch you or hurt you, but they clutch at you. It's almost like being in a zombie movie. When we finally made it inside the stadium we were greeted by the worst locker room in the SEC (aside from Mississippi State's). They have really low ceilings, and there's mold and mildew all over the place. Pipes everywhere. Some hot. Some not-so-hot. Some hissing with steam, like they might explode. Most players took a wide detour around the loudest hissing pipes. You could smell the swamp, and a decade's worth of stink left by teams that had been there before.

That morning I read up on the great traditions at LSU. The old dorms are still embedded into the stadium, with windows overlooking the field. I wished that I lived there. They had an old "H-shaped" goal-post in one endzone.

I also read about their mascot, the tiger, and how they'd

park its cage at the mouth of the tunnel to the opposing locker room. Amazingly, the story went on to describe how they'd use a stick with a nail on the end to poke the tiger, so he would roar at the opposing players as they came out of the locker room. They pointed out with sincere disappointment that the Humane Society stepped in, and they're not allowed to jab at their tiger with a stick any more.

Nowadays "Mike" the tiger is waiting for you at the end of the tunnel. I thought I had a pretty good sense of how big a Bengal Tiger is, but I had no idea. He's enormous. His eyes are the size of my fists. The bars on that cage they keep him in are no bigger than the thickness of my finger. There is no doubt in my mind that if that tiger wanted to get out of that cage, he's getting out. I went over to examine him. I felt like my chances of survival were high because he had lots of people to choose from for a snack. He looked a little bored.

It's one big, intense, hostile place. We were a double-digit underdog, but we beat LSU that day, 39–36. Couch threw for almost 400 yards and we ran for nearly 200 more. I imagine Big Fat Hairy Guy was pretty miserable that night.

Death Valley's actually not the loudest stadium I've been in. It's not even the loudest in the SEC. When we played Arkansas in Memorial Stadium in Little Rock, there were 45,000 people packed inside this giant, solid concrete amplifier. It creates an effect that's like a lot of kids screaming and yelling in an empty basement, where everything echoes. You're out there barking the cadence, "Go" and it's GO-GO-GO-GO-GO, or HIT-HIT-HIT-HIT-HIT. Everything you'd say would come back five times. If you multiply those 45,000 fans times four or five, it ends up sounding like 200,000 people are yelling at you. Then they'd shoot off a Howitzer at the start of each half, and anytime Arkansas scored. It was deafening.

In my opinion, the loudest place on Earth is the closed end zone at South Carolina. The distance from the back of that end zone to the crowd is about the length of my arm, and the stands go straight up. It's just this wall of people. The stadium overall isn't as loud, but that spot at Williams-Brice Stadium is like nothing else in college football. It's just sheer noise.

Little Rock was the loudest overall, but Florida is really loud too. I'm surprised you don't hear as much about Georgia, because Sanford Stadium is really loud, maybe just about as loud as Florida.

Big 12 stadiums aren't generally designed to be as loud as the stadiums in the SEC. You still need to use a silent count most places in the conference, but generally the fans are further from the field. Texas A&M is the loudest in the Big 12. Next, I'd say it's Nebraska or Oklahoma. These three are really loud. Texas is not as loud. Oklahoma State, their fans are more obnoxious than loud. That stadium has very small sidelines, though Colorado wins the award for having the smallest sidelines I've ever seen.

I've heard that in the Pac-10, other than at Oregon, you don't even need to use silent counts. In the SEC, you needed to use them every game, except maybe at Vanderbilt. The Big 12 is the same, you have to use them in most every game.

I don't actually like the travel part of playing away—the airports, the hotels, the change in the routine. But I love seeing the other stadiums and experiencing the other schools' traditions. Each place has its own personality. The SEC had so many fantastic places. I love hostile crowds, it reinforces how important the game is to everyone. Some crowds will say or do clever things. They all have their own memorable chants or fight songs, from Tennessee's "Rocky Top" to Arkansas's "Woo Pig Sooie!" Home field is an advantage because of the distractions created by the home fans. What they say, no matter how over the top, doesn't cause a problem, but the overall commotion can damage communication. That's the biggest problem, all that ruckus makes it tougher to communicate quickly, and it can break down your tempo.

I like mean, nasty crowds. A&M was my probably my favorite trip in the Big 12. They have a huge stadium, grand traditions, and good, old-fashioned, hostile fans. The student section was great.

It was always hot outside. There was an overwhelming sense of accomplishment for you and your team to win in such a hostile environment. Younger teams sometimes have trouble eliminating the distractions, but if your team has the right mentality, the atmosphere energizes them.

We finished the regular season 7-4, and earned a trip to play Penn State in the Outback Bowl in Florida. It marked the first time Kentucky had been invited to play in a New Year's Day bowl since Bear Bryant coached UK in 1951.

Tim finished fourth in the Heisman voting, the highest for a Kentucky player in over 30 years. My name was getting out in the coaching world.

Bob Stoops had just been hired to be the new head coach at the University of Oklahoma after working as Steve Spurrier's defensive coordinator at Florida. Hal told me Stoops was very interested in hiring me as his offensive coordinator. Bob came to several of our bowl practices in Tampa.

I'd toyed with the idea of leaving UK and Hal a year earlier, and I'd interviewed for jobs at Middle Tennessee, Louisiana-Lafayette, and talked briefly with Arkansas. Working for Bob at Oklahoma sound like a great deal. Stoops came up under three great coaching mentors: Hayden Fry at Iowa, where Bob was a terrific player; Bill Snyder at Kansas State, where he was a young assistant coach; and Steve Spurrier. When Bob spoke to me, he said that OU was a sleeping giant. I couldn't have agreed more.

Bob was a defensive guy who believed in what I did offensively, and he was going to let me run it as I saw it. We were talking about combining the top offense and top defense in the SEC at OU. We were both really excited. I could tell when we talked that Bob had a common sense approach to assembling a staff, to coaching, and to football in general. I wanted to be a head coach at some point, and I felt that learning from Bob and seeing how he adjusted to being a first-time head coach would be beneficial for me.

Hal was proud that Stoops wanted to hire me. He told me that he felt like I had to take the OU job. He knew the day would eventually come when we'd have to part ways, and for both our benefits, I'm glad I didn't make some dumb decision and just leave for the sake of leaving.

I accepted Bob's offer to come to Oklahoma and run the offense.

Hal let me coach UK in the bowl game. We lost to Penn State. Tim left after the game for the NFL draft. By then he owned a bunch of NCAA passing records. He was drafted with the first overall pick by the Cleveland Browns, who were essentially an expansion team. It was an awful situation for him to walk into, but he had this notion that Cleveland was close to home, to his family, and he liked that. The thing is, if you're a starting QB in the NFL, your world stops being some local thing. Your world becomes the whole wide world.

Tim did lead the Browns to the playoffs one year, but mostly he was running for his life. He had three different head coaches, and once he got injured he never really recovered. It's unfortunate because I was convinced he had the talent to be a great NFL quarterback, just like I was sure if I teamed up with Bob Stoops at Oklahoma, we could turn the Sooners into a national powerhouse.

Boomer Sooner

Leaving your mentor is tough, but I knew the day would come when I'd eventually leave Hal's staff. I'd been mentally preparing for it for some time. No matter what, I felt like I would always remain close to Hal, and I have.

Oklahoma was going to be different, and different—if you embrace it—can be really good for you. At Kentucky, I had a bond with Hal and the other guys on that staff. At Oklahoma, I was the one guy with no direct connection to anyone in the program. Cale Gundy and Jackie Shipp had played at OU. Mike Stoops (Bob's brother), Brent Venables, and Mark Mangino knew Bob from their time at K-State. Steve Spurrier Jr. knew Bob through his dad's days at Florida. Jonathan Hayes knew Bob because they both had played at Iowa. Bobby Jack Wright, who had come from Texas, had some previous connection to Bob and Mike. I never really felt like an outsider, though, because everybody on that staff was so fired up to be there. You knew right away that you were a part of something that was going to be special. You could feel it.

We had a month to put together our recruiting class. It was a mad rush. None of our wives were with us in Norman, and we were all staying at the Marriott right off the interstate. Mangino had the biggest room, so we'd have a staff meeting every night in his place. It was a lot of fun, with tons of energy in that room. The cell phones were going non-stop while we were calling recruits.

My focus was recruiting a quarterback that could play for us right away, because we didn't have a QB in the program who could run our offense. None. Emphasis on the word *none*. The closest we had was a small, scrappy guy who wasn't particularly dedicated.

The Sooners had gone 5-6 the previous season. They'd tried to run about four different offenses that year. I felt I needed a junior college quarterback who could come in at mid-year and be our starter right away, but we still needed to recruit two high school quarterbacks to fill out the roster. We had about a week to evaluate, target, and land the JC guy. I watched about 60 quarterbacks in all. Most of them I gonged right away for one reason or another. With mid-year JC quarterbacks, it's usually going to be a pretty shallow pool. I narrowed it down to two: Sean Stein, a big kid with a strong arm at Long Beach City College, and Josh Heupel, a lefty at Snow College in Ephraim, Utah.

A few of the OU assistants didn't like Heupel, but I really did. They didn't like the fact that he couldn't run well. He also had a weak arm, but he could throw it 45 yards without the ball fluttering. More importantly, he was deadly accurate, made great decisions, and had great command of the unit.

Heupel was originally from South Dakota. His dad was a college coach there at Division II Northern State. Josh started his career at Weber State, where he tore his ACL. A new staff came in that wanted to be more of a running team, and the old staff went to Utah State. Heupel transferred to Snow College so he could transfer freely to Utah State. He won the starting job at Snow only to find out that a QB from Hawaii was transferring in, and that guy's brother happened to be the offensive coordinator. Heupel and the other QB ended up splitting the job so they would each play a half.

I saw enough of Heupel's film that I was convinced he was our guy.

QB is a hard position to evaluate. There are so many examples in the NFL where people have invested a lot of money and time only to find out they've picked the wrong guy. Look at all the first-round quarterbacks they pay tens of millions of dollars to, who they eventually realize can't play. Meanwhile, Tom Brady and Kurt Warner, guys who weren't even close to being first-rounders, are going to be Hall of Famers. It's amazing. Personally, I feel like I do a good job at evaluating quarterbacks, though that doesn't mean I haven't been wrong from time to time.

The reason teams struggle when evaluating quarterbacks is that sometimes their priorities are out of order. They get caught up in arm strength, size, and speed. Things that are easy to measure. "Did you see the guy throw it through the goalposts while kneeling at midfield?" That's great, but last time I checked you don't throw passes in games from your knees. I've got defensive ends with great arm strength, but they aren't accurate. I bet they would love to play quarterback.

Arm strength is about sixth on the list of what I look for in a quarterback. First, I want to see how accurate he is, and if he can make good decisions. Then I want to see if he's tough, has good feet, and has leadership qualities. After all of that, then I'll consider how much arm strength and speed he has. If he isn't accurate and doesn't make good decisions, then he isn't going to be very good at bringing out the best in your other players. If his high school and college coaches couldn't get him to do these basic things, then it's unlikely he'd be able to do them in my program either.

Your quarterback is one of the core planks of leadership on your team. You have to be outright overpowering to win without a good QB. I don't necessarily think it's any more pivotal to have a good quarterback in my offense than it is to have in any other offense. But my guy had better be smart, because I'm going to let him check from goal-line to goal-line. I can't have a guy with a below-average intelligence.

It's very difficult to gauge a quarterback's intelligence from recruiting tape, but I know that guys who throw into double coverage aren't making good decisions. What I want to see is him throwing to his receivers right on the break, or just as they find themselves wide open. Of course, you don't know exactly what he's being taught. It always ticks me off when someone in the media talks about what kind of decisions so-and-so makes. How on Earth do they have any idea what kind of decision a guy is supposed to make? If he doesn't throw into coverage and throws to receivers on the break, then you can tell that whatever he's been coached to look for, he's finding. Once in a while you'll get to see a play develop where the quarterback checks from one receiver to the next to the next. Heupel showed on his film he could do that.

I invited him to Norman. I had four days to convince him to de-commit from Utah State, commit to us, and get him set to enroll.

> **"I had never heard of Leach. But I was aware of what they were doing at Kentucky, spreading the ball around. I was very intrigued, although it certainly wasn't the most entertaining trip any recruit ever took. I can guarantee that. Most of their staff was off recruiting and school was on Christmas vacation, so the place was dead. We spent the rest of the day I arrived on and the following day holed up in his little office, grinding away at film. He wanted to know how I fit in and I wanted to know how I fit in."**
> **—Josh Heupel, OU quarterback, 1999-2000**

All I had in my office was a TV, a VCR, two chairs, and a bunch of game tapes of the Kentucky offense. There was stuff all over the floor. I spent about seven hours straight with Josh, just watching film. He was sitting on the floor. We ordered out for food. I wanted to impress him to the point where he would come to Oklahoma and go to a nice place to eat. He didn't care about that. He wanted to watch the film. We sent out for sandwiches. He asked all of these intelligent questions. He was bringing up things at a level you usually don't bring up to a quarterback because it can be counter-productive if he doesn't understand. He's asking about coverages: "If they shift down here, do you read this guy over there?" I was hoping he would commit to us right on the spot. In typical Heupel fashion, he left us hanging. He doesn't really show you his cards. He went home. Drew the thing out. Then he committed. He came back to OU a few days later to enroll.

Most of our new players were excited about the schemes we were bringing in. The toughest things for them were the catching and route-running drills, which they really had to master on their own since coaches aren't allowed to work with players in the off-season outside of spring ball. Having Heupel there was huge. I don't think people around Oklahoma fully appreciated how instrumental he was.

The players get together and work out in the off-season, and you hope they come to spring with their skills in place. Josh got everybody on the same page and the guys came in reasonably sharp. That's a challenge for any quarterback, but Josh had to do it as an outsider in a team going through a coaching transition. He jump-started everything for us.

The rest of the staff was new to my offensive system as well. I had to teach everybody exactly what I wanted them to do in the offense, but also explain what the big picture was and why we were doing things a certain way. I didn't want to have a playbook, and hearing that an offense isn't going to have a playbook really shocks people, especially football coaches.

All a playbook does is document what you do. We, as coaches, know what we're running and how to teach it. We didn't have a playbook when I coached at Valdosta State or when I was at

Kentucky, and we really only had fragments of a playbook when I was at Iowa Wesleyan, which I never bothered to update.

I think playbooks are outdated. Now everything is on video, and your playbook is your cut-ups. We're past the era where it was tedious splicing film together. We're not sitting around for endless hours cutting up the one roll of 16-millimeter film anymore. It comes on DVD now.

If you're still a playbook guy, you're sitting there fussing about whether the X's and O's are drawn correctly, or if the lines are still straight enough if you make a slight adjustment. Then, you have some graduate assistant scurrying around, printing out pages for everyone. It all just seems counter-productive. The DVD image is more compelling, and easier to learn from anyway. I don't think a playbook is the best way to teach your offense.

We did make a playbook for our assistants at OU. It may have helped the coaches get on the same page early on, but in hindsight I think we should've just stuck with the video. I have not made a printed playbook since.

What I don't like is giving a playbook to the players. As a coach, there is a tendency to take short cuts and not be as precise in your teaching when you can lean on a playbook. As a player, there's a tendency to think you can just look it up in the playbook, study it like you're cramming for a science test. Well, if a player doesn't have a playbook, and as a coach you say, "We're working on these plays today," the players think, "OK, I'd better get this down now." It raises the level of focus. You're taking off their little swimming wings. We're going to be swimming in some pretty rough waters, so you'd better know how to stay afloat.

Even though I hadn't really known the rest of the staff for very long, I felt very comfortable there, and I have Bob Stoops to thank for that. He had my back from day one. His support was crucial.

Bob did a good job balancing his day-to-day with delegating responsibility to his staff. That's not so easy for a first-time head coach. It's rare for a head coach to give an assistant so much autonomy, especially one whose scheme and system is so different from what he's used to. Bob understood that you hire good people, and then you let them do their jobs. I realize that as a head coach the temptation to meddle is there, but you have to make a decision ahead of time that you won't. A lot of head coaches don't have the backbone to do that, and even if they do, they probably can't resist the temptation. Had I not been convinced that Bob wouldn't meddle, I wouldn't have taken the job.

> **"The reasons I hired Mike were good ones. 1) We didn't have a strong quarterback on offense and I knew his offense would attract quarterbacks. 2) At Kentucky, they moved the football, got first downs, scored a lot of points. They were great in all of these categories, so why couldn't we do the same here? I felt like we would be able to move the ball sooner that way than if we tried to beat people up and run it.**

> **"Mike was the only guy I brought in from that system. I hired several other coaches, and my point to all of them was, I did not want to blend all of these ways of doing something because I feel like then it would be disjointed. The one thing I did put my foot down on was, when I hired the other guys, I said 'This is what we're doing. I know you all have good ideas, but we're not going to mix all of this stuff. We're going with this, and this only. Somewhere down the road, we may evolve to something different once this has been established, but we're not going to have a hodge-podge offense, with this from that team and this from the team you**

came from. We're doing Mike's stuff and we're going to get great at it and that's what we'll do.' And I let Mike go with it. I trusted Mike. He did an awesome job."

—Bob Stoops

People think Bob and I are polar opposites, but we're actually quite similar. We were raised in places that have a lot in common. I'm from Cody, Wyoming. He is from Youngstown, Ohio. Both are blue-collar, gritty, back-to-the basics kind of places. Youngstown is a tough, steel mill, industrial town. Cody has mountains, trees, and cowboys. We both came from hardcore, no beating-around-the-bush, direct, honest-values places. Loyalty is incredibly important to us both. Bob is so much looser than the media and some of the outside world perceives him to be. If you're in Bob's circle and one of his guys, he's really a warm person and a lot of fun.

The scramble to get the team ready for that first spring practice after a coaching transition really helps you bond as a staff. You go from just getting off the road recruiting, to trying to get acquainted with your new players and analyzing who fits where, and then before you know it, spring is upon you.

After the first month or so at OU, most of the staff had found houses, but a few of us—Spurrier Jr., Mangino, Bobby Jack, and me—moved out of the hotel and were living in the office. I threw down an air mattress on the floor to sleep.

Mangino, the O-line coach, and I worked really closely together. There were some philosophical differences initially, but he did a really good job. He's a real common sense guy who constantly reinforced fundamentals. He can be gruff, but he's really got much more personality than some people imagine. He's a very entertaining guy with this biting sense of humor. Watching him get amused is contagious. His entire face gets red.

There was outside resistance to what we were planning offensively. Oklahoma has always had a lot of pride in its offense. This wasn't like Kentucky, where they'd been rock bottom. This was OU. When I was growing up, Barry Switzer was the coach of the Sooners and he was dominating Nebraska and Texas, two dynasty programs.

Oklahoma ran the wishbone. The attack was a thing of beauty the way it flowed. Every non-lineman got the ball in the wishbone, but the defense could never figure out who was going to get it. The wishbone was a big headache for defenses.

I love the wishbone. I know people think I'm so different from a "wishbone guy" because my teams throw the ball so much. In the wishbone they rarely throw it, but there is one huge common thread to my system and the wishbone. Whether it came from Emory Bellard, the old Texas A&M and Mississippi State coach, Barry Switzer, or Paul Johnson: the offenses were effective because they utilized every skill position. Those guys—Bellard and Switzer—hardly ever threw the ball, but they were still a very balanced team. Everybody touched the ball. Everybody contributed to the offense.

To a lot of folks around Oklahoma, throwing the ball just seemed completely foreign to what OU football was supposed to be. Before we even played a game, the two most wanted guys in the state were me for having the audacity to throw the ball, and Josh Heupel for being a QB that couldn't run.

On the first play we ran in the spring game that year, we lined up in the wishbone formation. We were paying homage to it. Then we shifted the backs out wide and ran our offense. I had run the idea past a local reporter, Dean Blevins, who'd been the Sooners quarterback in the '70s. Dean thought it was a good idea, so I went with it. People got a kick out of it.

What really helped turn back the criticism was that we got off to a fast start to the season, opening 3-0. We scored over 40 points in each game. The previous year OU had been held to 17 points or less in 6 of their 11 games. We averaged 44 points per game in the first month.

"Leach brought a breath of fresh air to the institution of college football. He just sees things a little differently from most people. He drew up this fake play list for the Texas game and left it on the field. The second play was listed as a 'double-reverse pass.' We didn't have a double-reverse pass. The second play of the game, if the defense was guessing for a double-reverse pass, he called the perfect play to counter it. Coach Leach was laughing because we could hear the defenders at the line-of-scrimmage yelling 'WATCH THE DOUBLE-REVERSE PASS!' We ended up scoring a touchdown in two plays on them."
—Trent Smith, OU tight end, 1999-2002

I never really thought they'd look at the fake call sheet. I just wanted them to think about it.

The sheet was laminated, so it looked like one of ours. We used terminology on it that sounded like ours, but we made it so it was still something they could understand.

Cale Gundy and I sat up one night and talked about doing it. The sheet said "Gundy" on top. We planted it with the equipment manager. He'd carry around this bag of balls before the game, going from one end of the field to give them to the kickers, and then back to the other end. He just stuck that fake script under the bag as he set it down, and when he picked the bag up, he just left the sheet lying there. One of Texas' GAs or assistant coaches picked up the sheet and looked at it for a few seconds. You could see the gears turning in his head: Is it? No, it can't be, can it? Wow! It is!

He walked very quickly over to Texas defensive coordinator, Carl Reese, who stuffed it in his pocket. It was funny. We just thought it would give them something else to think about. Instead, it gave us an easy touchdown and some momentum. They oversold, and we ran a crossing route. Anton Savage, a freshman receiver, was so worked up about scoring on that play; he actually dropped the ball two yards shy of the goal line. There wasn't a soul around him. But they still ruled it a touchdown.

Texas, ranked #23, still beat us 38–28. Then, Texas A&M came to Norman. The Aggies were ranked #13. They'd beaten OU 29-0 the year before. Our whole staff was excited before the game. R.C. Slocum, the Aggies coach, was a big deal. We young coaches were waiting in the tunnel to get a glimpse of him just so we could shake his hand. We had this line of OU assistants waiting to introduce ourselves to him. We weren't awed though. We beat the Aggies, 51–6. It was Texas A&M's worst loss in 98 years. Heupel accounted for six touchdowns. We had 14 different receivers catch at least one pass in the game.

> **"Ninety percent of teams today don't run an offense, they run plays. A goodly portion of football teams just run plays but without a concept.**
>
> **"With offense, you decide what you want to do. Then you decide, now, what is the best way to carry out that plan? So many people line up and then they try to decide what they want to do from that. It should be the other way around. The wishbone was all about balance. You can do it to the right or to the left, with this guy or with that guy. It's not a one- or two-threat offense. It's about constant threats. That's why I like Mike Leach's offense."**
>
> **—Emory Bellard, creator of the wishbone**

To me, a balanced offense is one where each skill position touches the ball, and every position contributes to the offensive output. There is nothing balanced about running it 50 percent of the time and throwing it 50 percent of the time if you are only utilizing two or three offensive skill positions and only attacking part of the field. A good offense has the ability to attack as much of the field as possible with as many people as possible. You want to put as much pressure on the defense as you can while utilizing all of the space and personnel that you have.

I think it's almost impossible to have a great offense if you have only one or two guys touching the ball. That one guy had better be really, really special, a Hall of Fame type of talent, like Herschel Walker was at Georgia in the early '80s, or Earl Campbell was for Texas in the mid '70s. But what if you break him? Then what? You've put all of your eggs in one basket. If you have a special player, you obviously want to get the most out of him. But are you really utilizing all of your resources then? Wouldn't you be better off as a team if everyone contributed to commanding the defense's attention so that special player could have the space to be even more effective?

Look at what Barry Switzer did when he had a great running back like Billy Sims. Sims was a fantastic runner. He broke the NCAA record for average yards per carry (for backs carrying the ball a minimum of 500 times.) In 1978, Sims won the Heisman Trophy and averaged 7.6 yards per carry. He ran for 1,762 yards. But he still only had 32 percent of the carries on a team that ran for almost 5,000 yards. Kenny King, one of the other OU backs, gained 779 yards that season and had an even higher average (7.9 yards per carry); QB Thomas Lott ran for 577 yards and 5.2 yards; and another running back, David Overstreet, ran for over 400 more and averaged 6.5 yards a carry. I loved how that offense attacked people. That is great distribution. That's balance.

In our offense, we made sure that all of the skill positions touched the ball. People get overly impressed by that artificial balance, where it's half run, half pass, but with only a couple of players touching the ball. You can run the ball every snap, but if you're in the wishbone, and everybody touches the ball, that's real balance. Or you can throw the ball every snap, and if everyone touches the ball, that's real balance.

I didn't think I'd like Barry Switzer. He seemed like a boisterous outlaw that coached renegades. Switzer had been the face of Oklahoma football. The Sooners won a ton under his leadership. He had the program really rocking and rolling for a good 10-year stretch. I thought I'd like Bobby Bowden and LaVell Edwards, I just didn't think I'd like Barry Switzer, although the more I watched his team from afar, the more I respected how they executed.

After I was hired by Bob, I went to Othello's, a cozy Italian restaurant in Norman near the OU campus. Switzer just happened to be there. I didn't know it at the time, but Othello's was one of the places he'd hold court. He saw me and asked if I'd like to come over to his table. Within five minutes of sitting down, I could just tell he was such a real, genuine, down-to-earth guy. I was surprised at how engaging he was. He was nice to everyone. He just has this innate ability to connect with people.

He'd been eating at the same red leather booth in the restaurant for decades. Usually he'd be surrounded by a real group of characters. It'd be Switzer; Patsy, the owner of Othello's, who was an old-world Italian guy in his '60s; Al Eschbach, a fast-talking, transplanted New Yorker who was a local radio host; a big guy everyone called Meatball, who was Patsy's son and just a total New York guy; and sometimes Larry Lacewell, Switzer's old assistant. Switzer is a great storyteller, and they'd all be hanging on his every word. The best was when Lacewell was there. They'd finish off each other's sentences and spawned one story after another.

> *"I did not know Bob Stoops' staff at all. I knew their names and where they came from. I had seen Oklahoma football through the '90s. Seen it go down hill. Seen it disintegrate. Lose*

its stature from what it had been and what it should be. Then Bob Stoops gets the job in '99. I went to the first game they played. Right from the beginning, I saw these guys knew what they were doing. The team played hard. They executed. On offense, I'm watching something that I'd never seen before. It was a triple-option offense; only it was throwing the ball instead of pitching the ball. It excited me. It was wide-open. Oklahoma fans had never seen it before.

"I found out that Mike Leach called the plays and that he had a background with Hal Mumme at Kentucky. Every down was a first down for him. There were no second or third or fourth downs. I got excited with it.

"One night I'm at my favorite haunt, Othello's, an Italian restaurant on campus corner. The guy that owns it is a friend I've known for over 30 years, named Patsy. He's an Italian immigrant. He speaks broken English. He can't read or write English, but he's a great chef, and tremendous personality. I'm there every night at what we call "The Table of Truth." You have to be invited to sit there because that's the table Patsy sits at. I'm at the Table of Truth. All of sudden Mike Leach walks in. I invite him over. I introduce myself. I admired Mike. I wanted to know more about his offense and more about him, but I found out right away the more I wanted to learn about him and his philosophy, the more

> **he wanted to know from me about the history**
> **and the tradition that I'd been a part of."**
> **—Barry Switzer**

I was interested in the whole history of OU football and Switzer's background, and pretty much everything else about the world of big-time football. You could ask him questions about any subject. What was Bear Bryant like? What was it like coaching against Darrell Royal? What was it like playing at Arkansas? Sometimes we'd all be chatting away for so long, the owner would toss him the keys and say "Just lock up," and this was usually around 2 a.m. He became an invaluable sounding board for me. We'd talk about handling staff, motivating players, getting people back on track if you lose, recruiting.

I picked up "the Wizard" magic trick from Barry Switzer. He asked me to pick a card and tell him what it was.

"Four of diamonds."

Then he said he was going to call the Wizard who would be able to identify the card I just selected. He would get on his cell phone.

"I'd like to speak to the Wizard," he said.

I looked around to see if there was someone else observing this, maybe somebody over my shoulder. There was no one. Switzer handed me the phone. A muffled voice on the other end said "four of diamonds." I was baffled. I wanted him to do it again. I picked another card. Switzer called the Wizard again. Again, the Wizard called out my card. It was after 2 a.m. I got him to do it a third time before he explained how the trick works.

"OK, so who was that?" I ask Switzer.

"That's my ex-wife," he said. "She lives in Arkansas. We get along great. I am her Wizard. She is mine.

The Wizard is great for recruiting. It gets the guy's attention and also relaxes him. It starts up a good dialogue and it's something they'll remember you for. It backfired once, though. I put the Wizard on the phone with this recruit from East Texas. I think he was superstitious or into voodoo. He just dropped the phone and sprinted out the door. He thought it was something supernatural. We didn't get him.

After hammering A&M, we turned around and lost on the road at Colorado before blowing out Missouri and Iowa State. We were getting better, but were still inconsistent. We weren't ranked in the top 25, although everyone around the program felt like we weren't far away from being a truly special team. The pieces were in place. I was sure Bob was the right guy to lead the program to a title. We'd stockpiled some promising talent. Heupel was going to push for All-American honors the next season and the two other quarterbacks we'd brought in that year, Jason White and Nate Hybl, a transfer from the University of Georgia, had the stuff to be future standout QBs.

Turns out my feeling about OU would prove to be right. The Sooners, in Bob's second season at Oklahoma, went 13-0 and won the national title. Heupel was the Heisman Trophy runner-up. White would later win the Heisman at OU, and he, Heupel, or Hybl would start every OU game at quarterback from 1999 through 2004. Late in that first season at OU, I got in the mix for the head-coaching job at Texas Tech, and it seemed like something I needed to consider.

RUNNING THE SHOW

Building the Team

I interviewed for the Texas Tech job three times in 1999. The school was looking to replace Spike Dykes, who was retiring after 13 seasons coaching the Red Raiders. I always respected Spike. He was a local hero. He was an example of what I thought a coach should be. I called up Spike to ask him about the job—I didn't want to be involved with Tech unless I got Spike's blessing. He gave it to me right away and was very supportive.

My first interview with Tech was at the Embassy Suites in Oklahoma City late in the season. I went over and talked to them for a bit. The interview was more about what the Tech brass thought the job was and what they were looking for rather than me telling them what I could bring. They said they wanted to improve the academics. They talked about how they were looking for an exciting, dynamic offense, how they were building new facilities, and that they wanted good energy around the changes.

As is the case with almost every coaching vacancy, there were issues. Texas Tech was on academic probation. They had one of the lowest graduation rates in the country. The football program was losing 18 scholarships over three years from 1999-2001 for academic certification improprieties.

I told them I could turn that around. I was honest.

"I believe in academics and education," I said. "If I didn't, I wouldn't have earned the degrees that I have."

They wanted to know what my recruiting plan would be if I was their head coach.

"We'll saturate the state of Texas," I said. "I'll use the junior colleges as a resource, but you don't want any more than five JC guys a year because you want the program built with high school kids.

"I'm not afraid to recruit anybody who's motivated to come, but I won't fly over a bunch of people to get to somebody that's not sure about the program when we've got plenty nearby that are just as good.

"We'll recruit JC guys to fill holes, or JC guys who could be difference makers. I'd like the JC guys to have three years of eligibility remaining or at least be mid-year guys so we'd have them for spring practice before their junior season. We'll recruit the state of Texas from top to bottom. We'll also recruit New Mexico if they have anybody, and Oklahoma, and Louisiana."

My point about not flying over a bunch of prospects to get to one who's not sure about the program meant I didn't believe in chasing ghosts or blindly throwing our hat into the ring for some "five-star," internet all-American who might not have much real interest in us. Instead, we could probably unearth someone closer by who would play twice as hard because he was excited to be at Texas Tech.

The Tech folks nodded their heads the whole time. They decided they wanted to do a second interview with me. We agreed to schedule it after the OU–Texas Tech game in Lubbock. I never, ever should've done it then. What a mess that day turned out to be. Bob was on the same page with me as far as the way I handled the process, but I didn't have much experience interviewing for a head coaching job and couldn't see all the pitfalls lying in wait.

We were playing at Texas Tech in their season finale late in

November. Texas Tech came into the game with a 5-5 record. The Red Raiders had just been beaten 58–7 by Texas the week before. We were 6-3. We'd scored at least 30 points seven times. Our offense had gone from 11th in the Big 12 to first in one season.

The idea was, we go to Lubbock to play Tech, and then after the game I'd stick around and have my second interview. Bad idea. It didn't take long for the media to hear that I'd be staying to interview for the Tech head coaching position. It turned out to be a total distraction for the OU team, which wasn't fair to our players. I didn't foresee that, and Bob didn't either. There's no way either of us would've wanted to cause that sort of ruckus around the team before the game.

We took the team down to Lubbock and people were talking about how I was the favorite to get the job, how Tech was going to rubber-stamp it after the game. We ended up playing poorly. We turned the ball over three times. Tech played their asses off. I'd heard that one of Tech's legends, E.J. Holub, gave a pep talk to the team about playing on behalf of Spike. The Red Raiders, with freshman QB Kliff Kingsbury starting the first game of his college career, rallied from being down in the third quarter to beat us 38–28.

I did wonder if the loss would affect my chances of being hired by Tech, but I was mostly just upset that we lost the game. You spend all week investing your whole mind, heart, and soul to win a football game. You coach them the best you can. I felt awful that we lost. I felt even worse that I caused a distraction that may have contributed to the loss.

I wasn't too worried about not landing the Texas Tech head coaching job. I knew we were doing great things at Oklahoma. The University of Oklahoma was the best job I had ever had. I knew that we were scratching the surface of something special. It was exciting to be a part of it. I loved working for Bob. I had a quarterback, Josh Heupel, who was incredibly smart. However, there are few opportunities for head coaching jobs and I felt like I could do some good things at Tech.

After we lost the Texas Tech game, I walked out of the Oklahoma locker room to find a group of reporters trying to get me to comment about the Tech job. I ducked them and went to the front of the building where the athletic director's office was, but the door was locked. I rattled the door, like I could tear it open.

Locked.

I couldn't get in.

I was stuck between some OU fans and a lot of Tech fans. They'd all read the newspaper. This was the worst-kept secret in history.

It was so awkward. I finally found my way into the building, and Gerald Myers, Tech's AD, took me to the hotel where the OU team was staying. I put on a suit. I slipped out the backdoor. The interview was held in a boardroom at a bank where I met a five-person committee from the Board of Regents, along with John Montford, the school's chancellor.

We had just lost, and my attitude was a mix of angry and somber. I was meeting with Tech's decision-makers no more than 90 minutes after the game, still ticked about the way we played. I didn't think the interview went well. They asked me some deadpan questions. Like I'd suspected, they wanted an OU win to help validate their decision. After the official business they dropped me off at the hotel so I could change before we went out to eat to get to know each other better. Gerald's wife was taking my wife around town. Then came the worst of it. It was 8 p.m. when I made it back to the hotel. Right in the lobby were the entire OU staff, the whole Sooner team, the president of OU, OU's AD—everybody.

The airplane charter service had called and told Oklahoma's football operations guy, "We're not coming to get you. We got a flat tire."

The football ops guy said, "Well, how are we supposed to get home?"

"I don't know. You're not getting home with us."

Well, I walked through the front door. Everyone turned and looked. They were going to be staring at anyone who walked through that door because they were hoping it was their ride back to Oklahoma, and here it was me.

I went up to change out of my suit. I felt so awkward about the whole deal. Worse yet, two OU players had been up in their room asleep and had missed the charter bus that ended up taking the team back to Norman. As I was getting ready to go to dinner, I was frantically trying to get someone on the phone from OU to figure out a way to get them back home. The whole evening was tense for me. I was upset about the game, worried about the stranded players, and trying to interview and make a good impression all at once.

I returned to Norman without the Tech job and focused on getting the offense ready to play Oklahoma State. Tech called a few weeks later. They wanted to do a third interview. We met in Dallas at one of their big boosters' offices. This time it was more to sell me on the job. I already knew that I wanted it. We flew back to Lubbock and I accepted the offer right there, knowing there was a lot of work ahead and not much time to do it. I was hired December 9, 1999, meaning I had less than two months to recruit before signing day.

I returned to Oklahoma to say goodbye to the team and the staff. It was emotional. Everybody there was so gracious. They knew it was a great opportunity for me. They also knew what being part of the Sooner program had meant to me. I'd only been at OU a year, but we'd accomplished quite a bit. I loved that staff and I loved that place.

Once I landed back in Lubbock, time just flew by. In my first full day in the office, I poured over the whole list of recruits Texas Tech had targeted. I recognized a bunch of the names. We'd looked at many of them at Oklahoma. I called as many as I could. By noon, I'd realized that the chances of getting many quality recruits wasn't going to be very high if I was doing all of the recruiting alone. I said, "Screw this!" and moved the pile of recruiting names to the corner of my desk. "I have to get the best staff in here now so I can get them on the road."

When you're hired to take over a program, the most important recruiting process is actually the one you do hiring your coaches. You've got to recruit them. You need to get the right coaches. You can't afford to be wrong on who you hire. You have to do it quickly because you've got to get them out there right away, otherwise you're going to have to recruit the incoming class by yourself.

After talking to some other coaches about it, I wasn't really tempted to keep the assistant coaches from the previous staff. Typically, retaining the old guys just doesn't work very well. Under one coaching staff, you're telling the players one thing. Under another coaching staff, you're telling the players something else. The guys I knew best from Spike Dykes's staff were offensive guys and I already had my own assistants in mind. Some of Spike's staff was not planning to stay. Some didn't fit what I was looking for. It was also my first step out of the blocks, so I wanted "my guys." I wanted as few other agendas as possible. I wanted people who were attached to me.

I had most of the staff I wanted to hire in mind long before I began interviewing at Tech. Robert Anae was an offensive lineman on the 1984 BYU national championship team during the golden age of LaVell Edwards. Robert played O-line for Roger French back when they were doing vertical sets—and this was during the time when I think Roger French was literally the best offensive line coach in the world. The core of what I knew as an offensive coordinator was learned visiting BYU. Robert had been an assistant at BYU, UNLV, and a few other places. I'd done some clinics with him. I liked him right away. Robert was working in academics and I knew he wanted to get back on the field. I'd even tried to hire him at Oklahoma, but Bob wanted his own guy.

Your most important asset as an offensive coordinator is your O-line coach, because he has your offense's life in his hands. Robert was the first guy I wanted to hire. He was really solid in so many ways. He had a great presence. When someone walked in the door, he drew their attention right away. He was incredibly loyal. He'd also worked as an NCAA Life Skills Director. I thought his experience would be invaluable in developing great O-linemen, as well as better students and better people.

I planned to use the wider line splits, and that was something Robert had done before. As simple and elementary as they may seem, the wider line splits are hard to get guys to believe in. Wide splits and vertical sets are usually the biggest sticking points, and Robert was on the same page as me with both of them.

Sonny Dykes, who was Spike's son, had been my GA at Kentucky. He knew the offense I was going to run. So did Dana Holgorsen, who'd been a wide receiver for me at Iowa Wesleyan and GA'd for me at Valdosta. Bill Bedenbaugh was another ex-player of mine at Iowa Wesleyan who I planned to bring in. I also wanted to hire a Texas high school coach, and a guy who threw the ball, so I reached out to Art Briles at Stephenville High School. I thought having a guy with contacts in the state of Texas would help our recruiting by strengthening the bond with the Texas high school football coaches.

On defense, I knew Greg McMackin was an experienced guy who'd been a defensive coordinator at the University of Miami and in the NFL with the Seattle Seahawks. He'd once told me he liked working with guys who throw the ball, because he'd worked with Dennis Erickson and June Jones in the past. He wanted to bring one of his guys with him—Ron Harris as his D-line coach—and that was fine with me as long as I liked him. Ron turned out to be a really good choice. I wanted Brian Norwood to be my secondary coach. I'd worked a clinic with him in Japan and I thought he was very bright. Ruffin McNeill, who Greg and I knew and liked, would be our linebackers coach.

Manny Matsakis had been the head coach at Emporia State in Kansas and started the magazine *American Football Quarterly*. I got to know him because I'd written some articles for the magazine when I was coaching at Valdosta State, Kentucky, and Oklahoma. I wanted him to be my assistant head coach and special teams coordinator. I thought Manny was someone I could rely on. He was a very organized guy. I also knew if we were going to build a new complex, I was going to need a guy who could help work on the building, go to meetings, and figure out what went where.

You also need guys in your program who are bonding influences, good at bringing people together. When things are good, that guy is excited too, but he's also the voice of reason. When things are bad, he keeps up the levels of enthusiasm and optimism. Dennis Simmons was this kind of guy. He'd played at BYU and graduated from there, so I knew he was intelligent. He'd also coached at Cornell.

We're all somewhat constrained by our backgrounds when trying to find common ground with other people. I've always tried to be as broad-minded as possible, and I've always been curious about people from different parts of the country and different parts of the world. That doesn't change the fact that I'm a middle-class white guy from Wyoming. I thought Dennis could be a really good cypher for a lot of things outside my sphere of experience. He was this inner-city black guy from Memphis who had gone to BYU, so you know he had to make a lot of adjustments. I hired Dennis to be a quality control assistant, which meant he'd help players with their day-to-day responsibilities away from football.

I wanted diversity, and not just in terms of the racial mix (though I think we had that with Brian, Ruffin, Robert, and Dennis), but from an ideological standpoint as well. I wanted people from a variety of backgrounds so that as we shared ideas about relating to our players, we'd have a lot of the bases covered. I wanted smart people. I also wanted people who knew things that I didn't know.

> **"I think a lot of coaches worry about compliance.**
> **For Mike, it was beyond compliance. He was**
> **sincerely worried about the kids. In medicine,**
> **we call it therapeutic milieu, which is more than**
> **worrying about the patient, the medicines, and**
> **the surgeries; it's about creating the environment**
> **around the patient to be able to maximize their**

health. Mike did the same thing when it came to student-athletes and in this case, it was an academic milieu by engendering the right values and the skill sets of these young men."
—Dr. David Smith, Texas Tech Chancellor, 2002-06

I kept the secretary, Patty Ross, who had been at Tech since she was 19, and the strength coach, Kelvin Clark. I wasn't 100 percent with Kelvin. He was a good man, but he was used to doing things a certain way, and I didn't think there was enough energy or enthusiasm with his approach. He wanted to do things differently than I did. He said, "This is my program. I'm going to do things my way." I replied, "This is our team. We're going to run the program the way that I and the rest of the coaches decide in our meetings. You didn't recruit any of these guys. You don't call any plays." He left. Bennie Wylie, who I'd brought in as an assistant strength coach, became my new head strength coach. I should've brought in my own guy from the beginning. Bennie viewed football and thought about personal accountability the way I did.

I hired Robert, Dana, Sonny, Greg, Bill, Ruffin, and Manny on the spot. Art interviewed for the job and I sold him on why coming to Tech would be a good move for the both of us. I basically did the same thing with the rest of the staff. We knew we really had to scramble. We had a little over a month to sign our first recruiting class. When I was hired, we only had one recruiting commitment from the old staff: Clay McGuire.

I didn't love McGuire athletically. He wasn't explosive. He wasn't strong. He didn't run very fast either. McGuire was from Crane, Texas, which is a town of about 3,000. He was a quarterback who'd played some defensive end, which is obviously an interesting combination. I thought he was probably 6-foot-1, 170 pounds. I can't say that I would've scholarshipped him but he was already offered one and had accepted.

"I'm not sure this is a good idea, but we're going to honor it," I thought.

Clay proved me wrong. I tried to replace him every year for four years and couldn't. We played him at tight end and fullback. We could find guys who were bigger, stronger, and faster, but he'd beat them all out. He was just a smart, instinctive player who could really catch the ball.

We were fortunate to already have Kliff Kingsbury, a quarterback, in the program. He had just finished his freshman season. He was a smart kid, really driven. He'd graduated third in his high school class of 450. Kliff threw the ball accurately, too. I remembered liking him in high school when I was at Kentucky. We didn't really go after him because we had a few other recruits who were closer to us, but we did like him. I knew that in Kliff we had someone we could win with.

We announced a class of 20 recruits on national signing day. Only three were junior college guys, and of the rest, only one was from out of state. I think it was the lowest-ranked recruiting class in the Big 12. We were just scrambling to get the best guys we could. Wes Welker, the recruit who would have the biggest impact for us in that first class, signed about two weeks after signing day. I remembered him from our camp at OU. He was this slow, short guy from Oklahoma City. You play games like touch football in those camp settings, and Wes Welker isn't going to show out in that. Even in real games he's a guy that a lot of people will touch. But he isn't going to get tackled very often. He's elusive, with a low center of gravity. He's a counter puncher who stays one step ahead and will outmaneuver you. His ability to focus may be better than anyone else's I have ever met.

Oklahoma didn't even want him as a walk-on. Oklahoma State said they'd only take him as a walk-on. Tulsa had offered him a scholarship but then backed off him. So two weeks after signing day Welker and his family made the six-hour drive to Lubbock.

Wes came into our office and said, "Listen, here's my tape, here's what I can do, I want to play for you. But Oklahoma State is close to my house. If I don't get a scholarship, I'm going to Oklahoma State, where I can get in-state tuition. If you decide to give me a scholarship, I'm going here and I'll be here as soon as school's out and be ready to play for the season."

We sent Wes out with one of our strength coaches to tour the facilities so we could talk about him as we watched his film.

It was the most impressive high school film I've ever seen. He did everything. His production was off the scale. He returned kicks, punts, and interceptions back for touchdowns. He caught touchdown passes. There's just play after play after play after play. We were of two minds in there, "Oh man, that's a great play! Look at that play. Oh, that's another great play! Wow! Yeah, but he's short and he's slow . . . he's a great high school player, but he probably won't be able to make the transition to college." Then, he finished the thing with an exclamation point, hitting a game-winning 52-yard field goal. He kicked the field goal. This is all in one playoff game.

We watched that film over and over, and talked, and finally figured, "Well, no matter what, we can find something to do with him. He can help us. He'll be a good team guy. Let's take him." We offered him a scholarship, and he started for us all four years. Welker caught 259 passes for 21 TDs, set an NCAA record with eight punt returns for TDs, and won the Mosi Tatupu Award for the nation's top special teams player. Of course, he's still short and slow, so the NFL didn't even invite him to the combine. He didn't get drafted. Instead, he signed as a free agent and ended up leading the NFL in receptions twice, along with making three Pro Bowls.

> **"When Wes came there that day, I thought, 'Oh my gosh, who is this little frat guy? Are you kidding me?' I thought it was some desperation move. It was two weeks after signing day. Even the coaches said, 'Maybe he could be a kicker if it doesn't work out.' But then you see him at practice the first day of camp, it was 'Wow!**

> This guy is our best player.' You knew we had
> something special. We called him 'The Natural'
> after one day of working with him."
> —Kliff Kingsbury, Texas Tech QB, 1998-2002

My first team meeting at Tech was longer than it should've been. I wanted to tell them everything all at once. It was a combination of introducing myself and my staff; explaining what we were going to do overall, what the off-season was going to be about, and what spring was going to be like; and explaining that we were looking for players of a certain type. I stressed an emphasis on the team. I didn't have it stated succinctly, but we covered the themes of our three overall goals: 1) Be a team; 2) Be the most excited to play; 3) Be the best at doing your job.

I think the guys felt the enthusiasm building, but it was too much, too fast. I should've spread it all out over several meetings.

In addition to completely changing the schemes, we had to overhaul the team's approach to school. Academics have always been important to me. How stupid and tragic is it for somebody to go to college and leave without a degree? When that happens, I think it's due to selfishness, laziness, or the failure of a good support group. In most cases, it's because of all three. I felt like I had a responsibility to help the guys through their academic issues so they could be the best people they could be, but as a coach there's also a practical aspect to it. If you want to be a good team, especially if you're playing with a short stick—which we were at Texas Tech—everything has to run as efficiently as possible. You don't have time to detour for academic issues. If you do a great job coaching a guy for a semester and he begins to develop as a player, but his academics are such that he's not going to be eligible, all that coaching is a complete waste of time. It all comes back to holding people accountable for themselves and emphasizing what is important over what is not.

We sat down the players who'd had legal problems or disciplinary problems in the past at Tech and gave it to them point blank: "Listen, here's how it is. This is your last shot. This is how we're going to do it. You've done this. You've done that. We'll get you right. We'll get you counseling. We'll pay for counseling. But if there is another mishap, you're gone."

Dorian Pitts, a linebacker who'd mostly been a special teams player, was suspended over some drug issues. Thing is, none of it happened under my watch. I didn't know what rules Pitts was under before I got there, so I said to him, "If you do this, this, and this, I'll give you another shot after an extended period of time. You're suspended this semester, and I'm going to drug-test the shit out of you. If you're dirty, you will never play here. If there's any NCAA drug test happening, any Big 12 drug test, or any school drug test, your name is automatically going to be added to the list."

As far as I know, he never stepped over the line again. Pitts busted his ass. He was enthusiastic. He was a big hitter, too. He was our third-leading tackler in my first season at Tech and led the team in tackles for losses. I think he ended up graduating early. He had a fantastic personality and spirit, and I enjoyed having him around.

It was always my hope that Dorian Pitts would leave Lubbock after he finished school. He was from East Lubbock and grew up around a rough crowd. Because he went to Tech, he never got enough distance between himself and his high school habits. A lot of times, if you've gotten in a tough situation in high school, that stuff can disappear when you go off to college. When you go away to school you're no longer anchored down by your high school mistakes. The people Dorian Pitts knew from East Lubbock were just blocks away from him at Texas Tech. I worried that he was too attached to the area where he'd have too many chances to fall back into bad patterns. He held up his end with me. He was great. I had another guy like Dorian who we also gave another chance to. He ended up dirty. We cut him.

"When my situation occurred, I thought, 'Am I even going to be able to continue my education here, much less play football?' But once I talked to Leach and realized what I was facing, I was grateful. I was a senior having to stay in the dorms for six months. My stipend was suspended. I had curfew. They were pretty intense stipulations that he set forth. I was just happy to be part of the team and I wanted to prove myself. I was willing to pay the price. I had put myself in that position. It had been my fault.

"Things were just so different under Leach. When Coach Dykes was there, shirts had to be tucked in. No earrings. He had a lot of good-ole-boy, country rules. Leach comes in. He's more business-oriented. He was about X's and O's. It was come-as-you-are but take care of your business. It made you relaxed. You didn't have to worry about the small things. You just worried about football and your duties. He had a pretty good system to ensure that they were getting the best out of you.

"After I was allowed back on the team, my dad, who had been out of the picture for a long time, started coming to the games. He got put on the will call list. I would have a great game. The stadium would empty out, I'd still be talking to reporters. I'd walk out to my car. My dad would be waiting by my car to talk to me. It was really cool. I graduated in December of

my senior year. I was actually the first one in
my family to walk across the stage and get a
degree."
—Dorian Pitts, Texas Tech LB, 1997-2000

Before I was hired at Tech, haircuts were important—or more specifically the length and style of a player's hair were important. Players weren't allowed to wear jewelry. I didn't worry about how long their hair was, if they wore dreadlocks, or had their ears pierced. Their time was their time. They could dress how they wanted to. But if they didn't go to class, the consequences were way more severe. If they tested positive for drugs, I cut them. One positive test after I told them the policy, and they were gone. I made sure they all knew that on the front end. If I found out they hit a woman or stole something, they were gone on the spot. If they missed a class or a study session, we'd roll them, meaning we'd make them roll on their sides all the way from one end zone to the other and back, over and over.

To help develop team chemistry, I had the guys compete in the "Super Games," a series of physical challenges we staged throughout the off-season. I broke the squad into eight groups to make sure I could mix as many different people together as possible. I wanted seniors rooting for freshmen, a black cornerback from the city cheering on a white O-lineman from the country. On Wednesdays, we'd have them playing anything from tug-of-war to arm wrestling, to dodgeball, to bowling, to water polo. If you missed a class, your team lost points. At mid-term and finals, your team would earn points for As or Bs. No points either way for Cs, but if you got Ds or Fs your team lost points. The players really got into it. We awarded the winning team workout gear that said "Super Games World Champions." Really though, if they were the right type of player, just winning the competition was its own reward.

The best teams that I've coached have always been those that are clear minded. That's tough to find, because it's very easy for people to get distracted. It's a mistake to look too far past the goal at hand. People would always come up and ask, "How do you think you're gonna do against Texas?" The truth is, I don't care about Texas right now. The only team I'm able to beat this week is New Mexico or Iowa State or whoever we are scheduled to play that Saturday. We wanna just win one game a week. That is all.

When I first got to Tech, I think the team had a problem understanding this concept. There was a mindset of how games that weren't against Texas, Oklahoma, or Texas A&M would be easy, and that the games against the supposed important schools would be really hard or impossible. That attitude created this sick sort of self-fulfilling prophecy.

Texas Tech had a losing record against North Texas when I arrived in 2000. The reason? North Texas has a major league hard-on to beat Texas Tech, and the Red Raiders just acted like they were too good to play them. How the hell can they not be excited to play North Texas?

I walked to our locker room the week we were preparing to play North Texas in my first season at Tech. Our record was 2-0. North Texas's record was 0-1. I overheard two of my players talking about the game. One of them said, "I'll be glad when we get on to the big games, instead of these little games that don't really count." The other guy said, "Yeah, I know. Tell me about it."

OK, I'll tell you about it, "Like how North Texas beat you last season in Lubbock? Or how they've owned your ass, beating you two of the last three times you played them?"

It infuriated me. That attitude is everything that's wrong with football. I am diametrically opposed to that way of thinking. It's an attitude of entitlement, and it's poison. We had a team meeting. I wanted this to cover not just North Texas, but all the teams we'd play. "You don't think North Texas is a big game? Try losing to them. Then you'll know what a big game is," I told the team. "If you're not excited about playing, well then you're in the wrong place, so get the hell out of here."

I thought it was very important to get that mindset out of there right away, and we did. We never lost to North Texas again.

You want a goal? Just win one game this week.

> **"One of his big deals when he got there was that you have to earn everything you get. We played a really close game against North Texas his first year, but we beat them. He made a big deal that you can't take anybody lightly. You have to have respect for everybody you play. From that first year on, every team that we were supposed to beat—North Texas's smaller programs—we not only beat, but we beat them convincingly. That was a major attitude adjustment he made in the program. He really was very big on accountability and focus and taking care of the details first."**
>
> **—Kliff Kingsbury**

Some coaches consider those teams that commit the fewest penalties to be the teams that are the most disciplined. I think that's misguided. You obviously want to avoid penalties, you want to have as few as possible, but there are very few teams that don't commit some penalties. If you're not pushing and playing on the edge and trying to make things happen, you're probably not going to be very good, but if you're going for it you're going to get flagged now and then.

In our last few seasons at Tech, we were near the bottom of the NCAA rankings in penalties committed. Then again, so were Florida, Oklahoma, Oregon, Texas, and USC. We may have been behind our opponents by 30 yards in penalties (which is not that much) but playing aggressively is worth a few flags. What's more, the teams that played against us would draw more flags than their season averages. I don't think it's because teams that played us all of a sudden got sloppy—they may have fouled more because we were tough to keep a lid on—but I think it had more to do with the individual match-ups we forced downfield.

Wide-open style teams do tend to get penalized more. If you're just sitting there running two yards in a pile or your offense revolves around a scrum, not much really happens outside the pile. If it's wide open, there's more explosive action, and you have a lot of individual match-ups in clear view, so the officials throw more penalties because they can see them better. I think it impacts both teams that way.

A lot of times, teams that have the fewest penalties are the worst teams in their leagues. They want to say how disciplined they are, but some of those guys are just afraid to play aggressively or they don't play hard enough to get penalties.

I used to make my players "roll" the field if they committed personal fouls or stupid penalties, same as when they missed a class. Some penalties are stupid, some are not. If an offensive lineman held, or a defensive back was called for pass interference, they didn't usually roll. Those are usually caused by bad technique rather than stupidity. A receiver, though, would have to roll twice as far if they were offsides because they're supposed to be looking at the ball, not go on sound. Most personal fouls are stupid.

Later in my days at Tech, I stopped making them roll. I got a more disciplined team and I didn't like the tediousness of the punishment. I thought it was more effective to call them out in front of their teammates in a team meeting. I'd show the penalties and how they each screwed the team, "Here's this play. Here's the result. It's coming back because you screwed us. It was this guy right here," and I would put the laser-pointer on the screen and highlight at the player.

"It was funny, when I was playing for the Dolphins in Miami and we were having problems with penalties, I told Coach (Nick) Saban, 'Let's make 'em roll.' All of the other

guys were kinda laughing. I was serious. I think it would've gotten the point across, but I guess you can't really do that in the League. In college, you have the scholarship hanging over their heads. You can make the guys roll and throw up. Coach Saban laughed. He thought it was funny, 'Are you shitting me? We're going to have Jason Taylor and Zach Thomas and these guys out here rolling? They'll tell me to go screw myself.'

"On the field Leach is very big on the details, being disciplined on your routes and how he wants you to do everything. Leach and coach (Bill) Belichick are actually a lot alike. They both have great attention to detail and want tough, smart football players. Coach Belichick has always said, in every move that I make, just know that I am doing what I think is in the best interest of our football team. Right or wrong, that's his outlook. Coach Leach is the same way."
—Wes Welker, Texas Tech WR, 2000-2003

People think you need to yell all the time to be a "discipline" guy. I don't think that could be more wrong. When we got to Tech in 2000, we had the lowest graduation rate in the Big 12. We were going to change that, and because we committed to our approach with great discipline. We had the highest graduation rate of any public institution in major college football at the time I was fired. To make such a transformation academically was truly a team effort. Our coaches and our academic administrators worked very hard at it. We were also fortunate that it snowed at some ideal times.

Once, at 4 a.m. in the spring, I brought our whole team,

coaches, and our entire academic staff outside because too many players were missing study halls. We could've just brought out the guys who'd been missing, but I wanted them all participating in an exercise we dubbed "The Tower of London," where everyone had to run—and crawl—carrying cinder blocks above their heads from one corner of campus to the next, from the math buildings to the science buildings. My attitude was, "You play with this guy. He plays right next to you and he's holding us back. You're going to class, but you're not doing anything about him not going.

"You're sitting here watching this guy not do his part and you haven't done anything to fix that. You're a senior and he may be a freshman. There's not just something wrong with him, there's something wrong with you, too. There's also something wrong with me as a coach, and the assistants, and our academic people."

We were lucky it snowed like hell that day. I wanted those academic administrators and those position coaches motivated to get the guys going to study hall. It's not like we had the academic people carrying cinder blocks, but I wanted the entire coaching staff and the entire academic staff aware of how seriously we were going to take academics.

There was a funny sort of camaraderie about it. Guys like our quarterback Graham Harrell, who never missed class, were out there running and rolling in the snow, cheering everyone on the whole time. We had a strength coach then who everyone called "Warden" because he looked and acted kinda like a prison warden. Graham barked, "C'mon, Warden, give us more!" as he was going for 100 push-ups. After that snowy dawn workout, they all went to study hall.

We came up with the Tower of London idea after my assistant Dennis Simmons and I went over to England to do a coaching clinic and tour the country. When I visit somewhere, I try to learn as much as I can about the place. There is so much to learn from different cultures, different parts of the world, and different eras. These things have always fascinated me. I wanted to visit every castle in England.

"Tours that would normally take two hours would take us eight. Leach would read every passage; every sign; every wall plaque on the freakin' tour. At one point, Leach stops and asks the guide, 'I don't wanna offend you, but it seems like the Earl's wife got around a bit, didn't she?' The guide starts laughing and goes, 'You know, mate, in my 40 years of working here, you're the first person to ever ask me that question. The only way one would know that is if someone had read all of these signs.'"
—Dennis Simmons, Texas Tech assistant, 2000-09

One of the places in England that I'd always wanted to see was the Tower of London, which was originally built by William the Conqueror. It served as a fortress, a palace, and a prison, and has been significant in England since before the eleventh century. The place is loaded with artifacts. On any visit to England, the Tower of London is a must.

In our first few years at Tech, we made the players roll to discipline them. We make an announcement at the end of practice, "OK, the following are going to visit the Chairman of Friendship and Fellowship . . . " The chairman was Ruffin McNeill, one of our defensive coaches, who'd sit in a chair on the field while the offending parties would roll across hundreds of yards.

They'd yell, "Man, Coach, this is messed up. Why they making us doing all of this?"

Ruffin would say, "Yeah, man, I know. I know. I just love y'all. If you go to class, you won't have to do this. I like watching you roll. I love you."

It was pretty effective, but I thought it was an unnecessary distraction for Ruffin. Unfortunately, at the time, we didn't have a strength coach, who would've been the ideal guy to handle that sort of discipline. Then we promoted Bennie Wylie, who'd been a college running back at Sam Houston State.

Bennie was a former assistant strength and conditioning coach with the Dallas Cowboys. He had a great presence about him. Bennie had a militaristic approach to things. He didn't tell the players to arrive at 4 a.m. Instead he'd say be there by 3:57 a.m. because he knew that'd stick in their minds better. His two best friends were Navy Seals, the Luttrell twins. One of the twins, Marcus, spoke to our team about commitment and accountability on the night before he was deployed to Afghanistan. Marcus was the only man to come away from Operation Redwing with his life, and his account of the mission, *Lone Survivor*, made it to the top of the *New York Times* Best Seller list.

> **"I'm a big English literature guy. We'd run by the English building and I'd say, 'Tell me the names of two of Shakespeare's plays.' Then, we'd move on. Everything we did had some rhyme or reason to it. And we had some fun with it as we reminded them about some of the choices they had made. You wanted them to understand that it was much easier to do things the right way than to have to do all of this extra. That's part of the reason why he was able to graduate 80 percent of the players."**
> **—Bennie Wylie, Tech strength coach, 2003-09**

There was no question that Bennie was a tough guy, but he also had a lot of common sense. I always felt that we needed the strength coach overseeing the physical discipline anyway. Bennie was the perfect man for the job.

> **"Our Tower of London was hilarious to sit there and watch. If we got to the math building, he'd say, tell me what is Pi? If you knew it, you'd**

move on. If not, you had to do some physical
activity. Bennie got a lot of his material from
Leach. The thing about it was, if you went to
class and did what you were supposed to, you
never had to do any of this stuff. If you didn't, it
was a great deterrent. It had the kids thinking,
'I know they're creative, I know they're going
to come up with something, who knows what
they'll come up with? Is this really worth me
not getting up and going to class?' That was the
whole thought process."

—**Dennis Simmons**

I had a sign in my office that said, "You're either coaching
it or allowing it to happen." Discipline is not just focusing on
the negative aspects and scolding your guys when they don't
do something the right way. Discipline requires encouragement.
Discipline requires support. Discipline requires sharing a new
perspective so the person can gain the confidence he needs to
be successful. Sometimes it's about making it more convenient
for your guys to perform the desired behavior rather than the
undesired one. Obviously, if a guy isn't giving great enough effort,
he needs to be called out. There will be times when you have to cut
people who simply refuse to change.

With every aspect of instilling discipline, there needs to be
some reflection on what your role has been as a coach. What
could you have done better? How could you have reached that
guy sooner? You can't fall back on, "Well, I told him a thousand
times and he still won't do it."

You told him a thousand times and he still won't do it? Then
you're not worth a damn as a coach. If I had to tell someone a
thousand times to do something, he ain't the problem. I'm the
problem.

"I missed one class. It was a communication class. Every day after practice one of the coaches read the names of anyone who missed a class in front of everybody. They called out my name. Leach called me into his office. He asked me what my problem was. I was a captain of the team. I was a junior. He said guys look up to me. He said he was sending me to the Tower of London.

"You had this big cinder block and you had to run around the entire campus with that thing held over your head the whole time. Texas Tech has the second-biggest campus in the country. It is so spread out that they have bus routes to take you to classes. You'd get done around 7 a.m. There were six other guys that did it with me that day. None of us ever missed another class again. I'd say 80 percent of the team did it once, but almost no one missed class twice. I told myself, halfway through I will never miss another class again. You were allowed to take a break to stop but the block had to stay above your head.

"I never missed another class again. I actually sat in the front row the rest of the year. It wasn't just because Tower of London was so grueling, but it was the guilt of knowing that I let him down. I looked at Mike like a father figure. He didn't yell at me, but he just gave me that look of disappointment that your parents give you, which is way worse.

"I think that's why so many guys are successful that left Tech. You get kids 18, 19, 20 years old, the time in their lives when they become men. You don't have to just be a coach; you have to be a father figure. You let these kids get away with doing whatever they want to do, not going to class; it just affects them in the long run when they get done with football. Mike refuses to cut anybody any slack. He demands perfection. I'll always be grateful. My dad told me he is totally in debt to Mike Leach for helping me become a man."

—Mike Smith, Texas Tech LB, 2000-03

A portion of teamwork is sacrifice. During the two-week winter conditioning circuit, I wanted them to sacrifice their evenings. We called it Midnight Maneuvers. We would actually start around 10 at night. The timing was perfect because that's roughly the time of day when we'd be playing a lot of fourth quarters. I've heard a lot of teams do their conditioning at dawn, but how many games are their players going to play before breakfast?

We'd have our guys do a bunch of stations, where they'd have to do everything from bear crawls, to dot drills for their footwork, to obstacle courses. Better still, we knew they weren't out with their buddies partying. Instead, they were with their team. They gave up their nights because it was a team endeavor. We were working together as a team—it was a good message to send.

One year, a few of our veteran players went out in town one night and we found out that they were involved in a fight. The team happened to be off that day, but we called in those "tough guys" to take part in our version of *Fight Club*. They reported to the football offices at 7 a.m., where we taped up their hands just like real fighters and put big boxing gloves on them. Then, Bennie trained them like boxers. They went into our sandpit and punched the stand-up dummies. We ran them all over campus while they wore the gloves. It was a lot like Rocky for a day. They probably had to go 30 rounds. Bennie and I were always on the same page with this stuff. We always tried to match the punishment to the offense. You were guilty of fighting; well, you're going to train like a fighter. You were guilty of not going to class; well, you're going to run by the academic buildings carrying cinder blocks while being quizzed on English Lit. We wanted our punishments to be a deterrent and an inconvenience, but we also wanted to have a little fun.

We tell everyone the team rules in the first meeting of the year at the start of training camp. They broke the team rules and they had to be held accountable.

This particular incident was one of those big crowd fights where no one knows who actually hit who. We punished them, but we reminded them how to handle these situations too. You do not throw punches. You leave. If a situation starts to go bad, you leave because that other guy out on the streets doesn't get to play in the stadium on Saturday, you do. When they write about it in the paper, it'll say so-and-so who plays this position for Texas Tech, who went to such-and-such high school and is from this town got into a fight with an unidentified male. They call him an unidentified male because he doesn't get to play in Jones Stadium. The unidentified male doesn't have anything to lose. He just goes back to his job at 7-Eleven or builds fences or lays bricks. You have a scholarship to lose. There's a different standard for you. I don't care if it's fair. I don't care what he said. I don't care what kind of names he called you or what he might've said about someone in your family. It doesn't matter. You leave.

I warned them about fighting. It was one of the first things I'd talk about every year when I first addressed the team. This was how I'd break down that initial meeting:

Introductions: I'd introduce the new staff, freshmen, and junior college players, and explain that there is no initiating of the freshmen. I'd explain that we have freshmen who are going to play this year, so don't treat them like freshmen. If you're a freshman, don't act like one.

Academics: I'd remind them that we have the number one graduation rate of any public institution in the nation. They were expected to uphold that standard.

Legacy: I'd tell them that we are going to require you to do things that other teams may not be required to do, because we expect our results to be different from theirs.

Communication: I reinforce that we must always have communication. There is never an excuse not to talk to one another. Communication is critical on the field to make plays. It is also critical off the field.

Respect: Respect the managers, trainers, secretaries, and all the support staff. No one works harder for less reward.

Then I would explain the team rules, which included no fighting. The rest were:

No Stealing: If you steal anything you will get kicked off the team. Trust is very important in football. If you are a thief, then you can't be trusted.

Don't Use Drugs: Drugs of any kind will get you kicked off the team. Drugs are selfish. No player's partying is more important than the team.

No Hitting Women: People who hit women are cowards. If you hit a woman, you will be immediately dismissed. We don't have cowards on this team.

No Drinking or going out after Wednesday night on game weeks.

Be On Time.

I'm not interested in rules for the sake of rules. Discipline doesn't have to mean having players cut their hair, wear collared shirts, and take off their jewelry. I didn't want them constantly looking over their shoulders worrying about the rule police. The football training complex is their sanctuary. I wanted them to feel comfortable and excited to be there. It's important for them to enjoy the company of their teammates and coaches. Discipline should be designed around necessary results, not unnecessary rules.

There were other points I'd bring up at the meeting. Some were training camp rules. Some focused on attitude. Some were tenets of the program, like how we were committed to playing the best player in his position regardless of age. I'd remind them that no one is entitled, and that they earned their positions every day.

I'd bring up the same principles throughout the rest of the year. We did things differently than a lot of other programs, and we expected our results to be different from theirs on the field and off.

A few years ago, right about the time that the NFL was realizing just what a talent Wes Welker was, *USA Today* did a huge story on him. In the piece was a quote from Welker that really jumped out at me: "I just try to concentrate on what I can control, and that is me going out and believing in myself."

That quote sums up his greatness better than anything I could've tried to say about him. It's a philosophy that really resonated with me. The words are simple to understand, but difficult to do, because most people don't have that level of focus. We spend a lot of time training our guys to focus, to be more clear minded. Some guys, like Welker—the biggest overachiever I've ever coached—are just born with the ability to focus. It's a talent, just like speed, quickness, or strength.

There's a catch-22 about self-confidence: You need confidence to be successful, but it's success that breeds confidence. There's this chicken-or-the-egg deal to the equation. At some point, you just have to decide you're going to be confident. Then, as you do, you're going to have more success. Some people come by it naturally. Wes was able to do things that people a lot more "talented" than him couldn't do because of his confidence, and the fact that he didn't allow a lot of distractions to get in the way. He didn't worry about how good the other guy might be or what the other guy was trying to do. He was just focused on himself.

Wes was a really good product of the principles and approaches that we were trying to teach. We spent four years packing that into him, and to see it work for him was a good example for everybody in the program.

I had signs made up of that Welker quote. We put them in every meeting room. I wanted those words within eyeshot of the coaches at all times so they'd draw their players' attention to it constantly.

Sometimes you believe that a certain way of doing things is best, only to find out later that it isn't.

When I took over at Tech I wanted a few guys with Texas contacts, which we obviously had with Sonny and Art. I felt like it was important to have guys with deep ties to the area. I bought into that idea back then, but I don't now. The most important quality in a recruiter is persistence. You want a guy who is willing to make hundreds of phone calls, who is a good conversationalist, and has the ability to establish relationships with people. I've had several assistants who on first look you'd think couldn't recruit, but give them time and you'd see they were great at it. Clay McGuire, who I ended up hiring as an assistant coach after he graduated, was that way. He wasn't necessarily the dynamic salesman type, but he landed three big-time recruits for our last recruiting class at Tech. McGuire stole two terrific recruits from big schools, Eric Ward and Will Ford, just because he was so persistent.

Another thing I came to realize is how vital it is for coaches and players to buy into the "team first" mentality. I've had players and coaches in the past that didn't buy in, and it didn't go very well. Selfishness is like a cancer. Football is infested with it. Between players, coaches, and staff, it's everywhere: "Well, I didn't select him . . . I don't coach him . . . They don't know how to use me right . . . Why did they make this call?" It's all just finger-pointing. You can't let that attitude find its way into your program. You could be the dumbest team in the league but if you're less selfish than the other team, you have a pretty good chance at winning.

If they say "me, me, me" or "I, I, I" and complain a lot, you need to get rid of them. If you can't change the problem, then you need to eliminate it. If it means firing or cutting people, it's better to do it sooner rather than later.

In old Westerns they'll talk about how killing changes a man. Well, firing or cutting someone does too.

My defensive coordinator Lyle Setencich gave me my first college coaching job at Cal Poly-San Luis Obispo for $3,000 a year. I brought him to Texas Tech in 2003, and we did some good things defensively and improved for a couple of years. Then his wife, Kathy, had a stroke. He split his time managing her care while attempting to put in the rigorous hours necessary to be a successful defensive coordinator. After attempting to do this for two-and-a-half years, we started to struggle on defense. As time went on, he developed an outward bitterness toward the hand life had dealt him, to the point where his attitude began rubbing off on the players and affecting their development. We became pessimistic and uninspired on defense. There were a lot of excuses and second-guessing.

After giving up 600 yards (366 yards rushing) to Oklahoma State, in a game that we lost 49–45, I realized that a change needed to be made. It had been pretty obvious to others that I'd been resistant to making the change for a long time. Ultimately, it was simple. He wasn't buying into the vision of the program, so he resigned for personal reasons.

As soon as Lyle left, I hung up that sign that said, "You're either coaching it or allowing it to happen." We improved quickly and went on to beat Virginia in the Gator Bowl.

In hindsight, I probably should've let two assistants go. We had another guy who was one of those eye-rolling, clock-watcher, second-guesser types, who was never a good X's and O's guy. When he became lazy at recruiting, he became obsolete. He'd developed this attitude over time along the lines of, "Well, you're the head coach, if you want him on the team, fine, but I'm not going to coach him." If you aren't going to contribute to developing the players then what do I need you for? Once Lyle left, we hit a point where it was obvious who wasn't buying in, and who was.

I felt that anyone insulted by the sign didn't belong on our team, coaches or players alike. I wanted people to buy into the program, and be accountable for their actions as a part of the team, as something bigger than themselves. I made the sign for my office four times as big as everyone else's. I had the biggest obligation since I was the head coach. I wanted to make sure that I didn't forget that philosophy. I wanted everyone to know that we, as a coaching staff, would be committed to abide by it.

I'd seen it when I worked for Hal Mumme, but I only experienced it when I was in the head coach role. You're beyond invested in the program—it's your head on the block. It's amazing the stuff you're able to remember, sort out, conceive, and anticipate. It's also amazing what you're blind to when you're rushing ahead at full speed toward your goal. You're just going, going, going, and with that, you assume everybody's behind you going at the same rate. Sometimes it's like Pickett's Charge in the Civil War; you're rushing up the hill to attack the enemy but your troops are scattered. You have to make sure you periodically check your flanks.

Setting the Tone

The title of this book emerged as the mantra of our program in the wake of a 2003 loss at Missouri. Their quarterback, Brad Smith, ran for almost 300 yards on us. Our team was really struggling. We had an overly aggressive offense and a timid defense, and it got to the point where they were starting to point fingers at one another. We were 5-3. We had just lost back-to-back games. The next day, I showed up at our team meeting with a sword. The blade was about three-feet long, and really glistened when the light hit it.

I'm pretty sure the players had no clue what was about to happen.

I'd thought a lot about what I was going to say before I entered the room. I jotted down a bunch of ideas on a scrap of paper, the same as I normally did before meetings. It's important for a team to be exposed to more than just football, and as I worked at it the pirates and the metaphor of the sword just sounded right.

I took that sword and laid it across the podium. The players were mesmerized, wondering what was going to happen after such a brutal loss. I've read about 20 books on pirates (the best is probably *Under the Black Flag*). I told them how England had the best pirates because they were the most adept at seafaring, and about how pirates came from all nationalities. You had all of these people who were tired of living in Europe, so they banded together. One may have been an Arawak Indian. One may have been an escaped African slave. Another guy might've come from the Orient. One or two guys could've come from England, dishonorably discharged from the Navy. In polite society back then there really wasn't diversity, but on pirate ships there was. All you had to be was a capable hand. Captains were voted into leadership. How is it that they were they so progressive in these ways? I imagine societal mores can go out the window pretty quickly when you're fighting for your life.

There are a lot of misconceptions about pirates. Pirates varied from the soldier/sailor type hired by the Queen Elizabeth I of England to help wage war against Spain, to ruthless outlaws with no direction but their own. Some pirates were actually pretty organized businessmen. Bartholomew Roberts, for example, didn't drink. He had a whole fleet of ships. He was a really efficient planner and organizer. Another pirate, Henry Morgan, eventually became the Governor of Jamaica. At some points in time it was illegal to be a pirate, but at other points it wasn't. Sir Francis Drake was paid by the Elizabeth I to plunder and pillage the Spanish and bring as many riches back to England as his fleet could carry. If you were an Englishman during the sixteenth century, you pretty much had a green light to do anything you wanted to the Spanish.

I told the team how pirates had a workman's comp deal, where if you lost your leg, you got a certain amount of additional treasure. Then, I told the team how similar football teams are to pirate crews, guys of all kinds of ethnicities coming from all corners of society, serving a gamut of roles onboard. I explained how the pirates viewed their swords the same way football players should view their bodies.

"They took great pride in their swords, sharpening them just like players do their bodies by lifting the weights and doing all of the drills we do," I said.

The players said nothing.

I swung this long sword through the air in front of them.

"Your body *is* your sword. Are you going to swing your sword aggressively, but really out of control like you're out there playing street ball?" I said as I began to haphazardly flail the sword around.

"If you're frantic, without being clear-minded, you put yourself into a vulnerable position. Are you going to duck your head and swing it timidly? Or are you going to have great technique and swing it without any hesitation?"

Some of 'em nodded their heads. Some laughed watching me flail around with the sword. Some couldn't wait till I stopped talking just so they could come up and touch the sword. But the point was made. We were pirates, and the next time we went into battle, our swords would be ready. "Swing Your Sword" became a battle cry for us.

We won our next two games, then lost on a last-minute touchdown pass at #6 Texas. We finished the season beating Navy 38–14 in the Houston Bowl. I know the pirates speech was unconventional, but you can't be insecure or let fear rule your life. You have to do what's in your heart.

Ego tends to have a negative connotation these days. But ego is so important. Ego doesn't help you when you win, but it protects you during the losses. When you get beat and thousands of people are disappointed and you're getting hammered from all directions—at home, nationally, in the media—ego allows you to stand up and say, "I'm the guy that can straighten this out. I'm the guy that can make this happen." If you don't have that inside you, then the people around you won't respond with confidence. I have never met a great player or an overachiever who does not have a big ego. That doesn't mean they're unpleasant. Their ego may be well covered with genuine modesty. Ego is why they know that they're the ones to get the job done.

Of course, it's not good for ego to manifest itself badly. I mean, there's a difference between narcissism and a healthy dose of ego. On some level, there needs to be something inside telling you, "I'm the guy that needs to coach this team, or I'm the guy that needs to get this ball."

It'd be ridiculous to say that Michael Crabtree, quiet as he was, didn't have an ego. He had a huge ego. No question. If you sat him down and asked him, do you think you're better than this other receiver, he would tell you without hesitation that he is. But Crabtree's not beating you over the head telling you that. Wes Welker is the exact same way. In his mind, and you can see this in his eyes, he is convinced he is the best receiver in the NFL.

Ego and confidence are wrapped together. They're not interchangeable, but they draw from each other. Ego is what drives you and makes it important for you to be successful. It's also the little voice telling you that being behind somebody else is unacceptable.

I don't think you can be a good coach without having some ego. There are some coaches who aren't as effective as they could be because they really don't possess it. Often as a coach you find yourself having to draw a line in the sand, and ego and firmness play into your ability to lay it down. I've met John Wooden. He was a caring, giving, confident person, but he had a huge ego. The fact is, he was an outwardly humble and very sincere guy, but he clearly had a lot of presence about him. He felt like if he worked hard, he would prevail over the other person, in part because he was John Wooden, and he was willing to work harder. Think about the core belief: Let's worry about us, not them. Our product is going to be superior to the point that it'll overcome everyone else's product.

Ego shouldn't come off as abrasive. Confidence should be genuine, not artificial. You can't help but respect a guy whose ego manifests itself through hard work, focus, determination, and the willingness to take his own path. In football there's a tendency to homogenize everything. Well, if everybody's like everybody else, then nobody is striving to be special or working to raise the bar. You need a touch of ego to step off the path and head your own way when everybody else is heading in another.

I've been accused a time or two of running up the score. People say "Well, the game's already been decided. Just kneel on the ball and call it a day." Screw that. I don't want the guys I send into the game thinking that way. Next year those third-team guys might be my starters. Heck, if we have an injury or two, they might become our starters next week. Running a team is an ongoing process. Even if it's the last game of the year, you still have another one next season. Regardless of the score, you've spent a long time teaching technique and lifting weights, and if there's some number-three left guard in the game out there yucking it up, I will rip him.

I've never cared if somebody else thinks the job is done and the game is over. You wanna be unique? You wanna be special? I truly believe everything is preparing you for something else. Be a team. Be the most excited to play. Do your job. That doesn't stop if you're down by 39 or up by 30. These are all valuable opportunities. You cannot just mail it in. How often do you get a chance to execute an onside kick? How many plays are you going to get in your whole life? It's all about making the most of it. This is an opportunity to get better, and every chance at getting better can help you down the road. The buses don't leave till the clock says 00:00. That means attitude and body language, and continuing to develop your skills until then.

In 2006, we played Minnesota in the Insight Bowl. We played about as bad a first half as any team I've ever coached. It wasn't that we weren't playing hard or giving a good enough effort. It just seemed like everyone on the team went out there trying to play perfectly and not make a mistake. We were playing constipated. It was exacerbated by the fact that Minnesota was hitting one big play after the next. Their quarterback connected on 11 of 13 passes for three touchdowns in the half. He was setting school records along the way. They had one big receiver, Jack Simmons, this big blonde kid who was having the game of his life. He caught five passes for over 100 yards in the first half. One of their running backs ran for 140 yards. Meanwhile, we turned the ball over three times. We were down 35–7 going into the locker room. Our team was discouraged. I had to find a way to put things in perspective at halftime. I'd already worked out what needed to be said to the team before we got inside.

There've been a few times in my coaching career when I haven't said much to the team during halftime. If you're really rolling along and playing well, you don't want to disrupt anything. You don't want to interrupt the momentum. Those are the times when the less said, the better. This was not one of those times.

One of the worst assumptions about coaching is that the further a team falls behind, the more their coach should rant and holler at them. That's not necessarily the case with me. Ripping is generally for situations when you don't have their attention or they're not playing hard. If you're not getting a good enough effort, that's when you rip into them.

There's a folklore around pep talks dating all the way back to Knute Rockne. There's an art to them, but great games generally aren't a byproduct of inspirational speeches. Usually, they're byproducts of a great week of preparation. Big wins usually start on Sunday in college.

I've always believed that the purpose of the pre-game speech is to generate energy without getting the guys too hyped. If they're already too hyped, you might want to calm them down. With halftime speeches, you're either staying the course or drawing their attention to other objectives. If the effort is not good, then you rip their ass. But within that context, there are many nuances to what you say and how you say it.

I approach the halftime talk by figuring out the objectives. I work up an outline in my mind. I want about three points, never more than five. If you're in a frustrating situation, you can't let your negative emotions cloud their minds. By the same token, you can't let your satisfaction allow them to become complacent as you go out to begin the second half.

At halftime during the Insight Bowl, the first thing I did when I entered the locker room was take the coaches into our individual locker room away from the team. "Get your players right," I told them. "We're not packing it in. We are not going out there in the second half with anybody that doesn't think we can win this game." Then I spoke to the team:

We may not be where we want to be, but this is still is an opportunity. I mean, we do not want to be in this position, but we are. So you now have this unique opportunity to make history. This can be the most memorable game of our lives or it can be a disaster.

We have had a lot of amazing comebacks here at Texas Tech. People thought they were impossible. I can think of game after game. I can think of several we've had against the Aggies. I can think of one against Texas. I can think of another one against Texas, which we barely lost. I can think of one against Mississippi. I can go right down the list. I can think of one against TCU, where we had one unanswered touchdown after the next. That is the identity of the school that you guys selected. That's the legacy that's been created here. Ok, so what are we gonna do?

What are we gonna do? Are we gonna be part of it? Are we gonna be part of it, or are we gonna be part of the one that quit because we didn't like the way stuff went and we got discouraged because of the way a play went so I'm gonna hang my head and pout?

Well, that plane ain't leavin' and that bus ain't leaving till the thing says 00:00, OK?

Long story short: Being excited to play is important. I think both teams were excited to play. We had some mishaps and then we got less excited to play and they got more excited to play.

So how do you make the comeback? Do your job. Do your job. Be great at doing your job.

O-line, hold them out a little longer.

Quarterbacks, make great reads.

Receivers, stick your routes. Make catches. Turn and go up field.

Running backs, finish off your runs hard.

Defensive line, you play with great pad level. You whip their asses.

Do not let them push you off that line of scrimmage.

Linebackers and secondary, you do a great job of making tackles.

The most important thing is blocking and tackling. What have they been doing better than us? The biggest thing is blocking and tackling. They are doing their jobs better than we are.

This is a team that is going to come out in the second half and try and use the clock. Defense, it's important for you to get three-and-outs, make 'em punt and get the ball. Offense, it's important for you to do your job. We do need to no-huddle, but we don't need some break-neck pace. Just go make routine plays. One after another after another. We finish drives. Then, kick-off and we do it all over again. That's all we need to do.

We need to block better than them. We need to tackle better than them. We need to do our job better than they do their job.

Ultimately, how's it going to turn out? I don't really know, except I do know that doing our job is the identity of this place. I also know that we have won a whole lot of games by doing just that when a whole lot of other people didn't have the balls to, when other people didn't have the guts to do that.

What team are we? We're going to find out this half. I

don't want to see anybody quit. Just keep bringing it to them. Make sure you're doing your job every snap.

They won the first half. Make sure we win the second half.

That was the entire speech. I'd like to say we came out and scored on the first play of the second half, but it didn't happen that way. In fact, Minnesota went on a 16-play drive to open the third quarter, but we won a moral victory by holding them to a field goal. We started taking some chances on defense by blitzing instead of sitting back and letting them bring the game to us. We trailed Minnesota, 38–7 with about eight minutes remaining in the third quarter. Then, we scored 31 unanswered points in less than 20 minutes.

A speech can kick start momentum, but a speech is pointless unless you get everyone to buy in and commit themselves. The speech might've put everybody on the same page, but it's about everybody committing to the effort. That's what made the comeback happen—everyone doing their jobs, together.

I think speeches are generally overrated, but good communication and having everybody on the same page is underrated. Dramatic little anecdotes, shouting, or emotional rants are overrated. The same approach isn't going to work every time. Over the long haul of the season, freshness is necessary. It needs to be stimulating, interesting, and exciting.

I think momentum is really important, but you have to remember that momentum relates to body language and mindset. Some really stupid things can spark momentum. A team can be way behind. They may kick a field goal right before halftime, then go running into the tunnel feeling like a million bucks. Well, they really didn't do much, but their mindset changed and it shows in their body language. The hard part is reaching the group, but if everybody decides to change their outlook, then all of a sudden you may have found some momentum. People want to believe, but sometimes they need a springboard to get going.

What was so special about us holding Minnesota to that little old field goal at the start of the second half? It helped us believe in who we were as a team, and that we could win. We ended up beating Minnesota 44–41 in overtime. Our 31-point comeback was the biggest margin overcome in Division I-A bowl history.

> "That was the best halftime speech I've ever heard. He wasn't negative. He gave everybody in that room the sense that a comeback was possible and encouraged us not to get our heads down, to believe in ourselves. That speech helped a lot. We were a young team at that point. Graham (Harrell) was a sophomore. We had a lot of young players who needed to hear that positive reinforcement.
>
> "In all my days of football, with my dad being a coach and me having been on a lot of teams, it did help that Leach was free and could get his point across in so many different and unique ways. He got his point across better than anyone I've ever seen. Sometimes in team meetings, we're talking about a football play, then the next thing you know, he's talking about pirates and swords or a dog peeing on his tent when he was a little kid. People would be looking around like, 'Where's he going with this one?' But he did a good job of giving your mind a break and not being so uptight. He could allow you to relax and get your mind off football for a little bit and then in the end, he'd get you re-focused."
> —Eric Morris, Texas Tech WR, 2004-08

Being a great communicator is something I constantly strive

to be. The central role of a coach is to reach his players. I believe that everyone is capable of great effort. Even if you're elderly or handicapped, you're capable of great effort. You may not always be capable of great results, but you are capable of great effort. Anybody can try hard. A coach has to be able to explain to his players how they can get the best out of themselves.

It really makes me ill whenever I hear a coach say, "To win, you gotta have great players," or "I told them to do it, but they didn't do it." That is sad. The best players give you a definite advantage, but if that's all there is to it, then let them watch a DVD and stick them out on the field with a chimpanzee wearing the headset. I want to have a role in the improvement of my players. I don't buy into the notion that whoever has the best players automatically wins. I've never believed that, and I never will.

That sign we had on the walls of all the coaching offices at Texas Tech is important for any leader to remember: "You're either coaching it or allowing it to happen." It's a copout whenever you hear a coach say that they told a player something over and over and over again, but the guy just won't do it. It's your job to hold the player and yourself accountable. It's your job to find a way to make him understand how to do it.

You have to be a great listener to be a great communicator. As tempting as it is to talk, you learn more by listening. You also have to observe body language and mannerisms—football really lends itself to this because there's so much film. When you watch practice film, you can better identify non-verbal cues you might not pick up on when just checking in with your guys:

> *"How's he walking around at practice? What's his body language like? Why's he suddenly pouting now? Is there something wrong in his life? I'm not sure, but he's not moving as fast. Well, maybe if we figure out why he's pouting, maybe we can get him to move faster."*

"I had never heard anything about Mike Leach before he was hired at Tech. He showed up at my high school. He was wearing jeans and a Tech shirt. He looked really young too. He wasn't like that traditional head coach coming over in khakis, wearing all of his bowl rings, with his hair to the side. He just sat and talked. He did a magic trick. He was so easy to talk to. I committed right there on the spot. I was sure I wanted to be a Red Raider after that.

I graduated, played in the NFL, and got into coaching. I still talk to him on the phone for hours. There's never a dull moment in a conversation with Mike Leach. What you see is what you get with him. He doesn't hold anything back. He says whatever he's thinking. He never changes. I remember when I was playing with the Baltimore Ravens. I'd be sitting there with my teammates Kelly Gregg, Dan Cody, and Kyle Boller. Leach would call. They'd be like, 'Your head coach calls you? Man, our head coach never calls us.' He'd send me a huge box of Texas Tech stuff every year. I haven't met one guy I played with who had a head coach who still calls his ex-players and does that kind of stuff for them, just to make sure that things are going alright or if you need anything."

—Mike Smith, Texas Tech LB 2000-03

It's a shame that coaches sometimes block out the rest of the world outside football. They're really missing out. Many of them think reading or hearing about something that doesn't directly relate to the game of football can foul up their focus. I've always felt like I'm lucky to have an interest in a variety of things, because if you have balance it will (hopefully) reduce the potential for burn out.

There is great value in living a life that balances the mental and the physical. There are so many more things to draw from and to teach your players that exist outside football. John Wooden always said he drew from his experience as an English teacher. Bud Wilkinson, the great Oklahoma coach, was once an English teacher too. Woody Hayes drew from his time teaching history. I majored in American Studies and minored in English, not football.

Wooden spoke about being an English teacher over and over in his books. I was given a DVD on Woody Hayes after winning the Woody Hayes Coach of the Year award. He talked constantly about military history and how he viewed life through that lens.

Football is obsessive. The game can lurk in the back of your mind and seem all-consuming, but it doesn't hurt to freshen it up a bit. I try to make a point of knowing a little bit about everything. The author Michael Lewis once said to me—and I hadn't given it much thought till he pointed it out—that I'm the most curious person he's ever met. I try to absorb as much as I can because there's so much out there besides football.

Of all the subjects I've studied over the years, the one people talk to me about the most is pirates. It's crazy how big this thing became. I think every kid is interested in pirates. After that "Swing Your Sword" speech, the players passed it on and spoke about it to reporters. Michael Lewis wrote about it in the *New York Times Magazine* and started a legend around it. The pirate thing became fun for the fans. People started sending pirate stuff from all over the place. Pretty soon, pirate flags began popping up all over our stadium. I think it helped add personality to our program. There are those who think it was my idea to become the "Pirate Team." It was really our fans' doing as much as anyone's, and the players liked the connection—a shared identity can be a powerful rallying call for any team.

> **"The players really got into the whole pirate thing. We were the 'Pirate Team.' I'll never forget that day Coach Leach came into the meeting with that sword and started explaining how pirates lived. It was wild, but it made so much sense as he got into it. We took three things from that speech: Don't hesitate. Be Smart. And be violent on the field. We were a young team and that pirate thing gave us an identity. We needed an attention-getter. We needed something to rally behind. That was it.**
>
> **"Whenever people find out I played at Texas Tech, they ask how the pirate thing came about. When I explain it, they go, 'You know that actually makes a lot of sense.' But I know they think it sounds crazy at first."**
> **—Antonio Huffman, Texas Tech CB, 2003-05**

Too many people reject anyone who doesn't conform to their manufactured, preconceived standards. If I like something, I like it. I don't get embarrassed or worried about how others might interpret it. I'm a Howard Stern fan. That's probably not something you hear from guys in a world full of stopwatches, khaki pants, and golf shirts. I started watching his show when he was on the E! channel. Stern fascinated me. He's extremely curious. His communication stems from his curiosity. He's curious to the point where he'll ask things that others aren't willing to ask. He'll go there. We're similar in that regard. The reaction to those kinds of questions is often as interesting as the answer.

It is a massive oversimplification to say that Stern is a guy who is just interested in crude, graphic material. He's hugely curious about human behavior, including things considered crude and graphic. Those things are a part of life too, and he doesn't shy away. It may not always be in good taste, but even in his wildest moments he can be very insightful. He's a keen observer of human nature. The other thing that I appreciate about Stern is his ability to laugh at himself, and to see the humor in things where others see only misery. Some people are too closed-minded to enjoy the differences and variety that other people can offer.

I've never been a sitcom guy. I didn't watch *Seinfeld* till it was in syndication. I didn't think that I'd even be able to stand it. I figured everything I ever wanted to know about life in New York City, I'd already picked up from some of my east coast classmates in law school. One day I was bored and channel surfing, and I watched the first 10 minutes of an episode. The four main characters were sitting around a table in a diner and made the strangest bet about which of them could go the longest without pleasuring themselves. I was hooked.

The characters were all over the top. They were all selfish—but a person's internal thoughts are often selfish. This was a sitcom about people who act the way they think.

Seinfeld was more realistic than most reality shows. Like any great television show, it was carried by the writing. There were four great characters that everyone, on some level, could identify with. Our daughter Janeen is Elaine.

The dialogue between the four main characters constantly mirrored what we all think and feel in our own lives. The difference was that we don't all have three like-minded friends who we can bounce this stuff off of. *Seinfeld* allowed everyone to share their thoughts vicariously through the characters. There was so much truth to the show. People often want to handle situations a particular way, or they notice the hypocrisy or the irony in certain actions. They have these thoughts roaming around in their head with no way out. *Seinfeld* provided that release for them.

I've always been a people watcher. I've been doing it professionally ever since I got into coaching. *Seinfeld* is a great people-watching show because of all their peculiar mannerisms, their characteristics, and their reactions. The plot of the show is reduced to almost no action, so everyone is just sitting around reflecting on a lot of points of view. Comedians would go out of business if they didn't have the eye for watching people. Same deal for football coaches.

Understanding the nuances of a person's behavior is quite a skill. Some of us are obviously more fascinated by those nuances than others. I'm sure Jerry Seinfeld and Larry David spend a lot more mental energy than most people on the little details. They have to. I heard that Seinfeld once said the main thing he and Larry David had in common was that they both had the ability to focus deeply on something very small, and they were able to blow the small things way out of proportion. As you watch that show, you realize it's purely a study in human nature. If there were too much plot or too much action, you wouldn't be able to see the subtlety in the characters' interactions. By minimizing the action and the plot, the nuance is revealed. You see how one person thinking one thing leads to someone else thinking—and doing—something else. It shows more than anything how self-interest affects a person's behavior.

I've literally stayed awake at night thinking about complete strangers. Why would he do this? Why would he say this? I didn't care if it was bizarre, I'm interested in motivation.

Seinfeld works because you get to observe the curious nuances of people and their interactions with one another. In order to coach effectively, you have to be a good people watcher. You have to study their nuances, how they represent themselves, and how they interact with others. All of your guys have different backgrounds, personalities, and things going on in their lives. Under the best of circumstances, it's a challenge.

Despite how great your scheme is or how great your technique, you have to understand that the players out there executing are people, and all people are different. The better you understand them, the more effective you can get them to be, the better you'll be as a team.

> "Leach's free association is epic. It really fascinates me. Nobody has the ability to free associate like this guy. He starts going and you're thinking, 'OK, where are you going with this?' I love his reset. His reset line is always, 'Well, the thing is.' Whenever he switches gears to another subject, that's his comma, it's, 'Well, the thing is . . .' And it's amazing to see how he always brings it back home.
>
> "He's one of the most unique people I've ever met. He's infinitely curious about everything. He doesn't come in there and meet new situations with an agenda. He likes to walk straight up and ask the tough questions. He loves it when someone is real as can be. He wants to learn something new. He wants to hear another point of view on something. He loves individuals."
>
> —Matthew McConaughey, friend

Discovering the ideal way to motivate someone is the ultimate challenge for any leader. It's gigantic. There is an art to it. Mistakes are always going to be made, but the closer you can come to the mark, the better you're going to be and the better they're going to be. When I was coach at Texas Tech, we had a few players you just couldn't be too nice to when it came to football matters. If you complimented them once, they eased up. You had to resist the temptation to be nice to them. I'd say to my assistant coaches, if we're pricks to them for four years, these guys are going to have better careers. But you can't assume that approach works with everyone. It won't. Some guys—just like Todd Frost back in Cody Little League—will fold or recoil. With some people you need a relaxed approach because they create enough of their own tension.

Once in a while, you come to the realization that nothing you do is going to motivate a player. On any number of levels, this type of player is going to hold the rest of team back, and in those cases the best thing you can do is get rid of him. As a coach you have to think about all the guys, not just one. I feel some failure on my part as a coach if I have to cut someone. It's always a last resort.

If a player is a really competitive person, it doesn't take long to get a good read on the guy. Michael Crabtree was so competitive, especially if you called him out. You might say, "Get off your ass! You haven't caught a pass in how many plays? How long are you going to let the cornerback kick your ass?"

After that, he'd physically pick up the defensive back and throw him around. He would run over the DB, around him, and through him. He'd literally put on a clinic. With Crabtree, it wasn't going to be one of those deals where he'd perform for three plays then say, "Now, are you happy?" He'd bust his ass the rest of the day.

I didn't care about embarrassing Crabtree when I'd call him out. If he was a guy who would go into a shell using that tactic, I would've used a different way to motivate him. Maybe I'd have brought him into the office to talk to him separately, so wouldn't lose face in front of his peers. We had a good running back at Texas Tech, Taurean Henderson, who we handled that way. Generally, quarterbacks need to be handled liked that too. Not that quarterbacks can't take it—most of them can. But because you call upon quarterbacks to lead the team, you have to be really careful about damaging their credibility with the rest of the team. As a coach, you're saying to the players, "Listen to the QB. Do what he says. Listen to him. Do what he says." But then if you jump on his ass in front of everyone, it may get some of the players thinking, "Hey, our quarterback's a total idiot and a screw-up. Why should I be listening to this guy? He doesn't know what he's doing."

However, if I'm going to rip the whole team, I'll start with the quarterback. I either start with him or I end with him. I don't want him to be lost in the shuffle. I want him distinguished. But if it's just the quarterback, I'll often do it separately. There is naturally more pressure on a quarterback because he knows more eyes are on him. He knows all of his teammates are listening to what he says. You don't want to make him feel insecure or lose credibility because his teammates have to respond to him.

Michael Crabtree wasn't going into the tank for anyone. When Crabtree arrived at Tech he was a bit tough to read. I didn't know what he was thinking because he never said anything. He'd have this look on his face. It was not really a smile. Not really a frown. It was more of a grimace. Plus he'd always mutter. As I got to know him better, I could finally hear him muttering about being happy, whether I was on him or not. When Crabtree said he wanted to be coached hard, he was dead serious, and he responded to it well. Once in a while, he would thank you for it.

I think everyone needs a push. If you're driven, you might find ways to push yourself, but you still need an outside nudge from time to time. Crabtree is a good example. He could push himself, but he periodically needed a reminder or a challenge. The downside with a guy as determined and as talented as Crabtree is that you actually had to be careful to not get him too motivated in practice, because it could have a negative impact on the guy he was going against. If it was a scout-team player, who was probably never going to play in a game for us and whose job was solely to get the starters ready, I didn't worry about it. If it was a defensive back who we were counting on to play, I didn't want Crabtree dismantling the guy with the whole team watching. It might crush him.

Balancing personalities is one of the trickiest jobs you have as a coach. It is important to listen to your players, observe them, really pay attention to the nuances in their actions and interactions. If you do this, you'll have your best shot at bringing all these guys from different walks of life together into one cohesive unit.

Life at Tech

On the night of November 1, 2008, my Texas Tech team hosted the Texas Longhorns in Lubbock. The game was supposed to be different from any other game I'd coached. Everyone outside the walls of my team said "different," but what they meant was bigger, more significant. What the outsiders didn't get was that the game was really not different at all.

Texas was ranked first in the nation. The Longhorns came to Tech as this great conquering team. They'd just beaten the #1, #11, and #7 teams in the nation. We were ranked #6 and had just beaten #19 Kansas, 63–21.

Cynics would say that Kansas was a lot more like us than we were like the Longhorns. But that didn't deter *College GameDay* from coming to Lubbock to see the Red Raiders host Texas. I suspect it was to continue the coronation process of the Longhorns as much as it was to take in the show in Lubbock. Still, I could sense there was a newness about Texas Tech being a Top 10 team that intrigued the national media. The media likes newness. There's an element of discovery there that they covet. They're curious. They want to poke at you. Sniff around. Get a better sense of what they think you are, kind of a "What have we here?" deal to it.

They hadn't gotten sick of us yet.

The media tends to have a short attention span. You can go from folksy to clichéd in a few heartbeats. The shelf life of this phenomenon varies, but since the press had already spent a month straight talking about Bevo, Colt McCoy, and Mack Brown, we made for a timely diversion.

The build up to the game had all the makings of a media spectacle. We were ranked #1 in the nation in passing. We led the country in fewest sacks allowed, and we were second in total offense. The reality was, that stuff had become business as usual for the Red Raiders. Never in its history had Texas Tech ever beaten a #1 team. Texas Tech wasn't supposed to play in games like this one, and Lord knows Texas Tech certainly wasn't supposed to win them.

As a coach, you have to fight the temptation to try and address everything when facing a program such as Texas. The Longhorns were big, fast, and powerful. They presented a lot of problems, so we had to have a fairly simple game plan that our guys could execute, while making sure we had enough variations to keep them off balance.

I thought it was vital to keep the team as focused as possible, and much of that involved keeping their heads out of the newspapers. We constantly reminded them that what really counted was our team and who we had on our sideline. Nothing written on the outside mattered—if we bought into that, we may as well not even play, because everyone was saying that #1 Texas was going to beat us.

People may have thought we'd get all worked up about the Longhorns' defensive line after they manhandled Oklahoma earlier in the year. But that Oklahoma game was Oklahoma's problem. Just because Oklahoma struggled with them didn't mean we would. We were confident in our offense. There were tactical adjustments we'd have to make, but way back in training camp was when we decided what plays were going to be in our package. That was when we determined how we were going to attack the field. Once we got into the Texas week, we just had to pick the plays that were going to fit the gameplan, and select the formations and techniques to counter what they presented.

About 3,000 students camped out in our parking lot the entire week before the game. We had 15,000 fans outside the stadium 12 hours before kickoff. Most people said it would be the biggest night in the history of Texas Tech football.

Honestly, I never viewed it that way. Every single game was big, and I did everything in my power to make sure our team believed it. After all, playing against #1 Texas wouldn't have been that big if we hadn't won the other games before it.

People loved to draw these David versus Goliath comparisons whenever we faced Texas or Oklahoma. They'd read about how those teams had all of these four- and five-star high school recruits and we didn't. These were many of the same people who thought we had to trick those teams to beat them. That was a mound of bull. That was not how our system worked. And it was not how we beat Texas.

> **"One of the biggest misconceptions about Coach's offense is that it's gimmicky or we're tricking people. We don't change it from week to week. We line up and we out-execute people. We line up in basic formations and out-execute them. We don't motion people. We try to put people in binds. We try to flood a zone. Or we try to beat people in man-to-man. We do throw it more than other people, and people try and make it like that's a gimmick. It's just that instead of running the ball, we throw short passes.**

> **"His whole deal is to out-leverage people. Take what people give you and attack with leverage, going where they're not. Attack them where they're weak. Make them defend the whole field. He analyzes everything. He never gets emotional about it. He looks at football from an outside source just watching the game, calling what he thinks he needs to do. He never acts on impulses."**
> **–Graham Harrell, Texas Tech QB 2005-08**

Our first offensive play of the Texas game—from our own 19-yard-line—was ACE RIP 30. The first part of the call—ACE RIP—was the formation. Ace meant we had one running back. The "Y" and "Z" receivers were on the right side of the formation with the "X" and "H" receivers on the left side. You want to be able to communicate a lot as quickly and efficiently as possible during the game.

We lined up in Ace Rip a lot. On this particular night we were in Ace Rip on 32 of 83 offensive plays. We ended up using eight different formations that night, but none as often as Ace Rip. I liked the formation because it's symmetrical: 2-by-2, meaning you're lining up with two receivers on each side. That would force the defense to spread out so they couldn't disguise who was covering who. It made it very difficult for them to hide their cards.

I like to start a game with something we are really good at—a bread-and-butter play. It's a good way to settle your players down. On that night, we didn't want Graham Harrell, our quarterback, to get ahead of himself and become impatient. We just wanted him to execute good, sound plays. There is an initial barrage of intensity when you start a game. You want to make it through this period without any hugely negative plays, especially if you're playing a team more talented that you. After the adrenaline subsides, teams settle in and are less likely to do as many erratic things.

We also wanted to leverage their defense in our favor. I tell my quarterbacks, draw a line down the center's ass, and if you see more defenders on one side of that line than the other, you probably need to go where there are fewer of them.

Sounds simple, right? I've had people tell me I coach a football game like a 14-year-old runs his offense on X-Box. There's probably some truth to that. I've had the benefit of not having been institutionalized by the coaching caste system, and that lets me think my own way. Within the coaching world, there's an element that wants tactics to be this complicated, impenetrable discipline, like it's some badge of honor for a package to be difficult to understand. It's like some think there's something noble about doing something that others don't have the expertise to grasp. The only thing that does is make communication complicated and cumbersome among your staff and your players. It is critical to constantly simplify concepts and the way they're communicated. It also eliminates hesitation.

We were well prepared for Texas. We knew Graham wouldn't have to check very often. Maybe he checked 10 percent of the game. The quarterback really doesn't have to check much if you're facing a team that is really basic in their scheme. Against New Mexico, at least when Rocky Long was coaching the Lobos, it was a completely different story. Our QBs would probably check 60 percent of the game. You knew what they were going to run, but you didn't know when they were going to run it.

For the Texas game, just like every other game, we broke down our call sheet into seven categories: For the "Open" field, we had plays that we could call anywhere and at any time; "Red Zone," "Goal line," and "2-Point Plays"; "Special" plays; "Screens"; "Big Plays," which were our plays for third-and-long situations; and "Short Yardage" plays. Several of the plays were listed in multiple categories.

When Michael Lewis wrote a cover story on me for the *New*

York Times Magazine, he wrote about how my call sheet, which we tweaked for every game, was the only written record of our offense. That article drew a ton of attention because the *Times* is an international newspaper with a high-brow following. People were intrigued by our offense, how we managed it, particularly our view of time and space (as it relates to football, of course). That might be what got *60 Minutes* to come to Lubbock.

In a game of football, you really only have three resources— time, space, and personnel. How much space do you have? Well, you have 52 yards by 100 yards, but you really don't have that whole area available at the same time. You only have about 30 yards in front of you or till you hit the end zone. People like to talk about how some quarterback can chuck it 70 yards downfield. OK, but do you have a guy that can run a 70-yard dash in 2.9 seconds? We figure our receivers have to complete their route in 3.5 seconds, because we measure play time in terms of pass protection. The NFL guys sometimes say an offense has about 2.7 or 2.9 seconds. Since none of my guys have been able to run a 2.9 second 70-yard dash, I haven't spent a lot of time working up plays in that model. That doesn't mean the ball won't go further than 30 yards though, because if you're on the left hash and you throw a fade route, the ball will travel farther than 30 yards. I see it as having 30 yards in front of us with 52 yards of width. The trick is to figure out how to use all of that space, because if you're just going to restrict your game to the middle of the field, then the defense has the advantage. They can pinch you in and tee off on you.

When it comes to personnel, you need to have everybody contributing. There are five skill guys, six including the quarterback, and all of these positions have to contribute.

With time, it's about determining how quickly you can get there. In football, there's a temptation to try and block everybody, but it just can't be done. If the defense is determined they can always bring one more guy than you can account for since one of your guys will be busy carrying the football. At times, you have to get the ball dealt off to somebody before they can get there. In order to do that, you have to make sure the guy who is not accounted for is the one that is the farthest from the quarterback or the ball carrier.

I'm one of a few head coaches who still calls the plays during the game. I love it. I've heard people talk about the play-calling game between the offensive coach and the other team's defensive coach as a "chess match." I don't see it that way. To me, chess is too stagnant. I also hate when people compare football to war. That's disrespectful to war. It's nothing like war. I haven't been in a war, but I know football's not like that. It may be fun to pretend it is, but pretending is where it ends.

Calling plays in a football game is more like boxing. You're trying to anticipate what they're going to throw at you, but you have to remain focused on your own abilities if you're going to counter-punch effectively. The most important thing isn't *what* they're doing, but *recognizing* what they're doing. They can only run so many things. Is it Man or Zone? Are they gonna blitz or drop? Just recognize it and play fundamental football.

Calling plays means managing a lot of moving parts, all complicated by strengths, weaknesses, imperfections, and a lot of diversity. On top of all that, you're going up against another group that's trying to disrupt everything you want to accomplish. I find it incredibly fulfilling.

I don't think everybody has it in them to be a good play caller, yet I do think it's a learned skill that improves with practice. You have to be even-tempered and clear-minded. All hell is breaking loose out there, whether that means you're way up on somebody or they're knocking your teeth in. As a play caller, you don't have the time to celebrate or mope around. It takes discipline to maintain that even keel. It's a lot like having some flex in your knees when you're skiing. You can't go down the mountain stiff-legged, you have to be able to react to and absorb the bumps as they come. On top of it all, your players respond to your attitude, and regardless of whether you just had a great play or a bad one, it's the next play that counts.

Play-calling starts early in the game week. You want to start rehearsing it in your mind, and the best way to do that is to specifically practice what you want to call. Choices have to be made. There's no "a little of this" or "a little of that."

There's a certain amount of risk involved with play-calling, so you need to have faith in yourself and the people around you. Mistakes are going to happen—live with them and work through them. In boxing, you're not going to be able to knock somebody else out unless you throw some punches. Don't be afraid to throw 'em. Don't save your "big play" for third-and-long.

You have to maintain focus, for yourself and for your team. There are always a bunch of things out there that you can see, but it's important to not overload your players. For instance, you tell your quarterback, "I like this and I like this," that's it. There are probably three other things I could tell him, but he doesn't need to know that. You can't give him too many things to keep track of out there. You have to channel it to him in digestible portions.

You're juggling tendencies, vulnerabilities that you can see, and playing hunches when calling plays. But you can't just pull your plays out of the air based on your gut. You don't want guesses. "I just know it." "I feel it." No, you don't. You don't make decisions based on feelings you can't verify.

At some point you get into the rhythm of what they're doing defensively. By the second quarter, I usually had a feel for what they were inclined to do. Starting with the script we worked on all week, and which we'd already been using through the first quarter, we would run through our options and make adjustments. We'd have kind of a party line conversation on our sideline. I would first and foremost talk to the coach up top in the coaching box. It used to be (inside receivers coach) Dana Holgorsen. Then it was Lincoln Riley (who replaced Dana.) He was my spotter. He'd tell me what he saw about how the play just unfolded: "OK, the safety jumped on the crossing route."

I'd ask if the post was open. The answer may have been, "Well, I couldn't tell because the wide receiver got jammed up and tripped," or "That corner's playing really loose. If we did the post, it would take a while for him to get there."

"O.K, how about the curl if he's playing that loose?"

"Yeah, the curl would be real good."

We'd talk back and forth. "How are they when we're in two-backs?"

"They seem to be having trouble with it. The safety stays back and he does this."

This conversation continued while the players were getting up and walking back to the huddle. Meanwhile, our other offensive coaches might throw in a little input if they saw something, but it had better be important. The priority was talking to the coach in the press box and him telling me what he was seeing so we could make a decision. The other coaches were not to interrupt that—only if there was a break in the action. The offensive line coach would also be talking to a guy up top, but they were on a separate set of headphones. If they needed to tell me something, then my line coach would tell his coach up top, who would tell my coach up top, who would then tell me. If I had a question, it would go that route in the opposite direction. Much of the conversation was to confirm with one another that we were seeing the same thing, and how to address it.

I watched two games at Valdosta from up in the booth. You can see the game better, but it's not like you can't still see the game pretty clearly from the sideline. The biggest element I felt like I lost being up in the booth was the emotional connection to the players. There are guys that need to be picked up, guys that need to be settled down. Football is a very emotional game. I wasn't able to address the human element up there in the box.

It's important to have patience as a play caller, but you also need to have the nuts to pull the trigger. There are teams that you have to be patient against. You run basic stuff and let their game plan unfold. That works best against teams that aren't the most talented, because the super-talented teams tend to be the most basic in their approach.

I find that the most difficult teams to play against are the ones that operate under a similar philosophy to mine. They don't try to make too much happen in any one play. They're about executing good plays with good technique. This mindset usually comes from the medium-talent teams. With the super-talented teams, it's most important to withstand their initial barrage. They're usually explosive, and you don't want to let them hurt you right at the beginning of the game. Teams with top talent force your margin of error to become very narrow. Routine plays that will get you 12 yards against an average team are only getting you four yards because of how quickly they can chase you down. Super-talented teams can recruit great players at most positions. As a result, they sometimes rely on talent more than scheme, and stay basic.

Don't make the mistake of holding onto your best stuff thinking that you'll be "saving it." Fire it at them. Throw your best pitches.

People tend to overestimate how quickly they're going to catch on to what you're doing. Stonewall Jackson once said, "Never take counsel of your fears." I didn't talk to Stonewall about it, but I think that's just a fancy way of saying, worry about what you're gonna do, not what the other guy might do.

There is this perception out there that play-calling needs to change from season to season. People think, "Well, everybody knows your stuff, they've seen it over and over again and now they've adjusted to it." Teams often overcompensate based on this idea. Your opponent is still playing with 18-to-22 year-olds, and they get new ones every year. I know I have new guys every year who make the same mistakes as the previous crop. They need to grow and develop. Their coaches may have seen what we're going to do, but the players probably don't know how to cope with adjustments that are too elaborate. Adjustments are one of the most important parts of football, but first you make your opponent prove they're necessary. Don't just guess that they're necessary and change your whole system.

We played Kansas in 2008. We lined up in double tight end formation. On film, whenever they played someone in a double tight formation, they always rolled to one safety. They'd start out with two safeties deep, and just prior to the snap they would move one safety down to the line of scrimmage and shift the other one into the deep middle of the field. (Against passing teams, a lot of defenses will typically play two safeties deep.)

Going into the game, I said they probably wouldn't roll to one safety against us because they feared the pass more than they feared the run, but if they did roll to one safety, we'd give (wide receiver) Ed Britton a post pattern. Sure enough, just as Graham got behind center, they rolled to one safety, so he gave Easy Ed a post. It was a pass I probably could've completed myself. Touchdown, Red Raiders, on our second offensive play of the game.

Sometimes you call plays to set something up for later in the game. There is a probing nature to play-calling, but, like boxing again, you have to keep body-punching until things start to open up. Once you loosen them up, then you attack the head. There might be a guy on the opposing defense who you target. We'd run "4-Verticals" out of three different formations on three consecutive plays at the same cornerback. We'd just want to wear his butt out.

On the first play, we'd go vertical. After that, my receiver got to run off the field. I'd bring in a new receiver for the next play because we were going vertical again. The cornerback would still be out there. By third down, that DB would be out of gas. We'd give it a different look each time and no-huddle for good measure. We might've run it out of trips formation, two-by-two, out of two backs—it didn't matter. We were wearing out that corner physically and mentally. We wanted him to second-guess himself, to stop believing in himself. If you can push it to the point where they get him over to the sideline and are yelling at him and drawing stuff up real fast, you know they're in trouble. Psychological damage has even more of an impact than the physical damage. If you get on a roll and make the other team's coaches frantic, then they'll help unravel their own players for you.

Texas only lined up with five men in the box on that first play from scrimmage, so our quarterback, Graham Harrell, opted for the run, which went off left tackle. I liked the call because there was only one level of the defense to pierce. We gained five yards. Our next three plays were all passes, which included picking up a third-and-five and then hitting a 29-yard completion to Tremain Swindall on a variation of 4-Verticals, or what we call "6"—as in six points. I've heard a bunch of different names used for 4-Verticals. "All Go." "999." "All Verticals."

There is nothing simpler in the whole world of football than 4-Verticals, or "6." Since the game of football was invented, since the days of the cavemen, they ran this play. Back then it was called "Everybody Go Deep." At Tech we'd run it a bit differently than most teams did. We'd settle our receivers down and throw it behind them. When the DB turned and flipped his hips, our receiver would look back to the quarterback, but he still ran fast. We coached our receivers to "let the ball take you to the play."

Our guys looked for the ball often, and we wanted them to. We drilled it over and over and over again to hit it at all points along the way. You could stick great defensive backs at every position in the defensive secondary and they would have a difficult time stopping it. Now, a great DB might be able to narrow your margin for error, but he couldn't stop it. Of course, the tricky part is that the quarterback and the wide receiver have to be on the same page. It has to be precisely executed or else you end up stopping it yourself.

The upside is that our QB could hit his receiver at any point, starting from right on the line of scrimmage all the way to 35 yards downfield. Somewhere along that path he's bound to be open. And that's just one guy. Multiply that by four. Then, for good measure, we'd stick a back underneath and release him right or left or through the line by the center and tell him to "Get open!" after we'd blown the top of their coverage. It's a beautiful thing to see all that space open up for a back.

The downside is that "6" becomes a game of execution and anticipation. The quarterback and his receivers have to be on the same page as those windows come open. It has to be in the quarterback's head, "He's about to hit a window, I have to throw this thing right *now*."

At Tech, we were big on looking at the quarterback. People say, "Well, that's going to slow you down." Well, not very much. Michael Crabtree, who caught 134 passes for 1,962 yards and 22 touchdowns in his freshman season at Tech, was always looking at the QB, and he would never quit working on a play. He might be the fifth read, but without breaking the integrity of the play, he'd keep working, keep working, keep working—and we're talking about a guy that was a ridiculously marked player—but he'd still make a ton of mop-up plays because he kept hustling.

A turning point for us came in my third season at Tech, which was also Kliff Kingsbury's third year as our starting quarterback. We got to thinking about all of this space we weren't utilizing. Why weren't we using it? I saw all this real estate out there that was just being wasted. Run or pass, it's a constant effort to best utilize the space on the field.

We told our players to work on verticals all off-season, but when we came back they clearly hadn't worked on them that much. So in the first couple of days of camp, we decided to throw verticals all the time. The first day we completed about 30 percent, and I said, "That's bad. We need to do a better job of getting on the same page and this is something we really need to look at it." So we talked about it. "If he's open here, you need to throw it. If he's open now, you need to look. You guys aren't on the same page, but we need to get on the same page because there's space everywhere."

I love the curl route, but even if you have great technique you can only be open at the tail end of the route. The corner route is the same way. With vertical routes, there are a lot of chances to be open between the point where you start and 35 yards downfield. There's going to be a learning curve with a vertical route that's more severe than there is with a horizontal route, like a dig route or a curl route.

The receiver runs the route and looks to the quarterback as the defender adjusts. The receiver keeps running. The quarterback decides when and where to throw the ball. On the throw, the receiver adjusts to the ball. If the receiver stops or settles because he guesses, then he is wrong. If the ball is thrown to the wrong place, where there is no space, then the quarterback is wrong. Where the ball is caught is based upon how the defender chooses to play the route. Simply stated: Throw it where they are not. The execution of this requires months and even years of practice. However, the space itself is always there, and it's impossible for the defense to cover.

In Kliff's first two seasons as a starter, he averaged 23 TD passes and around 3,450 passing yards. His third season, after we changed our approach on "6," he threw for 41 TDs and 4,500 passing yards. Kliff was really good at throwing slants and the really quick stuff.

Kliff wanted to be sure, and wouldn't throw the ball if the receiver wasn't looking. He'd say, "Well, he wasn't looking, so I didn't throw it." B.J. Symons, the quarterback who took over after Kliff went to the NFL, had a different attitude all together. He'd say, "Screw that," and he'd fire it in—the receiver had better be ready. B.J. didn't care. He'd throw a laser shot and hit the guy in the side of the helmet if he wasn't looking. During the season, he put on a clinic running "6." He broke Ty Detmer's record for most passing yards in a 12-game season. He broke Kliff's Big 12 record for single-season touchdown passes (52). When we went to Ole Miss to play the Rebels, he upstaged Eli Manning, who is a great quarterback. B.J. threw for 661 yards and we beat them, 49–45.

There was some initial staff resistance to running "6" this way. It faded pretty quickly. We'd always been in the mid 40 percent range with it, and then we reached 56 percent while averaging 9.5 yards per attempt. Not per completion. Per attempt.

One of the more challenging parts of the passing game is finding a running back who can run a great option route. A typical running back's solutions to most obstacles are speed and power. You have to develop their vision and work with them so they can conceptualize the route. The simplest way of putting it is to say, "Run to your hole, turn your butt away from coverage and adjust to the biggest open spot." Inevitably he'll ask, "Well, what if the guy follows you?" OK, then keep running laterally. Basically, it's just "get open."

The Texas Longhorns do not like to defend verticals. They like routes that are more clearly defined so they can pounce on them with their speed.

After we hit Texas for 29 yards on our fourth play from scrimmage to move into UT territory, I wanted to see how the Longhorns would respond to a variety of sets. The next play we called Blue Flip, a two-back set. Texas had a tendency to keep the tackle box (the area between the tackles near the line of scrimmage) filled versus two running backs, to defend against the run. Against most teams, they used one safety against two backs, but against us they used two safeties. The play we ran was "34 Lead." The Longhorns' front ate it up. We gained one yard. What I took from the play was that if they played with two safeties deep, we still had to run it. Even if we were limited by what their talent could do to us physically up front, I felt like we could run it somewhat effectively because we were gonna have our seven against their six. You needed to get them coming and going a bit so they're not rushing straight upfield and teeing off on your quarterback.

I try to put together plays that are multi-faceted enough to work even if the defense shifts into something we didn't expect.

For example, if the defense is playing Cover-2, you expect the Y-receiver to get the ball on "Y-Cross" most of the time, but if the defense ends up in Cover-3, instead of the Y-receiver getting the ball, the Z-receiver ends up with it most of the time. That's fine by me. You don't want it to become a situation where you're just trying to out-guess the other guy. A pass play should always provide you with a variety of options.

If you are outnumbered or out-leveraged (the vulnerability based on where offensive and defensive players line up) on a run play, then you need to check to a different play where the numbers and leverage are in your favor.

Football teams have all sorts of breakdowns and research about what an opposing defense likes to do—or not do—based on its history. You really can amass quite a bit of data: The Longhorns blitzed 27 percent of the time against Blue Rip, but only 18 percent of the time against Ace Rip, and played Cover-1 17 percent of the time on third-and-long.

Everyone has their GA's (graduate assistants) breaking down numbers on more situations than you could imagine. This intel either ends up on your grease board, or on some print-out with these little rectangular boxes separating each category. You hope the numbers will reveal a pattern that will help you get a feel for what the other side is thinking. If someone is just random—22 percent of the time they do this, 19 percent of the time they do that, 17 percent of the time they do something else—well, that just means they're pulling it out of a hat. They're just trying to change it up to keep you off balance. Odds are they aren't going to be great at any one thing because they're in a constant state of transition. You want to have stuff that is versatile enough to have a chance against anything.

If there is a tendency that you've identified, then you can specifically select the plays you want to run against it. Those are the plays that you've repped all week during practice. You are really best at what you do the most, rather than constantly changing what you do. That holds true on both sides of the ball.

Our first drive against Texas fizzled after we took a sack. However, we did get deep enough into their territory that our punt pinned them back at their 2-yard-line. We forced a safety when our defensive tackle, Colby Whitlock, sacked quarterback Colt McCoy in the end zone and took a 2–0 lead. On our next play from scrimmage we came out in slot formation. I wanted to see how Texas would respond. We ran a draw play. They'd been putting a lot of pressure on us—the added pressure from their defense was that primal reaction a lot of defenses have after you knick them. It makes them want to come after you harder because it's like you hit them in the face. They were pissed.

The draw got us five yards. We called a naked bootleg, which was a misdirection rollout pass by our quarterback. The Longhorns were bringing more and more pressure, but they were not doing it with blitzes. Instead, it was with twists and stunts by their defensive line. Their edges were soft. On the play—35 Naked—Graham got outside and completed a 15-yard pass to Detron Lewis to put us back into UT territory. We ended up moving the ball into the Red Zone, but only got a field goal out of the drive.

Our defense was feeding off all of the energy of the game. They were playing great. Texas managed to pick up one first down, but had to punt the ball back to us. This was the worst any team had made their quarterback look all season.

We began our next offensive series at our own 4-yard-line. We dented them with a few running plays and mixed in a couple of screens that we'd seen work for Oklahoma. The misdirection gave them problems because they were so aggressive. We also called a few plays that made their D-linemen run laterally, which wore them out and started to make them second guess themselves. Teams that have all of these really good athletes, like Texas, Oklahoma, or USC, tend to be big momentum teams used to steady success, so when things aren't going quite their way they become uncertain and get frustrated.

I am a big believer in screens. We had a lot of different kinds of screens in our offense. There were receiver screens, tunnel screens, the slow-RB screen, the fast-RB screen, and the flare screen to name a few. I think a shuttle pass is also a screen. The screen is just such a great off-speed pitch.

There are a lot of plays where I don't worry if I get busted calling them, but I don't want to get busted calling a screen. Most screens are designed to use a team's own aggression against them, but if they sense it, they won't get upfield. Instead, they'll sit at the point of attack to blow it up.

A lot of people think you want the defense to blitz to make a screen effective. I don't really care that much. You just want them to declare. You want them to blitz and come forward, or you want them dropping back. You don't care which, you just want them going somewhere and going somewhere fast. You don't want some guy sitting there, lurking around, spying on you, mucking things up. Lazy defensive players kill you on screens even though they help you on everything else.

The variety of plays not only kept Texas off balance, it helped us get into a rhythm and quicken the tempo. We drove 96 yards and into their end zone in just over four minutes.

By halftime, we were up 22–6, but the Longhorns worked their way back into the game. Texas burned us on a long punt return for one touchdown and then a 91-yard pass play for another. Still, everything we did offensively was working. About the only thing that went wrong for our offense happened with about six minutes remaining in the game. We were up, 29–26 and driving for another touchdown. It was first-and-goal inside their 10-yard-line. We threw a ball to Crabtree near the 2-yard-line, but the ref tossed a flag. Offensive pass interference. It was a brutally bad call. Crabtree never even touched the guy. He just came out of his cut, stuck his toe in the ground and the DB fell over because he lost his balance. They backed us up 15 yards to the 25. We went from what should've been a spot on the 2 to practically out of field goal range. We settled for a long field goal, which we made, but we let the penalty affect our composure. Then, Texas marched down and scored with nothing but token resistance on our part.

Suddenly, instead of being up 36–26, we're down 33–32 with 1:29 left in the game.

Before sending the offense back onto the field, I pulled Graham aside.

Graham is the son of a Texas high school football coach. In fact, he is the son of the son of a Texas high school football coach. Lots of college quarterbacks have dreamed of the very scenario he was about to step into. Less than two minutes on the clock. Facing the #1 team in the nation. National television. Graham Harrell hadn't just dreamt of this day all his life, he'd been coached for it from the moment he was born.

I've seen it go both ways with these guys who grew up with football in their blood. Some take the game for granted, but a lot of my best quarterbacks have been sons of coaches. Graham had an incredible level of awareness about him. The guy was really good at transferring what was going in my mind onto the field. He just had a sense of what I was after. He was calm under fire, and he could keep the rest of the unit calm.

I said to him, "Talk to them and make sure that they're settled down and ready to play. Now all we have to do is march down there and win this thing. They might be playing off. Don't be afraid to throw it underneath. And, early in the drive, don't be afraid to throw it over the middle."

I also probably said something about shoving it up their ass.

He just looked at me and nodded.

"No doubt. I got it."

It wasn't exactly a moment of back-and-forth dialogue like Christopher Walken and Dennis Hopper had in *True Romance*. Truth is, on the football field, these exchanges seldom are. Graham trotted onto the field and marched us deep into their territory, to the Texas's 28-yard-line. Only eight seconds remained on the clock. We'd run "6" on four of the fives plays on the drive. Of course we were going to run it again.

Crabtree took off up the right sideline. The Texas DB spun. He tried to run with Crabtree and turned to keep up. The DB was not looking at Graham. Crabtree was.

We always coached our quarterbacks to throw the ball at the receiver's ass check away from coverage if the DB wasn't looking and overplaying the receiver deep. Graham did just that. Crabtree snatched the ball, then ran past the Longhorn defender to go into the end zone. Our fans poured from their seats and rushed the field.

We beat the Longhorns, 39–33. It was the first time Texas Tech had ever beaten the #1 team in the country. We gained 579 yards of total offense, which was over 200 more than they'd gained on us. That night we were 9 of 11 for 173 yards when we ran "6." In hindsight, I wish I'd run it 20 times.

A few days after the game, someone gave me a picture.

Crabtree is just about to cross the goal line. Behind him in the photo is Chris Fowler, the host of *College GameDay*. Fowler's jaw is open so wide, it's almost on the turf. He looks like he's screaming the loudest of anybody in the Jones Stadium. I don't know if he was rooting for us. I hope he was. He was certainly surprised. I guess a lot of people were that night.

Sticking to Your Guns

A few months before we beat top-ranked Texas in 2008, my agent at IMG, Gary O'Hagan, told me that he'd been speaking to *60 Minutes*. Gary said they wanted to do a piece on me.

I was excited. I remember thinking, "Wow! *60 Minutes*? Really?" It was such an honor since they don't do many features on coaches. I also figured that kind of exposure would be great for recruiting and fund raising. As I kept thinking about it my mind was racing: "OK, this is *60 Minutes*. It's probably not going to be like any media experience I've ever had. This isn't sports. This is news. They're investigative reporters. If they find a bunch of dirt, they're going with it." But you know, I didn't have anything to hide. I didn't have secrets. I was fully prepared to stand behind my record and all the hard work that I, my staff, and my players had put into elevating the program.

60 Minutes reporter Scott Pelley, who grew up in Lubbock, was going to do the piece. I was concerned about the logistics of the thing because it sounded like the producers wanted all of this time in the middle of our season.

About five years earlier, Gary, who'd worked with Michael

Lewis in the early '80s when they were both at Salomon Brothers, told Michael about me. That resulted in the feature Michael wrote for the *New York Times Magazine* about our team and what we were doing at Tech. Gary told Scott a lot of the same things about me that he'd pitched to Michael Lewis.

Gary assured me that *60 Minutes* would work around our schedule. He didn't say what the angle was going to be. I knew it'd be about some football stuff and our graduation rates at Tech, and that they'd probably touch on some parts of my career. I also knew *60 Minutes* wasn't coming all the way to Lubbock to talk about some middle linebacker's pulled hamstring.

The *60 Minutes* crew came down to Lubbock early in the season. They interviewed me briefly and then went all over the place. I figured I'd see them hovering around our football complex all the time, but I barely saw them at all. They might've done some of the background before they got there. I don't know.

The second day they were there, Kent Hance, the chancellor at Tech, showed up at our football practice. Hance never came to practice. Ever. I cannot recall any other time he showed up at one of our practices other than that day that *60 Minutes* was in town. But there he was. He came over to me, "Mike, I called up *60 Minutes* and told 'em to do a story on our football program."

Oh, really?

He told me that he had known the producers over there for years because of all his contacts, and that they owed him one.

He wanted me to think he set the *60 Minutes* piece in motion. I knew that Gary had been in discussions with them for weeks.

I know why Hance showed up at practice. I knew that Hance loved the microphone and the spotlight, and I knew he could get jealous of others getting the spotlight. He may have thought they were going to be filming that day.

I said to the producer of the *60 Minutes* piece, "Do me a favor. Whatever you do, go get a comment from Kent Hance and make sure that his face is in the story."

I later found out that Gary had called the producers, too,

asking them to get a comment from Hance.

A day went by and the producer says, "Your chancellor is kind of a strange guy."

Why? Was he negative?

"No, it was positive," the producer said. "We went over there to talk for 10 minutes. He shut the door and kept us there for almost two hours. He just kept talking."

I was just relieved that they spoke to him.

The whole *60 Minutes* process is fascinating. It's like being on *This is Your Life*. It's amazing the effort they must go through to track down some of these people. You can tell the producers like the element of surprise: "Well, so-and-so told me da-da-da. What were you like back then when you . . . " and then they leave this dramatic pause hanging in the air so you feel like you have to fill in the blanks. I wasn't concerned, but if you're an embezzler, I imagine that technique could rile you to the point of panic.

When they left Lubbock, they said they didn't know when they were going to run the piece. Initially, they'd told me December. They ended up putting it on the air in January, after our 2008 season. I was with my family in Colorado on a ski vacation. I watched the thing and there was not a comment from Hance. I said to Sharon. "This is going to be trouble."

She said, "Why is that? It's very positive."

"There's nothing in there from Hance," I said.

She said you don't have any control over *60 Minutes*. I said, "He'll be jealous of the attention I got and there'll be negative ramifications. He's going to take it out on me."

You know that you can't get too caught up in things you have no control over, but for a lot of folks, football coaches especially, that's a lot easier said than done.

I don't mind being called an "outside-the-box" thinker. I guess that's a compliment in this age of shameless conformity. Although I do find the term "outside the box" lame, overused, and non-descript.

Really, I'm just striving to be open-minded in my search for solutions. My mindset is no guts, no glory.

Innovation only happens when somebody bucks the norm and tries doing things a different way. I suspect most people are reluctant to step outside conventions because they don't want to open themselves up to criticism. It's unfortunate. If there is honor and nobility in what you're doing, you shouldn't fear anyone's opinions.

After the 2008 season, we came up with what some might consider an unconventional way to address a problem we were having with one of our best receivers, Ed Britton.

Easy Ed was a fun guy to coach, but at times he could be high-maintenance. He was very intelligent, and very well read. He always had some science-fiction book with him. The guy also had a good sense of humor and a great spirit. But he lacked common sense and he was easily distracted. He'd also decided that he wasn't going to be very diligent about going to class. I felt like we needed to remedy that situation immediately.

The situation went beyond just affecting Ed. If Ed missed practice because we sat him for having missed classes, it also affected the quarterbacks, the offensive linemen, and our entire team. The whole team preparing together is crucial for creating a cohesive unit. Furthermore, Ed wasn't someone who couldn't do the work. If Easy Ed was limited mentally and wasn't achieving, that'd be one thing. That wasn't Easy Ed. Instead, he was making a conscious decision to blow off class.

I believe either people want to graduate or they don't. Either they're doing their part or they're not. We give guys a lot of money in scholarships to go to class and do what they're supposed to do. We are essentially paying them money to work on football, and a big part of that is academics. Ed was one of my favorite players, but that didn't mean I wouldn't hammer him.

I asked Dennis Simmons, one of our receiver coaches, what he thought we ought to do with Easy Ed. Dennis did not disappoint me with his answer.

"What we ought to do is get a desk, stick it right there on the sidelines, and put him out there during practice to do his homework."

"That is a brilliant idea," I said. "Actually, what we really ought to do is stick ol' Easy Ed on the 50-yard line on the Double-T (Texas Tech logo) in the middle of our stadium where everybody can see him."

Dennis's mom actually deserves credit for the idea. She made Dennis do something similar when he wasn't performing academically. She'd make him sit there on stage doing his homework while his basketball teammates were practicing on the court next to him. I figured if it was good enough for Dennis, and Dennis turned out pretty well, it was certainly good enough for Ed.

I was envious that I hadn't thought of it myself. We were fortunate that it happened to snow in West Texas that day. Snow always helped drive home our point a little bit better.

I wanted Ed to be able to draw the correlation between the football field and the classroom. What better way than to put a desk on the 50-yard line? I also wanted his teammates to get the point, so that we wouldn't have to teach them each the same lesson individually. Having Easy Ed, one of our best players, out there at midfield on the Texas Tech logo, studying at that desk while the snow was coming down, was a lot of fun for everybody, except Ed. It was hugely positive for the team, and for Ed specifically. And if Ed didn't like it, all he had to do was go to class.

I couldn't imagine Easy Ed got a lot of studying done outside at midfield, but I was sure that study hall seemed a lot more appealing.

"I was thinking we were gonna get blasted that it was cruel when this story got out, but I looked at all of the comments posted online after the story and not one person said anything negative about it. They loved it. Even Edward's own dad

posted on there, saying, 'Do what you guys gotta do.' A few weeks later, I was at an academic conference in Miami. The first question I got asked was 'Did your coach really do that with that player?' And I said, yep. They go, 'Wow, I wish my coach would think like that.'"
—Victoria Simonoff, Texas Tech Academic Counselor

Meeting the real Wizard, John Wooden, is one of the greatest thrills I've ever had. I was invited to go his apartment in Encino, California, a few years back. It was an incredible experience. I don't think it's possible to cram more awards, books, and knowledge—a whole lifetime of achievements and wisdom—into such a small space as he had there. Being in his presence, I was overwhelmed by his love for his wife, whom he lost years ago, and for his understanding of life. This was a man who won more awards than you can imagine, more than any coach in any sport, but he valued his books and the pictures of his family more than any of those awards. I was with him for a few hours on a spring afternoon. When you were around John Wooden, you knew you were in the presence of greatness. He was the guy who had all of the virtues that Jimmy Stewart tried to portray in a Frank Capra movie.

I read Coach Wooden a lot. I cite him more than anyone, which is ironic because basketball is the sport I'm least interested in. With Wooden, you marvel at the focus he demanded from those around him. "Make each day your masterpiece," he'd say. His ability to consistently focus and perform at such a high level was inspiring.

I asked Coach Wooden what he attributed his success to, and then as he was explaining, he told me he was fascinated by the success we were having at Tech. He asked me how we prepared our players to play against teams we knew had superior talent to ours.

He had a lot of questions about our preparation and skill development. He was one of the most curious people I've ever come across. Here was this guy in his 90s, who once said, "It's what you learn after you know it all that counts," and if anyone knew it all, it was him, and he was still searching for knowledge.

Throughout the four hours I was with him, his phone was constantly ringing from all of these former players of his. He even got a call from a former NBA player who he hadn't coached, asking if Coach Wooden would introduce him at the Basketball Hall of Fame ceremony. (He told the guy he couldn't because of travel issues.)

There are so many great principles any leader can learn from Coach Wooden. He's the person who taught me that it's always more important to worry about what you do, not what they might do. He's the one who said the thing that's going to impact the score is you doing the best you can, and if you want to change the score, change yourself. Borrowing from great minds like his helps you grow your own philosophy in a positive fashion.

John Wooden's wisdom extended far beyond basketball. I'm never impressed when people from athletics think they can step into the business world and solve some company's problems. That doesn't make any more sense than some vice president of IBM telling me what to run on third-and-long. Wooden had a broadness to him that other people don't. He was so inspirational. He knew so much about how to create structure in life and how to be a well-rounded person while never comprising oneself. His greatness had to do with what was within: It was apparent in how he carried himself, how he spoke, how he thought.

Wooden once said, "Be more concerned with your character than your reputation." I've always tried to keep that idea in my mind as a coach, and it's a virtue that was really tested at the end of my time at Texas Tech and the weeks following. I'd dealt with some individuals in that situation whose agendas were based on lies. I refused to play that game. Reputations fluctuate based on what people think, and you can't control what people think any more than you can control the weather. But you can control who you are and find satisfaction in knowing that you did your best. The most important question you can ask yourself is, is this the right thing to do? You can't let what somebody else thinks or might think cloud your own judgment.

When you're a leader, you open yourself up to all sorts of shots, and it's your responsibility to stand up for all of your people. You'll get most of the glory when things go well, and you'll take most of the blame when things don't. It's common sense, but until you have some experience with both, it can be tough to process.

Criticism can be inspiring, if it's valid. If it's over something I've already worked through mentally or don't buy into, I ignore it. But if I think the criticism is valid, I will try to correct the problem. I like the fact that there's another set of eyes on the situation, but a lot of criticism is just yammering.

Coaches typically spend too much time dealing with criticism. Much of it comes from the media. I think the media are like realtors. My dad, my brother, and my sister are realtors. They don't care if the market is up or down, they just want property moving. Action is good for business. That's the way it is with the media, too.

People always talk about how the media are so negative. I think they get a bad rap. They haven't usually been negative with me. At times, yes, but for the most part they've been pretty positive.

My wife reads a lot more of the articles than I do. Sometimes she'll give me the verbal rundown. Other people sometimes come up saying, "Here, you have to read this. This is hilarious."

The only time I ever read newspaper articles is if someone brings one to me and says, "Here, read this!" Typically, those articles are either very complimentary or incredibly negative. Either way, the truth is somewhere in the middle. Looking at that stuff too much just distracts you from the task at hand. I try to follow what

I tell my players and keep my head out of the media. Sometimes, if it's something that might be good for recruiting, I'll read it quickly and file it away. If it's ridiculously unfair, then we may not give that reporter as much access as they used to receive. I try to cooperate with the media. I realize they have the pen. But if they're not being fair, I can impact their access. The reporter doesn't have to agree with me, but should be fair about it.

Misconceptions sprout like weeds from ignorance. The media says that you were wrong because you ran a certain play, or a player got burned because he busted his assignment. Really? How would you know what the assignments were, or what the call really was? You were not in our meeting room. That doesn't stop the "experts" from popping off. That kind of attitude is everywhere you look now. Every other channel seems to have two guys in suits in a split screen shouting at each other. In a lot of cases, neither guy actually has a clue what he's pontificating about. Just being outspoken is apparently good enough. Whatever the issue, it has to be the worst-ever this, or the best-ever that. The middle ground isn't good enough any more. Sometimes accuracy doesn't even matter. Instead, it's about being first or being loudest. That is a shame.

The media, in this microwave society we live in now, has become more reckless and irresponsible. I saw that first hand with the "reporting" on my situation with Craig James and his family, and with the way Texas Tech fired me.

"I think there was tremendous irony in the fact that the school that hired Bob Knight after all of his abuse issues fired a coach for alleged mistreatment of a student athlete. Kent Hance and Gerald Myers were huge protectors of Bob Knight. I left Tech over the fact that I didn't tolerate Knight's behavior and I wasn't going to be forced by the board to hire his

son, so I walked away.

"Kent Hance was very critical of me during some challenges I had with Knight. One phone call I got from Hance was irate, threatening, and irrational. Hance said, 'If there was an election tomorrow between you and Bob Knight, he would be elected.' I said, 'Is that how we're going to be selecting chancellors going forward?' There always had been politics with a small "p" among academics, but it became Politics with a capital "P" with this current administration. The rules changed. It became more of a politics office rather than an academic office. The de facto board, and the shadow board of Jim Sowell and some of these folks hold sway because of their donations to the Governor and because they probably helped Hance get that job.

"Gerald Myers is also an interesting character in all of this. Gerald felt at the end that the only thing saving his career at Texas Tech with the board and the shadow board was Bob Knight. Bob was brought in to create an ego for the organization and deal with their sense of inferiority. At one point when I was being attacked by Bob Knight, Marsha Sharp—our Hall-of-Fame women's basketball coach—and Mike held a recognition for me, and that clearly created a lot of animosity with Gerald. I'm sure that Gerald was looking to do some things here because Mike wasn't always playing ball

> **with him, and Gerald saw his star rising with Bob Knight, not Mike Leach. There's old roots here."**
> **—David Smith, Texas Tech Chancellor, 2002–06**

I admire Bob Knight, his 900-plus wins, and his contributions to the field of coaching. He is clearly one of the greatest basketball coaches that the sport has ever produced. I have learned a lot from him and have enjoyed the conversations that I've had with him. None of this material is an indictment on how he chose to coach. However, there are obvious contradictions in how he was handled and the situation with which I was confronted. The following is intended only to illustrate the political environment and the impact of outside influences that exist at Texas Tech. I hope this helps shed some light on how things got to where they were in the administration.

Pat Knight, the former Texas Tech basketball coach, is my favorite basketball coach. I consider him to be a close friend and wish him the very best.

A lot of times, the most revered person at a school is the football coach. At Tech, the most revered person was the women's basketball coach, Marsha Sharp. She won a national championship, donated $100,000 to the school for a new academic center, and had graduated almost 100 percent of her players. She even had a freeway named after her in Lubbock. Her games would outdraw the men's games. So when Bob Knight came to town all he was hearing was Marsha Sharp, Marsha Sharp, Marsha Sharp.

The athletic director, Gerald Myers, and the president at the time, David Schmidly, who had once been a walk-on basketball player, were going to let Bob do anything he wanted. The president was really excited about Bob Knight. He'd come to me and say, "Well, Bob Knight says it should be like this."

I thought, "Well, maybe you'd better tell Bob Knight to worry about his basketball team."

Knight schmoozed all of the big Tech boosters. He and Gerald, who was once the Tech basketball coach, would go on junkets every couple of months. They'd meet the boosters, take them out to dinner, take them hunting, and so on. That's why, when he had the infamous salad bar fight with Chancellor Smith, he was able to rally those guys against him.

Knight wanted to get David Smith out and replace him with Kent Hance. With Smith out of the way, Knight could have total control. Hance was beholden to the same people who wanted to oust Smith.

I never swore at the chancellor or threw salad at him in public like Bob did. If I had, I would've expected some sort of disciplinary action to take place, but Bob didn't even get his hand slapped, let alone face a suspension. Nothing happened because some regents and the hotshots in Dallas trumped Chancellor Smith and threatened him with his job.

Bob Knight deliberately left two players behind in Austin after Tech lost to UT. The players were still talking to the media and he was upset because they'd lost, so he left them behind. He flew home without those two players, and that was the start of the bad blood between the chancellor and Knight. Chancellor Smith asked, "What were you thinking? You don't leave student athletes behind."

There was an incident where Knight dropped numerous F-bombs on live national television while sitting next to Steve Alford. Another time, Coach Knight got into a confrontation with a janitor in Houston. During a game, he slapped a player on the chin who wouldn't look him in the eye during a time-out. They would just cover it all up. Nothing happened with him.

Marsha and I didn't want Chancellor Smith to go anywhere because he was a voice of reason and balance. We held a fundraiser for him that would not only help the school financially, but would also spark some positive publicity and show a strong indication of our support for him. We threw it together in a month and raised $65,000. Bob Knight, Gerald Myers, and several regent members tried to get us to nix it. Hance, who was not chancellor then, actually called me and told me not to do it. I said, "Why wouldn't I do it? He's my boss and the chancellor of the school."

Imagine school administrators trying to nix a fundraiser on behalf of the chancellor. Gerald actually called me in to his office. He said, don't do this. I said, "This is the chancellor of the university. I work for him and so do you. I'm happy to help him."

Marsha and I headlined the event because we wanted to give Chancellor Smith our support. He survived for a year, but they got him one year later. Smith was a good chancellor, but he just got tired of fighting them.

We didn't want them to railroad the chancellor, but they eventually did. When Marsha resigned, she told me, "They're going to get you next."

I said, 'Well, they've been trying for a few years. I guess if I don't get out of here soon, they probably will." It was always my hope that an environment of cooperation would develop eventually at Tech. We'd built a great program and I knew we would continue to grow. I didn't want to go anywhere unless it was a great situation.

The environment at Texas Tech was insanely tense at times. It required a lot more than just being the winningest football coach in the history of Texas Tech University to keep the program afloat. I had to make sure I didn't stick to the wrong part of the political spider web when I walked into work some days.

Myers, Hance, Jim Sowell, and that whole crew wanted Bob Knight to be the star of the show, even though my teams had better seasons every year. They made Marsha's life miserable. She was fighting Tech brass the whole time. Gerald cut her budget. She had scheduling issues to work through. It was one item after another.

As a coach, you understand that politics are a part of the job, but I was surprised at the level of ruthlessness, and at the lying, just for the sake of obtaining power at Texas Tech. The pettiness and the pointlessness of it was shocking. These guys went out of their way to cause damage. To call it dysfunctional would be an understatement.

The Power Play

The events that led to my dismissal from Tech at the end of 2009 actually began before the 2008 season started. My contract was set to expire in two years, so, at Tech's invitation, my agents started negotiations with Tech president Guy Bailey for a contract extension. Negotiations were going well. We'd actually agreed to a contract in principle, and Tech was going to get back to my agent in the next couple of days with a written version, but the call never came. In March 2008, after all of the head coaching vacancies had been filled for that year, Tech athletic director Gerald Myers sent my agent a letter. It said they were not planning to do anything at the time and he encouraged me to find another job.

During the 2008 season, we end up going 11-1 in the regular season, beat the #1 team in the country, had *College GameDay* set up shop in Lubbock twice, and had the highest graduation rate of all public institutions in the nation for Division I. I wasn't asking for Mack Brown or Bob Stoops pay, but I felt my salary should befit the coach of the third-best program in the conference. Tech, however, wanted to pay me a salary comparable to the ninth-best program in the conference.

I said I'd just continue to work with the contract I already had. When I refused to sign the contract they'd put in front of me, they threatened to fire me. At the time, I was one of the lowest-paid head coaches in the Big 12, even though we'd won more games than any program outside of UT and OU. Kent Hance, Tech's chancellor, and a couple of members of the board of regents, Larry Anders, chairman, and Jerry Turner, vice chairman, became frustrated by my refusal to sign. They said I was overpaid.

In the Texas state university system, the universities have a chancellor and a president. The chancellor is in charge of the university and all of the satellite campuses. For example, Kent Hance oversees Texas Tech and all of its campuses outside of Lubbock. The primary role of the chancellor is fund-raising.

The president oversees the day-to-day operations at the main campus. Guy Bailey was the president of Texas Tech. This setup had made for some pretty unhealthy situations over the years. In my 10 years at Texas Tech, we had five different presidents and three chancellors. It was a revolving door. During my time in Lubbock, I got along really well with four presidents and two chancellors. This is a pretty high percentage when you consider how many new faces we had to adjust to. Inevitably, the offices of chancellor and president would become locked in a battle for control and power. The friction between the two positions is the reason there was so much turnover. Any time someone in either office changed, there was a ripple effect. As a head football coach, it was a delicate situation. If you paid too much attention to one, the other may get jealous. If you didn't pay attention to either one, you risked having them both feel neglected.

All responsibilities regarding the head football coach's contract and his hiring and firing fell to the offices of the president and the athletic director. According to Tech policies and procedures, the chancellor and the board of regents were forbidden to be involved in the day-to-day operations of the main campus, or with interfering in the president and athletic director's dealings with the head football coach. They were also forbidden to allow interference from boosters and any other outside influence. In 2006-2007, Auburn University almost lost its accreditation after the Southern Association of Colleges and Schools, the regional accrediting agency, cited the micromanagement by Auburn's top booster and trustee Bobby Lowder over the rest of the board, claiming Auburn failed to prove the university president's "ultimate control over the athletics program."

Even though Tech president Bailey and AD Myers were the only people authorized by university policies and procedures to conduct my negotiations, the others interfered with the talks. When negotiations finally resumed, Bailey was cut out of them. All negotiations were conducted with Hance's office. At one point, during the conference calls with my agents, there was even an attorney there who was sent by a booster. I didn't realize the degree of interference until the *Dallas Morning News* published a bunch of emails from Jim Sowell, one of Tech's biggest boosters, to Hance. It was clear from the emails' contents that an outside booster was directly meddling with the day-to-day operations on campus, which is illegal.[1] The emails also made it clear that, after we agreed in principle to a new contract with the president, Sowell and Hance obstructed the entire thing.[2]

It was vintage Kent Hance. This is a guy whose whole persona stems from the time he beat George W. Bush for Congress way back in the good ol' days of the late '70s. Hance hit below the belt like crazy during the campaign. He ripped on Bush's drinking and preached about instituting dry counties and oppressive self-righteous values. But if you track the money, Hance opened a bar, Fat Dawg's, when he was in law school and only sold it when he was getting ready to run for Congress. But that's Kent Hance. He'd tell anyone with ears, "I'm the only one to beat a Bush in an election in the state of Texas." OK, well, Bush went on to become the President of the United States. You, well . . .

As a congressman, Hance was elected by the Democrats and yet was one of the first guys to step across the aisle and jump in Ronald Reagan's lap when things started turning his way.

Regardless of your politics, if Hance believed in anything he had ever said, what was he doing over there with Reagan so quickly if he ran as a Democrat?

When he switched his allegiance to the Republican Party, his announcement came just two weeks after he'd dismissed rumors suggesting he was in fact about to switch parties. The defection drew national attention, along with outrage from Democratic leaders. The county Democratic chair, Harvey Morton, accused him of "blind ambition." Then Hance proceeded to campaign for governor, which prompted 68-year-old former governor Bill Clements to come out of retirement to oppose him in the primary. Clements slaughtered him in the race, getting 58 percent of the vote to Hance's 20 percent. The good people of Texas saw right through what Hance was selling.

Hance loved to tell everybody how much power he had, but he was like the Wizard of Oz. If you pulled back the curtain, you'd realize there was only this little man pulling levers.

After months of contentious negotiations, we agreed to a new five-year contract in February of 2009. In my opinion, the Tech brass resented that it looked like they were outmaneuvered and that they'd caved to public pressure. A couple of regents and the chancellor (Hance) were particularly upset. If Hance didn't like the contract, he shouldn't have agreed to it, though he really shouldn't have been involved in the negotiations to begin with.

The day after the contract was signed, Hance, Turner, and Anders began looking for an out, a way to fire me before the end of 2009 to avoid paying me significant contractual bonuses.[3] They planned to hide behind the shield of sovereign immunity, a law that basically puts any actions of the state outside the realm of legal recourse. That means they can't be sued unless they agree to allow themselves to be sued. Tech's main legal argument was, "We're a state institution and we have sovereign immunity." The state of Texas has sovereign immunity. They argued that as a state institution they were protected by the same condition. My contract stipulated that the university gave me the right to sue Tech in state court, but they were trying to strip me of that right. If a state institution was able to hide behind sovereign immunity, this would make all negotiated contracts with a state institution unenforceable. Most states in the country, excluding Texas, have withdrawn the doctrine of sovereign immunity because they understand that the key component of any contract is mutuality of obligation, which is the backbone of capitalism. What is the point of having a contract with a state institution if it is unenforceable? If you don't have that, you have nothing. Is this the type of government oppression that rolls through anybody's head as they listen to the "Star-Spangled Banner" or recite the Pledge of Allegiance?

We obtained copies of emails from Turner advising Hance and Tech board members that they should terminate me by November 30, 2009, to avoid paying me my $800,000 bonus due on December 31, 2009.[4] Shockingly, this email was sent the day *after* I signed my new contract. The bonus was for completing six years of service. Twice in prior contract negotiations they'd moved the date I was supposed to receive this bonus. It appeared that they never had any intention of paying it. If that seems far-fetched, keep in mind we had all sorts of documentation to back it up. We had another email from former Tech regent Windy Sitton, which she wrote the day Tech fired me. She acknowledged the fact that my firing had been "in the works" since I "outmaneuvered" them in contract negotiations during February 2009.[5]

Tech's solution came in the form of player Adam James, who had become known amongst his teammates and coaches for his unjustified sense of entitlement and bad attitude. He was also the son of former SMU football player and ESPN announcer Craig James, the ultimate little-league dad.

In August 2009, Craig James told me he was in business with Chancellor Hance. No doubt Craig was telling me this because he thought it might influence me into giving his son more playing time. Craig had become infamous around our football office for this sort of thing. My staff and I received more phone calls from Craig James regarding his son's playing time than from all of our other players' parents combined.

In the first month of the 2009 season, Lincoln Riley, one of our receivers coaches, met with Adam to tell him his effort at practice wasn't good enough and that he was getting dropped to third team. James stormed out of the office. He shouted, "Fuck this!" in our lobby full of secretaries and players. He rammed his way through the door of the football office so hard that the door split and came off the hinges. It cost us $1,100 to fix.

He immediately called his dad. Craig James then called up a bunch of guys on the staff. He called our football operations director Tommy McVay. He told him, "You coaches are crazy. You're screwing my kid!" Then he called Lincoln and left an enraged voicemail, "You don't know what you're doing! Adam James is the best player at the wide receiver position." He concluded his message to Coach Riley by stating, "If you've got the balls to call me back, and I don't think you do, call me back."[6]

Lincoln brought me the voicemail, so I met with Adam James.

"If we were interested in what your dad has to say, we'd invite him to the meetings," I told him. "We didn't invite him to the meetings. We've got 12 people that evaluate everything you do. Once in a while we might be wrong, but it's not very often. We arrive at a decision based on the wisdom of those 12 people, not your dad, who is totally biased. We coach you, not your father. If he ever calls here again, we're going to play it over the speakers to the entire team."

He said, "Well, I can't do anything about it."

I said, "Well, maybe you can't. But you'd better do something because I will play it in front of the team. What do you think the guys on our team who don't even have a dad are going to think when you're sitting here putting pressure on us for playing time, rather than going out there and trying hard and earning your spot?"

He didn't appear to care about that. He just didn't say anything. I was hoping he'd turn the corner. It didn't happen. I discovered later that Craig went around bad-mouthing our coaching, our program, and later complained to upper administration.

> "Before Adam James ever entered the football locker room at Texas Tech, I had heard how spoiled and selfish he acted in a team atmosphere from many of my baseball friends. Adam was on the baseball team his true freshman year at Tech, before he ever joined the football team, and did not make it through the baseball season because of his selfish attitude. After a baseball game in which he felt like he did not get enough playing time, but the team still won 20–1, he came into the locker room after the game and 'pouted and threw a big fit,' according to another player on the baseball team. A few weeks later in the middle of the season, he just stopped showing up to practices or games and quit because he was not happy about how he was being treated. One of my roommates was a baseball player on the team and many of my friends were a part of the team that witnessed all of this. These baseball players told me he was 'spoiled and selfish' before he ever came to the football team.
>
> "After quitting baseball he came out for football and his selfish attitude was very evident, as was his laziness. During off-season workouts he would often be caught skipping

lifts in the weight room or finding ways to cut corners and get out of conditioning exercises. When we had player-organized seven-on-seven throwing in the summer, when he would show up, he was much more interested in playing his own games on the side of the field or telling people that he wasn't going to run any routes because the coaches do not give him a 'fair opportunity' anyway. During the season he was often 'injured' (it usually seemed like a very minor injury that could keep him out of practice but never out of any other activity, including games), so he would not participate in some drills in practice. None of these acts were productive for our team, but the most detrimental part of Adam was his off-field attitude and actions.

"In the locker room and away from the facility, Adam used any opportunity he had to tell other players how he was being treated unfairly, how the coaches did not give him a fair chance and how we did not have to do everything the coaches told us to because they had no option but to play some of us. When I heard these kinds of things I usually tried to put an end to them, but Adam pretty consistently talked bad about the coaches or downplayed the importance of working hard when he was off the field. When he talked to young players or players who were usually on the scout team, he would explain how the coaches were not fair to certain players and only played favorites.

When he talked to players that did get some playing time he would talk about how we didn't really have to do what the coaches asked of us because the coaches had to play us anyway. And it almost always tied back to how he was not getting a chance to play just because the coaches were unfair.

"The coaches were always more than fair to Adam, I felt, because he came into the game during certain formations and situations during the season, but because of his work ethic and attitude many of the players on the team had a hard time trusting him or relying on him. He was not always practicing and we had seen his laziness during the off-season. Adam was a kid who seemed like he had been given everything he wanted his whole life and acted like if things did not go exactly how he wanted, then it was because someone was treating him unfairly or his failures were somebody else's fault. He was a selfish player on and off the field who was counterproductive for our team and would be for any other team.
—Graham Harrell, Texas Tech, QB, 2004-2008

Bad effort is the kiss of death when you're evaluating someone. Unless you can convince yourself that you're the one who can change the guy's mentality, you don't need to have him on your team. If it's a recruit, his high school coach had probably been telling him that he needed to make a better effort for four years. You have to try to figure out if you can coach him through it. Typically, really lazy people don't become hard workers. Avoid underachievers. Sometimes a young player needs the opportunity to mature. Speculating on this is risky—while anyone is capable of great effort, results may vary.

Staffs debate their players' merits all the time. When Adam James was a receiver prospect from Celina, Texas, most of the Tech staff was against recruiting him. They didn't think he could play. I thought Adam could develop into a contributor. Our DB coach, Carlos Mainord, who'd been coaching and recruiting for four decades, didn't think he'd help significantly, but that'd he'd be OK. Maybe a special teams guy.

Adam's daddy, Craig, came around and campaigned for his son. He talked about how good Adam was. It all started when we beat Cal in the Holiday Bowl. Craig, who was there to announce the game, came up to our hospitality room. He started talking about how great his kid was and how great the bloodlines of the James family were. I later found out that he tried giving the same sales pitch to the Nevada staff after calling their bowl game too. It was quite a turn for Craig, considering just a year earlier he'd announced he would never let his son play for Texas Tech. At the time Craig was calling the Houston Bowl, where we were playing Navy. One of our players scored a touchdown and then celebrated by throwing the ball into the air. When the ball landed, his teammates hit the ground as if they'd been washed over by a wave. They called it the Nestea Plunge. Craig apparently thought it was a fake bomb or something, and he went on a rant about how he'd never let his son become a Red Raider. That must've been before he realized Adam's phone wasn't going to be ringing off the hook from college coaches.

Our staff thoroughly researched whether Adam James had any other scholarship offers. We didn't find any. We offered him a grayshirt, which meant that his scholarship wouldn't go into effect until January. He needed as much time as he could to develop. He was the last guy we signed in that recruiting class. Craig used to rattle off the names of all his relatives who had played. I bought in, thinking, "OK, the genetics are on his side. Maybe he'll blossom.

We've had good luck developing gray shirts in the past."

The thing about it is, Adam was big enough and moved decently. He was not fast, but he had pretty good hands. He could've fit into the role of tight end for us, but because he didn't work hard he was only marginally effective. We could never get him to move out from behind his father's coattails. Together, they believed that playing time was determined by politics and influence rather than hard work. Craig may have expected his son to get some level of preferential treatment. I disagreed. That's not how I ran the program at Tech. As a head coach, I believed in making people earn their way, and I wouldn't put the interests of an individual above the whole team.

Adam wanted to be handed his position and playing time, as opposed to going out and earning it. Craig would constantly call and try to talk to me. I'd avoid him. Just because he's a celebrity parent didn't mean we were going to have a bunch of face time on how much his kid should play. It was a non-stop struggle. When I wouldn't talk to him, he would try to twist the arms of assistants and support staff.

My biggest regret was not cutting Adam James. I kept hoping he'd develop a work ethic. He had two position coaches, first Dana Holgorsen, then Lincoln Riley. He didn't get along with either one.

As a coach, you want it to work out. We invested a lot of time in coaching Adam James. We worked hard to try to rehabilitate him to make him a working part of the team. We thought he may have simply been the victim of his dad's little-league father tendencies, and that he'd eventually find a way to be his own, independent person. But that didn't turn out to be the case. I should've cut my losses, but I was really hoping that he'd improve and stuck with him.

There are always going to be people that don't immediately jive with the way you want things done. You've got mean kids you need to loosen up. You've got soft kids you need to toughen up. One way or another, you're trying to figure out how to maximize their talents. With Adam James, we were trying to figure out how to move him beyond being a spoiled child and get some cooperation out of him. He had some talent and could've helped. But as long as he wanted to fall back and use his father as a substitute for hard work and achievement, we weren't going to get anywhere. Sadly, he continued in the same vein.

There've been several people that I regret not cutting, but I've never made a cut that I regret. There's a definite quality of addition by subtraction. It's not only about having the biggest, strongest, and fastest guys, it's also about having people believe in what they're doing and forming a cohesive unit. If someone is doing something you don't like, can you change them? If you decide you can't change them, then you ask yourself, "Can I live with it?" If the answer to that is no, you have to cut them.

On December 14, 2009, as we began to prepare for the Alamo Bowl, I noticed Adam James nonchalantly going through our first period of practice. I told him if he didn't improve his effort, I was going to send him to "Muscle Beach," which is the area designated for injured players and for lifting weights that Bennie Wylie, our strength coach, oversees. Adam ignored the warning, so we sent him along with two other players over to Muscle Beach. Bennie told the three players they had to run laps and stairs. According to Bennie, Adam gave him attitude. Adam was the last one to finish each exercise and he danced through the discipline like he was mocking it. After the session at Muscle Beach, the other two players admitted their effort on the field had been unacceptable. They said they would work harder. Adam told Bennie that his effort had been fine and that the Tech coaches didn't know what they were doing.

Three days later, on December 17, Adam James again displayed his contempt for team rules and the coaching staff. He arrived at practice twenty minutes late, in street clothes, wearing sunglasses. He said he had a concussion. The team physician acknowledged that James had a mild concussion and limited him from physical activity until he was symptom free. The team policy dictated that all players, including injured players, attend practice in practice attire and participate in the manner permissible given the nature of their injury.

According to Steve Pincock, the team trainer, James was "walking the field" in an indifferent way. James was wearing street clothes and had a baseball cap on backwards, which, injured or not, he knew was against team rules. I asked Pincock why Adam wasn't dressed appropriately for practice. Pincock said he didn't know. This was the first he'd seen him because Adam was late. I asked him why Adam was wearing sunglasses. Pincock said Adam's eyes were sensitive to light because he had a concussion. I told Pincock to remove James from the field since he wasn't dressed properly, was late, and had a bad attitude while the rest of the team was practicing hard. I swore in frustration. I told Pincock to put him somewhere dark and have him do something.

We continued to practice.

At no point did I say to lock him in a room. I never told Pincock what he should do with Adam beyond getting him off the field and putting him somewhere dark since his eyes were sensitive to light. The training staff handled the injured players. The coaches did not. The training staff decided to put Adam James in the equipment garage, where the O-line enjoyed hanging out during our special teams period. I didn't have a problem with it because he was not in any danger. I wanted him off the field so he wouldn't be a distraction.

Months later, when Adam James was deposed under oath, he said he found the incident "funny" and that he did not believe that I should have been fired.[7] In fact, he texted his father about the incident while in the equipment garage because he thought he would "like" it, since they both have the same sense of humor.

On December 19 we held practice on our game field inside Jones Stadium. Before practice, Pincock gave me a rundown of the injured players. He asked me what I wanted him to do with Adam James. I told him do whatever he did last practice.[8] Then, as I went down the tunnel to start practice, another one of our trainers told me Adam was in the media room, which was the same place we have the opposing coaches hold their post-game press conferences. I continued on to practice to get ready for the bowl game.

According to Pincock's statement, he specifically told James not to go into the electrical closet by the media room. James admitted under oath that he ignored Pincock's instuctions. He admitted that he let himself into that closet and that he shot a video—a video that would start a firestorm of allegations—because he thought it was funny. Those were his words. Even having that phone with him during practice time was against team policy, but he ignored that rule, too, and used it to make his own little *Blair Witch Project* where he was seen whispering and scanning the electrical closet. He was specifically told *not* to be in that area, but there he was, acting like a captive.

Craig James told Hance that Adam had spent three hours in that electrical closet based on instructions from Pincock. That night, Craig called Larry Anders (chairman of the Tech board of regents) and complained that Adam had been forced to practice with a concussion and had been locked in an electrical closet. How absurd is that? To even suggest that I wanted this guy, who is in for five plays a game, to practice hurt because we so desperately need him is just ridiculous. We'd already held out the starting quarterback for a month that season because he had a concussion—*the starting quarterback*. Adam was forbidden to practice because he had a concussion. We wanted him away from the field.

According to both his and Anders's depositions, Craig demanded that I be fired. Hance called me and said that Craig had phoned Anders to complain about his son being forced to play before his concussion was healed, which was simply not true. I explained the situation to Hance, and also told him how often Craig called up the Tech coaches to lobby for more playing time for his son. I told him that Adam had been a constant discipline problem and that I planned on cutting him from the team. Hance told me not to cut Adam.

During the conversation Hance said he was going to give the Jameses three options: Adam could stay at Tech, and that we, as coaches, would help him become the best that he could be; he could transfer and we'd release him to any school he wanted; or he could stay at Tech, be a regular student and we'd continue to pay his scholarship, even though we didn't do this for any other student.

On December 20, Pincock put Adam in the training room and instructed him to ride a stationary bike because his symptoms had subsided sufficiently to do physical activities. I was not informed of how he was being treated until after practice. I was not concerned, because this was the trainer's job.

After speaking with Anders and Jerry Turner (vice chairman of the board of regents) Hance ordered an investigation into the Adam James matter, to be conducted by university attorney Charlotte Bingham. Interestingly, Bingham worked for Hance, not the president's office. Later that night she interviewed Craig James, who told her that Adam was required to stand in an electrical closet for hours.

She interviewed Adam, who told her that he had been forced to stand in the closet for five minutes. Neither of these statements were true. Adam was never told to stand in the electrical closet. Pincock had specifically told Adam *not* to go into the electrical closet.

Turner contacted Bingham on December 21, before she'd interviewed a single witness outside the James family. Turner instructed Bingham, Tech president Bailey, and AD Myers that the investigation should be used to terminate me.[9] Neither Turner, Hance, nor any of the regents should've been involved or interfered with any of this. It is strictly prohibited by university policies and procedures. The entire matter should've been handled exclusively by the president and the athletic director.

Despite that, Bailey advised me that same day that while the investigation was no big deal, he was concerned that Hance was going to "railroad" me because of his business connections to Craig James. Bailey was so concerned that he had his assistant attend and keep a record of the investigation interviews.

When Bingham interviewed me, I told her about Adam James's poor work habits, that he showed up late for practice, that he did not have workout gear on, and that I did not want him loafing while his teammates were working hard. I also told her that I wanted the trainers to take him away from the field and put him in a dark place because he was sensitive to light, and that the trainers had handled him from there.

Bingham reported her findings to Anders, Bailey, Myers, Turner, and Hance, and did not recommend that I be fired. Hance called me to say that some members of the board of regents wanted me fired because of Craig James' complaints. Hance said they were going to take some sort of disciplinary action against me even though he couldn't explain what I'd done wrong. Hance wanted to fine me as much as $100,000 and demand a letter of apology. He said he would call after the board meeting to take place on December 23. He never did. Even though they never spoke to me beforehand, Turner and Anders announced at their board meeting that they intended to fire me over the James affair.

According to Anders and Hance's depositions, Hance told Anders and Turner that the clause in my contract giving me the right to a 10-business day cure period for a violation warranting termination was meaningless. A cure period is intended to give a person the chance to fix a problem instead of being outright fired. We specifically negotiated for this clause in my contract for exactly this type of situation. Hance (and boosters interfering from the outside) had proven to be untrustworthy during contract negotiations. We felt that clause was necessary to prevent any shady behavior on their part. Ignoring this 10-day cure clause, Hance pressured Bailey and Myers to suspend or fire me immediately.

The day after Christmas, two days after Hance told Anders and Turner he was going to fire me, I met with Myers and Bailey.

I told them I was happy to cooperate with the investigation. They handed me a letter dated December 23, signed by Bailey, acknowledging "the allegations by the James family had not been substantiated" despite, or perhaps as a result of, Ms. Bingham's investigation. They then told me I needed to sign a letter admitting wrongdoing on my part in the "mistreatment" of a student athlete. I told them I was innocent and I would not sign that letter.

We went back and forth for over an hour. They kept trying to get me to sign the letter and admit that I did something wrong, when they knew that I didn't. As this was going on, I couldn't help but think that it was an attempt to cheat me out of the $800,000 completion bonus they would owe me at the end of the calendar year. It was clear that I was being railroaded.

At that point I suggested a way out. I said, "Listen, if you don't want me here, then why don't we negotiate an exit strategy. We have committed the best recruiting class in the history of Texas Tech. It was ranked 14th in the nation by the online recruiting analysts. We have a great team coming back next season. We have a great chance to have an even more successful team than we did in 2008. If I'm not your guy and you don't want me here, let's negotiate an exit strategy. We'll sign a great class, have a great season, and I'll resign in December. I will find another job and you can hire somebody that you're more pleased with, but you're not going to railroad me with false charges." It would've been a good deal for all of us, because I wasn't interested in being in a place where I clearly wasn't wanted. But they were not going to cheat me out of my $800,000 bonus, or my salary for the coming season that we'd already agreed on.

Bailey and Myers assured me that they wanted me to be their coach, that this was not about getting rid of me, that they were not trying to fire me, that this incident was only a little thing, and that if I would just sign this letter it would all go away. This obviously turned out not to be the case. All the correspondence we discovered between Hance, Turner, and Anders prior to this meeting made it clear that they were planning to fire me shortly after I'd signed my contract. In my opinion, they never had any intention of honoring my contract. I didn't trust them because all the signs leading up to this meeting told me otherwise, and I refused to sign their letter that falsely suggested I'd mistreated a student athlete.

That same day, Craig James wrote to Hance again claiming his son had been placed in an electrical closet and that he'd been forced to play with a concussion. Ms. Bingham knew that the statement was inaccurate but said nothing to the board, Hance, Bailey, or Myers.

On December 27, Ms. Bingham left a voicemail for my attorney, saying that "outside pressures" were affecting the situation. Bingham later testified that those "outside pressures" were the James family. She left a voicemail because she was heading to Peru for a couple of weeks.

According to depositions by Anders and Hance, Bailey and Myers recommended that the Adam James matter be closed by my paying a fine and receiving a letter of reprimand. Bailey and Myers, under Tech policies, are the two people with "sole authority" to determine the disciplinary measures for me as Texas Tech's head football coach. They are supposed to make their decisions without any outside interference. But according to an email we obtained, Anders and Turner instructed Hance that Myers and Bailey were not to issue a letter of reprimand. Anders and Turner wanted to keep the Adam James incident open and "use it to [their] advantage" to terminate me so payment could be avoided.[10]

Instead of issuing me a letter of reprimand and closing the Adam James matter, Hance claimed that he declared that I had until noon on December 28 to provide a signed copy of the letter presented to me on December 26, plus a letter of apology, or I would be suspended. Even before the deadline, Anders told Hance that it was already too late for me to avoid suspension and termination.

At no point was I offered the letter of reprimand. And I was never told that I would be suspended for not signing the

December 26 letter, nor was I asked for a letter of apology. One can only assume that this was because they'd already planned to terminate me.

Our team left Lubbock for San Antonio on December 28 to continue preparing for the Alamo Bowl against Michigan State. When we arrived in San Antonio, I received a call from Myers. He told me I was suspended.

Myers told me the decision had been made by Hance and some of the board of regents and said there was nothing he could do. He told me that I would not be coaching the team in the Alamo Bowl and also barred me from speaking to my team. That tells you something about the people I was dealing with. The only reason for the suspension was that Texas Tech had received a complaint from a player and that the investigation was not complete. Myers suggested that I was insubordinate for refusing to sign the letter admitting to mistreating a student athlete. I told him that refusing to sign a letter is no justification for a suspension. There was no contractual basis for Tech to suspend me, nor was there any evidence of wrongdoing to support such a disciplinary measure. I reminded him that my contract did not obligate me to sign a letter. I asked how my exercising the right not to sign a letter constituted insubordination.

Turner told Hance and Anders that if I tried to seek an injunction allowing me to coach in the bowl game, they would fire me. Anders agreed. Another Tech board of regents member, Nancy Neal, recognized that they were attempting to avoid payment of the $800,000 bonus owed to me on December 31, and said it should be paid and that Tech "should not be cheap about it."[11]

On December 29, I filed suit seeking a temporary restraining order to lift the suspension and coach the bowl game. This was within my rights as part of the Texas Constitution and Tech bylaw 70.10, which stated specifically that a non-faculty employee of Texas Tech, which I was, had the absolute right to file suit as an appeal of a suspension and a claim for violation of any law without fear of retaliation. Bailey and Bingham later testified that I had the absolute right to file suit without fear of retaliation.

On the morning of December 30, at a pre-hearing meeting in the court's chambers, my attorney, Ted Liggett, informed Tech officials that we intended to proceed with the hearing. At that point, the Tech representatives handed my counsel a letter of termination effective December 30, 2009. Tech then released a "Statement from Texas Tech on Termination of Football Coach Mike Leach" in which Tech admitted that the termination was due to my filing the restraining order against Texas Tech.

I found it interesting that Tech publicly stated that the investigation was ongoing, despite the fact that the head of the investigation, Charlotte Bingham, had been out of the country on vacation since the morning of December 27. Yet, during her absence, they had both suspended and fired me. Also, on the day of my firing, former regent Windy Sitton confirmed that my termination had nothing to do with the Adam James situation, but resulted from the ill will generated by the 2009 contract negotiations.

She wrote an email to Jerry Turner that we obtained:

> *"Jerry, I know his firing has been in the works since the Chancellor and the AD were outmaneuvered by Leach. That is our problem.*

> *"The problem rests with the arrogance of the Chancellor and the ineptness of the AD. Everyone sees through this injustice to Mike Leach and Texas Tech. The Sitton family has given scholarships and have had multiple seats since 1976. We will not renew our options [on] our 12 seats or for that matter our PSLs for Basketball. This whole thing smells, and we do not want to be a part of this blight on Texas Tech."*

Later, when Turner was asked in his deposition if he was aware of any former regent who said the firing was a result of ill will left over from the 2009 contract negotiations, he denied having any such knowledge. As part of their conspiracy to hide their true reason for firing me, Bingham, Anders, Turner, Hance, Bailey, and Myers began the process of changing the investigation report on the James incident. According to Bingham's deposition, Hance directed Bingham to change her investigation report because it was too "mild" and "too milk toast." (*sic*)

We also discovered that at some time before Craig James had made any complaints about the treatment of his son, he'd hired Spaeth Communications, a public relations firm. Tech representatives worked with Spaeth Communications in an effort to get Pincock and the team physician to change their stories. As Merrie Spaeth, the president of Spaeth Communications, put it in an email exchange with Sally Post, Tech's director of communications and broadcast media, the doctor needed to "recant" part of his statement.[12] Meanwhile, Hance made statements along the lines of, "If you sue your boss, you are going to get fired." Turner admitted in four emails he sent to Anders on January 4 that I was fired for the restraining order against Texas Tech.

From the moment Tech suspended me to the time my firing was announced, there was a flood of media reports revealing all these "details" about things I'd supposedly done. ESPN's Joe Schad was just spewing this stuff that Craig James and Spaeth Communications were feeding him: "Alleged electrical closet" . . . "Alleged electrical closet" . . . "YouTube video of Adam James in the alleged electrical closet is available" . . . "I'm told the alleged electrical closet is approximately 4 x 10 feet."[13]

Then *SportsCenter* showed Adam's YouTube video from the electrical closet. Too bad they never said Adam went in that electrical closet after he was specifically told *not* to go in there.

Merrie Spaeth distributed the video. We obtained documents where Spaeth and people at Tech were talking about the best way to distribute it so it would be as inflammatory as possible.[14] There was an email saying Spaeth had people use online pseudonyms to smear me in the comments at the bottom of news stories, on blogs, and in message boards.[15] Kent Hance had been a lobbyist.

He used every weapon available in his campaign against me.

Spaeth Communications was specifically hired by Craig James and used by Tech to smear my reputation. It's alarming, but not all that surprising, considering how some administrators at Texas Tech operated. There were emails where Sally Post was taking cues from Merrie Spaeth. The emails suggest that it was not an "investigation" at all but more of an effort to sell me down the river.[16] They knew the facts weren't on their side so they used Spaeth Communications to spread misinformation and try to turn public opinion.

In those emails, Spaeth talks about writing up the new statements by the trainer and the doctor. Then, Tech would say sign 'em or else. This while Pincock, the trainer, is seeing the national coach of the year get the axe. It's not hard to imagine what was going through his mind. I think he's an honest guy, but I suspect he was very conflicted. He had to be afraid for his job and his family. So Pincock signed off on their statement, which omitted pertinent details so it would appear more favorable to Tech.

On top of that, you had all these analysts, who were colleagues of Craig James, weighing in on ESPN. They had no knowledge of the facts. Obviously, they weren't even concerned about the facts. They just took everything that Craig James, through Spaeth Communications, was feeding them, and kept repeating it over and over, during every pre-game show, every halftime show, every post-game show, and during *SportsCenter*. This went on for days.

There were a number of exchanges between my agents and ESPN. But ESPN was more interested in presenting the fantastical story by Spaeth Communications. They weren't just showing one side of the story, they were perpetuating falsehoods.

There were statements out there from Adam James's two position coaches, Dana Holgorsen and Lincoln Riley. There was a statement from the strength coach, Bennie Wylie. There were statements from three of James's teammates—players that had been successful in the program and had witnessed Adam's behavior, as well as mine. CBSSports.com and other media outlets chose to run those statements. ESPN, which also had them, chose not to. When one of my agents asked Joe Schad, the ESPN reporter, why they neglected to report those statements, he said he didn't see how they were relevant to the story. But when Craig James gave Schad Adam's cell number so he could hand the phone over to his roommate Chris Perry, a back-up lineman whom we'd suspended twice, his statement was considered relevant.[17]

It was worse than hypocrisy. It was malicious.[18]

I waited a little while before going out in Lubbock. I figured that, as is the case with most stories, half the people would believe Tech's tale and half the people would be skeptical. However, when I went out in the middle of all of this, it turned out none of them bought what the Jameses were selling. I had complete strangers come up to me to say, "Great job" or "You got screwed." I would show up at a restaurant and I'd get a standing ovation.

My Texas Tech cell phone had been cut off, but people still found a way to reach me. Coaches in the business, some retired, some still active, called to offer their support. Hal Mumme, Bob Stoops, Barry Switzer, Dennis Franchione, Urban Meyer, and Kyle Whittingham all reached out to me. I heard from a ton of my ex-players. I tried to get back to all of them as fast as I could. People who I barely knew, fans who had actually done their own detective work, were reaching out to me. The overall reaction was really touching.

People know what I'm like. They knew I'd never abused players, and they knew about Adam James being a malcontent. They knew that his dad was meddlesome. There were even these people from Celina, Texas, where the Jameses live, who would tell me, "Adam's been a spoiled brat since the beginning." I heard from guys who had played in the NFL who would say what a smug jerk his dad had been in college and in the NFL.

My approach was the same one we preached to our players all the time at Tech, "Play the next play." I wasn't sitting riveted to the

TV, watching commentary from Craig James's buddies at ESPN. I was too busy on the phone, combating the situation. I knew I was dealing with some bad characters, but the fact that they would be dirty to the point where they could actually injure themselves legally? That illustrated not only a level of ruthlessness, but also a level of poorly founded, even stupid, arrogance.

Keep in mind, I was not the one who hired a PR firm. Craig James did. He hired Spaeth, the Swift Boat PR firm. I didn't think I needed to hire a PR firm. I felt like the truth was enough because I didn't have anything to hide. All of the "Team Leach" members rallied on my behalf, and I'm grateful to them. The truth of the matter is, I believed the facts would actually come out, which they did for the most part, except for one media entity that appeared ridiculously biased. The other outlets had portrayed things more accurately, but they were overshadowed by the magnitude of ESPN. NBC had it right. CBS had it right. The *New York Times* had it right. Fox had it right.

As much as irresponsible reporting was a problem, the bigger issue was Texas Tech and ESPN's refusal to reign in Craig James. It was insane. There's not a person who walks the face of the Earth that thought we wouldn't have been in that position were it not for Craig James. This whole mess was not about Adam James's injury, or his treatment after the injury. It was about administrative corruption. They used Adam James as an excuse. His father got in the middle of it and made it about favoritism, nepotism, and undue influence.

Then I heard that Craig James was planning a run for the Senate. I believe he consulted with Hance on his potential campaign effort. American politics already have enough people like him. We should be trying to clean guys like him out of the Capitol, not bring in more of them. The reason we were in this situation to begin with was because these guys had no integrity. They didn't even trust one another, and because their whole story was a lie, they were scared to death about who might someday tell the truth. They weren't friends, some were enemies, and they were stuck in a pickle together.

Guy Bailey didn't trust any of them. Gerald Myers didn't trust any of them. There were a lot of them that Kent Hance didn't trust.

They were in a very vulnerable position. Hance, to a point, used Craig James, but did he trust Craig James? Did James trust Kent Hance?

A year and a half after Tech fired me, they'd still only paid me about 15 percent of what I was owed from 2009. They paid me $300,000 in base salary, but my guaranteed outside income was $1.6 million. My bonuses were $25,000, which came from Tech playing in a bowl game, another $25,000 because we finished the season ranked in the top 25, another $25,000 because we won five Big 12 games, and an additional $25,000 for having a graduation rate above 65 percent. Plus, they owed me $800,000 for the completion bonus, which was six years in the making. At the time I write this, I have still not been paid for the 2009 season.

In March, I flew from Florida to Lubbock for my deposition. I also wanted to be in the room when Craig James was deposed under oath. I wanted to sit there and see how well he could lie to my face.

Craig walked into the room like he was already a senator. He was shaking everybody's hands, saying things like, "Hey, howya doin'? Boy, I love those boots! So, Dr. Bailey, now, where's your family from?" I didn't go near him.

In Craig's mind, everybody thinks he's the greatest thing ever, and we should all be honored to be in his presence. Apparently, he didn't get around to reading any of the blogs that bashed him. He was the one person with nearly a 100 percent disapproval rating. I sat there and looked at him while he told his lies under oath. He'd look down whenever I looked at him. It was awkward because I was sitting in the same room with this individual who tried so hard to get me fired, and who had a PR firm go to such lengths to smear my reputation. Then again, by the time Craig had his deposition, I had already sat across from Hance while he was deposed. I made him look at me every time. I just stared at Hance thinking, "Everything about this man is unclean." The type of unclean where if you got too close, it would never wash off.

Craig seemed like he had no sense of what was happening. He talked to my attorney Paul Dobrowski like the man was a child. This, after Paul had destroyed him in the deposition for several hours. Paul was the most dominant figure in the room. Craig was very evasive, which is a bad way to do depositions because you look like a sleazy liar. He would try to qualify everything. On numerous occasions, there were total contradictions between him and Hance. Obviously one of them was lying. Or was it both? They would take these long breaks, where I suspect he was being coached. You knew somebody was going to throw somebody else under the bus, because we were dealing with two people who really lacked any sense of loyalty. It didn't take long for them to step on one another.

Craig said he was shocked that I was fired. Then Paul showed him all of these memos written by him demanding that I be fired. He said he never threatened to sue Tech, but then we showed him the memo where he threatened to sue Tech.[19] He said he never called the administration or the chancellor. We proved that they had contact around 30 times. He said that Spaeth worked for his attorneys, yet we showed him the memo where Spaeth was apologizing to James for how much his bill was.

He said that Spaeth had nothing to do with putting out Adam's video, but Spaeth had everything to do with putting out Adam's video. The memo specifically detailed doing it, how it would be most effective to orchestrate, and how to get the most views.[20] Nobody bought that he would pay this big bill without knowing what it was for.

Craig would just sit there and get this screwy little smile whenever he was caught in lie. It's the same look an infant gets when he's just messed in his diaper. Yet he continued to carry himself like he was pulling it off. Meanwhile, the other people in the room had to be thinking, "You are a total idiot.'"

Craig waited down the hall while Adam was being deposed. When my attorney walked out, Craig gave him this big ol' smile. He shook his hand.

"How's it goin' in there?" Craig asked him. "Shoot, you're doin' a great job, you know. I really like those boots. You know, I'm a boot guy. It's like walkin' in sand. I love your shirt. I love western clothing."

It was incredible. I made sure I didn't walk near him, so I wouldn't have to hear the same sappy drivel. "How've you been? How's your family? Great to see you!" It reminded me of when he came around our offices with his transparent agenda.

Quite frankly, I had tried to stay away from him for the past two years because I knew that the hand you weren't shaking held an ulterior motive.

Adam's deposition was taken on a Saturday. The Thursday before he'd been punished for discipline issues at Tech by the new coaching staff. He admitted it. It's in his deposition, which I read, but didn't attend. We wanted him to be isolated. This was someone who'd never done anything on his own. His parents were always there to prop him up. We didn't want his father to be in the room because we didn't want them to be able to compare stories.

Adam admitted that it was his idea to go into that electrical closet after the trainer specifically told him not to. He admitted that he disobeyed the trainer and shot his cell-phone video, and he even texted his father saying, "You're going to like this."[21] My attorney Ted Liggett asked Adam why his father would "like this," and Adam said, "Well, we have the same sense of humor and personality, and I thought—we thought it was funny. So I said 'you're going to like this.'" Adam went on to say while being deposed under oath that he did not believe that I should have been fired. He also talked about how he felt like a slave and a prisoner.

How could he say he felt like a prisoner or a slave? It illustrated how much he vacillated on things. He also said he was never scared or harmed. He said he thought it was funny. He joked about it with his friends. Furthermore, he said he didn't think I should've been fired for anything. Compared to Craig's deposition, you would've thought Adam was testifying on my behalf.

Right around the same time that Tech was appealing to have my case thrown out of court, the school hired a new head trainer. Tommy Tuberville, who was brought in as the new head coach after Tech fired me, wanted his old trainer from his days at Auburn. This trainer was at the time being sued by a former Auburn player for mishandling the player's rehab from back surgery and ending his career.

He was the only trainer in the entire country who was being sued for mistreatment of a student athlete, and this is who Texas Tech hired after what they'd alleged about me? It's beyond ironic. This action alone validates every point that I've made. It reveals that Tech's original motive was not the health and well-being of their student athletes, it was about them trying to keep from having to pay the money they owed me. They knew I didn't do anything wrong with Adam James, and if they truly believed that I had done something wrong they would never even have considered hiring a trainer who was in the middle of a federal lawsuit.

The player that Tuberville's trainer allegedly injured wasn't even a guy who'd made complaints about playing time. The player was a starting lineman and was a Freshman All-American. This wasn't a player with a screwy motive who was in for only five plays a game. The attorney for the former Auburn player said his jaw almost hit the floor when he heard that Texas Tech was hiring this guy as its new trainer. I'd like to say I was equally shocked, but I wasn't. It was par for the course.

> **"No man has a good enough memory to be a successful liar."**
>
> **–Abraham Lincoln**

Gone Fishin'

I'd never been fired from anything in my life until Texas Tech canned me at the end of the 2009 regular season. The whole situation was pretty surreal. It all went so fast. I was trying to get counsel from my agents and attorneys and figure out the best way to address all these moving parts: how to handle the media, how to defend myself, setting our legal action in motion, and, most importantly, the future of my family.

My kids were due back in school within days. I was under fire by the media. My family and I decided we'd go to Colorado on a trip that we'd already planned. By the time we arrived it was apparent there was going to be a life change for all of us—me, my family, and the families of my staff.

Through it all, I was thinking about the impact the situation was going to have on all of our staff and their families. I'd been with a lot of these people for almost a decade. My assistants' wives would come to our recruiting dinners. They'd get to know our players and their parents. As a head coach, you grow close to the wives and their kids, especially through all of the bowl weeks, when our families hang out in the hospitality rooms and attend all the events together. You see families grow and children get bigger. They become your family too.

Any time my contract was up at Tech, I never signed a new one until my assistants were taken care of first. Any time I ever got a raise, my assistants got a raise too.

I had to make several calls about possible jobs for a few of my assistants, but fortunately most of the staff landed positions pretty quickly. Two of my coaches, Carlos Mainord and Charlie Sadler, retired. A few others were retained by Tech. When Ruffin McNeill got the head coaching job at East Carolina, he hired a lot of the old staff. Dave Emerick went to Arizona, and after a coaching change at Tennessee two more coaches were hired on in Knoxville.

I moved my family to Key West. I've always loved it down there. In the last 22 years, I'd visited Key West as many as three times a year. I'd bring my staff from Tech down there every year for our retreat. We paid for it out of our camp money. It's just such a relaxing environment with all sorts of interesting characters. The whole place is beautiful.

"One year we're out in a boat in the ocean. It was me, (fellow Texas Tech assistants) Dennis (Simmons), Charlie Sadler, and Dennis' cousin. Leach and one of his buddies, Joe Clements, hop out to go for a swim. All of a sudden, this shark appears near the boat. It was at least eight feet for sure. It was a huge shark. All of us, except Leach, thought they were in danger. Leach was the only one who wasn't really, really worried. The shark was longer than us. This thing is circling. Leach and his buddy move closer together. He later explained to us that they did that so they'd give the shark the impression they were bigger than he was. I guess it worked, although he

was about two seconds away from having his leg chomped off."
-Bennie Wylie, Texas Tech strength coach

I didn't think the shark was quite that big. I thought it was maybe six feet. I'm convinced the shock of seeing it enlarged it in people's minds, and I don't think it helped that Dennis had just watched *When Sharks Attack*. I know it definitely didn't help that he was throwing his chicken bones into the water after he finished lunch.

"I was thinking, 'This is bad. This is really bad. I'm going to lose my job. I can see the headline tomorrow: Texas Tech Head Coach Eaten by Shark.'"

-Dennis Simmons

I never really saw a sense of urgency in that shark. It looked like he was just strolling through his neighborhood. It's not that I wasn't concerned about his presence. I was, but I just figured the smart thing to do was to try to fool him into thinking we were bigger than he was and get into the boat as quickly as possible.

I'm not even sure what kind of shark it was. I've caught a bunch of lemon sharks, but they're usually more of a tannish color. This shark looked gray. You don't see that many sharks when you're swimming around Key West, and even with the occasional visit from one, it's a great place to live.

My wife and I had bought a house there in August 2009. Prices were down and it seemed like a good time to buy. We planned to rent it—and did rent it out during the football season—but then the Tech situation exploded, and Key West seemed like the perfect place to settle down.

Leaving Lubbock was bittersweet. My family and I liked living there. All of the fans there were terrific. After my dismissal, I'd walk into restaurants in Lubbock and receive standing ovations.

People I'd never met before would come up and hug me. But even with all the positive reactions from the people of Lubbock, it was too much of an emotional roller coaster being there. I am grateful for the support we had. A bunch of them created "Team Leach" on Facebook and it grew pretty fast. There were about 65,000 members. That blew me away. It was the spirit of those people that made everything we'd accomplished at Tech over the ten years so worthwhile.

> **"His story resonates because everyone feels like they've been screwed at one time or another in their lives, and we think he got screwed by Texas Tech University. Texas is used to a typical football coach who talks in coachspeak: 'We gave it 110 percent . . . We tried real hard . . . We'll come back next week.' That kind of crap. The establishment in Texas loves that crap. Mike's not that. He is educated, thinks outside the box. He believes in accountability. He is also a rebel and a lot of folks like that. They like that his kids graduate, that he controls the kids and that he's not a typical football coach, because typical football has never worked at Texas Tech."**
> **-Charlie Hodges, founder, Team Leach**

Relocating to Key West was one of the smartest things I could've done. Living in Lubbock with all that was going on with Texas Tech was a constant distraction. I was right in the middle of it. In Key West, I could think independently but could still stay connected to the lawsuits. It also kept my family out of the chaos.

"He'd been coming here for so long and meeting people, he had instant family and friends. As quirky as he can be, it's a good fit because we're pretty quirky too. Living in Key West is not for everybody. A lot of people come here and they're mesmerized by the things they see. Island living is a different thing. We're so secluded from everything. We're closer to Cuba than we are to Miami. We get along with everybody. Mike loves to talk to people. They love to talk to him. He'll talk to anybody. He's not pretentious. And here, it's just so nonchalant."

-Joe Clements, Key West resident

The Key West lifestyle is great. We didn't need a car. My wife and I bought bikes for ourselves and our two youngest kids. They'd ride their bikes to school. We'd ride all over town. When we needed to go grocery shopping, we'd bike the three miles over to the store. We'd do our shopping and then call for a cab with a bike rack.

Key West is a two- by four-mile island with roughly 33,000 residents. It has a lively, touristy main street, but other than that it's quiet and laid-back—small town enough that you really get to know the locals. There are a lot of activities centered around the ocean. It's historical, unique, and the food is great. Most importantly, it is one of the greatest people-watching locations in the world.

During the year we spent in Key West, I figured I might as well take the time to do some things I never could have done while running the program at Tech. In the spring, I visited coaching buddies at Oklahoma State, Oklahoma, Florida, Utah, and BYU. The support of my coaching colleagues has been huge. I flew over to France for two weeks to be a consultant for a French football team, watched lacrosse in Maryland, and had a chance to spend some time with Matthew McConaughey and Peter Berg, two friends in Los Angeles. It was really fascinating to see how those guys work.

Whenever I visit with coaches these days, I'm more curious about structure than I am about scheme. I haven't made any wholesale changes in a long time, but there may be a technique or a drill that I can apply to what I'm doing.

The things I'm really asking about are along the lines of: How do you break down and analyze film of an opponent? How do you manage your day? How do you organize practice? How do you handle your players and coaches? The most beneficial thing for me is to watch how they operate, because it stimulates my mind. Turns out it was the same thing with the movie guys. Sitting in on Peter Berg's production meetings while he was working on the movie *Battleship* was really an eye-opener for me.

They have two-hour meetings where they discuss all the aspects of the film with every entity involved in the production. Peter had characters in the movie from outer space and would drill down into every detail: "What's he going to look like? What's he going to move like? What's his personality like? How are we going to convey that? This guy has a moustache. Should he also have a scar on his face? Why is this here and not there?"

Peter may end up with no more than two minutes of film a day, but an amazing amount of focus and detail goes into those two minutes. In football, we draw up scripts, watch cut-ups, and debate within our coaching staff whether a certain play would work better if the receiver pushes his route to 13 yards instead of nine. We gnaw at the details so when it comes time to perform, the operation can run as precisely as possible.

Peter takes input from a lot of people. I'm like that, too. Anybody in the room is free to say whatever they want. Sometimes, when you don't use their idea, they get upset. However, that doesn't mean their contribution wasn't valuable. That idea may prompt another idea that makes the cut. I'm the kind of guy who will ask the janitor what he thinks about a certain subject. If he says something I feel is worthwhile, I'll consider changing my own opinion. I had student assistants sit in on meetings all the time at Tech. They're entitled to say what they think. I know that's irregular at most schools, but a fresh set of eyes can be invaluable.

In the summer, I flew up to the Northeast to spend some time at the Jets' and Eagles' training camps. I loved being around Jets head coach Rex Ryan. He is one of the truly fun people in football. If you love football, chances are Rex Ryan will love you. His team is built on positivity, confidence, and aggression.

Rex said something while I was with him that I think really makes a lot of sense. He told me, "I did the best in classes that I enjoyed, which is why it's important to me that my coaches have the ability to make our players enjoy practices and meetings."

He has an acronym he likes to operate by, "KILL"—Keep It Likable and Learnable. That's how it really seems to be around his camp. Everybody was excited to be part of his program because they knew they were going to be aggressive and play on the edge. If somebody made a play, they were excited. They weren't bogged down keeping track of a lot of extra rules.

Rex seemed like a defensive version of me. His defense acts like the meat is on the table and they're the ones who are gonna take it. They're not going to see who picks at it and then take what's left over. Forget that. They're gonna make something happen. Critics say, "You can't give up the big play! You can't give up the big play!" Well, you might get beat for six because you're in man coverage. You might, but you might pick one off instead. You might knock the hell out of the quarterback. You might rattle him to the point where he can't play very well the rest of the game. In my offense, we try to get the ball in everybody's hands. In Rex's defense, he tries to hit you from every position.

With my offense, we try to create space. As a defense, the Jets do a good job of eliminating your space. They crowd the box or disguise their intentions.

I was impressed with the things Rex did to foster the team's identity. The Jets pointed to their helmet decals a lot for motivation. "You're a Jet!" "Play like a Jet!" My thought was, you could practice with no decals on the helmets, and have the players earn them with hard work. If they had a bad effort in practice, the decal on their helmet would be gone when they came into the locker room the next day. You're letting them know where they stand.

Urban Meyer is a good friend of mine, and I know he did something similar with his true freshmen when they went through camp. In his first head coaching job at Bowling Green, he would place an inch-wide black stripe on each newcomer's helmet, stretching from the top of their facemask to the back of their neck. Those stripes would stay on the helmets of his freshmen and transfer players until they proved they belonged.

Urban explained that he did it to "de-recruit," to get rid of the recruiting nonsense that now often comes with being a top prospect. He wanted them to understand that they weren't special recruits any more. Instead, they were just like anybody else trying to make the team, and the stripe wouldn't come off until they made a big enough impression on their teammates or the coaching staff. Then, there'd be an impromptu ceremony when a successful new player would either walk in front of the team on the practice field or walk into a team meeting, and they'd yank off the tape so his helmet would be the same as the guys who'd already proven themselves. He said it was all about "The Power of a Unit."

Visiting with Andy Reid and the Eagles staff was fascinating too. I've known Andy for years. Like me, he's a BYU grad who met his wife at BYU. Like me, he's drawn a lot from BYU offensively. Our practices and philosophy are very similar. Everything builds on something else. It was all about teaching skill and teaching in small pieces. We really think a lot alike. He has said that in his mind, the whole field is the Red Zone.

Andy's a talker, not a shouter. If he saw something he didn't like, it was, "Listen man, I'm not into that." He has an offensive lineman's mentality in terms of accountability, and that really resonates with me. Andy's roots are as an O-line coach—same as mine. As an O-line coach, you have to be very committed to coaching technique, more than for any other position, and you have to choreograph the action of your five guys with that of the running backs and the tight ends.

I was sitting in the conference room one day at the Eagles' training camp facility waiting for practice to start. One of their assistant coaches came in and introduced himself. His name was Juan Castillo, and he was the offensive line coach of the Eagles. He started telling me his story and his path to coaching. NFL Films did a big piece on him called "Living the American Dream."

He had been a linebacker at Texas A&I in Kingsville, and after playing a season in the USFL, he really wanted to get into coaching. He'd been a high school defensive coordinator, but the only position that was open at his alma mater was offensive line coach. An entrepreneurial friend of his told him that anytime he wanted to set up a new business, he'd visit three or four similar businesses so he could learn the good and the bad of their operations. Juan took that model to heart, and set out driving all over the country every year, visiting four or five different line coaches who would teach him their technique. He visited Tony Wise at the Chicago Bears, Tom Bresnahan at the Buffalo Bills, Joe Moore at Notre Dame, Jerry Hanlon at Michigan, Jim Hanifan at the Washington Redskins. He crisscrossed the country in his car for five straight years. He would sleep in his car and live on McDonald's, all of it to learn how to coach the position better.

Juan became a great college line coach and produced a bunch of NFL players, and he's proven to be one of the NFL's best assistants over the past decade. He's coached Pro Bowlers and developed six undrafted players into starters. From a humble background, he worked and worked some more to reach the top of his profession. Now Andy has shifted him over to defensive coordinator for the Eagles. You can be certain he'll apply the same diligence to his new role that he has throughout every step of his career. Guys like him are an inspiration.

"Mike and I had so much in common because we're both small-school guys who take pride in developing kids. For me, it always came down to, 'What do I have to do to get my guy better?' Not everybody's like that, but Coach Leach is like that. It's easier to say, 'Well, this guy can't play.' But in Division II, you have to deal with what you've got. When I was at Kingsville, I thought I had a better line than the University of Texas and people would laugh [when they heard that], but four out of my five guys went on to play in the NFL. There is a confidence factor in me and I see it in Coach Leach. We're not scared of being underdogs. We both have the 'Why not me?' attitude and know that when you work hard, good things happen.

—Juan Castillo, Philadelphia Eagles
assistant coach

I've realized from my time with the NFL teams and these coaches that I need to find a way to connect with my defense better. Our offense overshadowed our defense at Tech, so people forget that we were in the top half of the conference in scoring D in 2007, 2008, and 2009, and that was while playing against the high powered offenses of the Big 12 South. I also realized that I should assert myself more when deciding who plays on defense and special teams. Despite the fact that my defensive coaches will still oversee the day-to-day and I'll let them run what they want, I'll give more input on who plays. Andy Reid does it that way. So does Rex. It is helpful to observe these two guys, who I respect and admire.

In my year away from coaching, my representatives and I have heard from a lot of different people with all sorts of offers, from appearing as a guest on talk shows to reality shows, one even suggesting *Dancing with the Stars.* I'm not against dancing, I was just never very interested in it. It doesn't matter what they pay. I can't dance for anything, so attempting to learn the foxtrot on national TV in some sequined costume? Nah, I think I'll pass.

When I was in grade school, they had a phase in P.E. where we had to do some type of dancing. It was like square dancing. It was impossible for me to hide my dissatisfaction. I was asked to sit down in two-thirds of the classes. I did not have a very good attitude. I've always been insecure about dancing. I'm not putting on tights and stretching. When I'm 88, maybe I'll re-think it, but not now.

I was invited to speak at clinics all over the country and even got to speak at MIT's Sports Analytics Conference, which was an honor. I appreciated the chance to see the quality of the people taking part in that. The topic I was speaking on was about the decision-making process, which they dubbed "Gut vs. Data." Everybody there was determined to look at sports with as much dimension as they could. You could tell you were among some really intelligent people.

CBS approached me about being an analyst on their college football telecasts. I was intrigued by their offer. It's a job that would keep me close to football, though it wasn't something I'd ever thought about before, because I figured I'd always be coaching.

They flew me to New York for a broadcasting seminar. My biggest challenge: being expeditious with my commentary. You have to deliver your message in a short period of time, and it has to make sense. Spontaneity is a good thing in these situations, and in my career I've routinely acted off-script. By the same token, I needed to artfully squeeze my words into a 20- or 30-second window.

My broadcast partner, Roger Twibell, pulled me aside and said, "You already know this stuff. Just relax and be yourself."

I know more about football than most guys do. But I also know some great coaches who turned out to be poor announcers. Some guys can look at football on a technical level, but have a hard time breaking it down and communicating it in a digestible fashion. They never quite translate what they see into terms the audience can understand. It is, after all, a lot easier to communicate with a senior than a freshman.

Jason Sehorn, the former NFL defensive back-turned-CBS announcer, told me to pretend that I was talking to the dumbest guy in the audience, which is certainly an interesting perspective to have. He said it is not a two-way conversation, but a three-way conversation between you, the play-by-play announcer, and the audience.

It seemed really hectic at first, but once I got into it the time between plays seemed to get longer. As a coach, you're pressed for time between plays too, and there's a whole lot going on around you. Eventually you figure out how to get what you need done within that time span. It's a juggling act in the broadcast booth, too. I had a small earpiece in my ear to hear cues from the booth while I watched the play. Then, while I'm talking, I'd be looking at a monitor out of the corner of one eye so I know what's on the screen. At the same time, I'm looking out of the corner of my other eye, trying to figure out where the spotter's pointing. The more I did it, the easier it got.

In addition to working for CBS, I also agreed to host a daily, three-hour radio show on Sirius with Jack Arute. The talk show was a blast. Still is. Jack has more of the pirate spirit in him than anyone I know. He used to own a boat, is a very independent thinker, and his name is Jack—same as Jack Sparrow and Callico Jack—which is about as close to a pirate name as a guy can have these days. Even his last name has a pirate flair to it. Arute. It sounds like it needs an exclamation point at the end of it—*JACK AROOT!* He's got this loud, bellowing voice that sounds like a pirate's voice should sound.

Time flies by while we're doing the radio show. I love the back-

and-forth we have. And it gives me a chance to view the other side. I've always been pretty accessible to the media. I've always tried to appreciate their point of view, and this gave me a chance to see it firsthand.

I never thought I'd have the chance to be on the other side of the microphone. You learn from all of your experiences, and my latest have been no exception. I've been given an insider's view of a whole different, though related, industry within football. Ultimately, I believe these experiences will broaden my skills as a coach.

Back when I was in law school, everything was a blur. Two years after graduation, that whirlwind of information settled down and made a lot more sense. I felt like I knew much more about the law after I had a chance to step back and view it from afar. The same thing has happened with football. My perspective has been broadened and my ideas about coaching have become more refined. I've gotten rid of some of the clutter and now I have more precise ways to teach. I have a stronger sense of how to keep the entire staff on the same page philosophically.

I knew commenting on college football had the potential to rile some people. I've always been willing to speak my mind on any subject. It didn't take long to stir up some folks in Alabama after I said the Crimson Tide, which was everyone's number one team at the time, wasn't my top team. I had a lot of respect for Alabama, but considering the players they'd lost from their national title team the previous season, and how their schedule played out, I didn't see them making it through the year undefeated. They had the toughest schedule in the country, not only because they had a lot of good teams to play, but because many of their opponents were coming off open weeks to face Alabama. They went on to lose three games.

CBS said it didn't mind me talking about Texas Tech, but I wasn't going to throw the Red Raider team under the bus. I recruited every one of those guys. I was booted out by a few bad actors, not by the players or the fans.

I felt like they had the chance to have a great season. We had 16 starters back—the most in the Big 12. We were one of the few teams in the league who had our starting QB back, and we didn't have only one experienced quarterback returning, we had two. When I was a part of the staff, we felt like it would be our most talented team yet. We had one quarterback who had beaten Oklahoma, another quarterback who'd beaten Nebraska. We had a good stable of running backs returning. All of the receivers were back except for one. We had all of the key players from the team that went into Austin and rolled up over 400 yards of total offense. We had our most talented front seven and had recruited two of the best junior college defensive linemen in the country. It was frustrating to see them go flat several times.

Watching Tech play is a little weird for me, but I've been occupied with other things, especially since I'm worrying about my own games on Saturdays.

Being around football is different from being *in* football. I miss coaching. I find myself missing many of the little things that are a part of a coach's life—the opportunity to teach young players, to develop them as they hone their technique, the discussion of the elements you consider when building the game plan, and just the energy around the team as it gets ready for game day. There is nothing like the relationships you have with the players and the other coaches, and the camaraderie of everyone battling for the common cause. I would've liked the opportunity to get back into coaching after the 2010 season, but only if it was the right situation. I'm happy now. My life is different from what it was when I was coaching, but it's still fulfilling. I still have the desire to coach, but I'm going to make sure I go back for the right reasons, which means finding a school that is committed to football, values academic excellence, and wants to work as a team so that everyone can win together.

Epilogue

The reaction to *Swing Your Sword* after it was published in the summer of 2011 was amazing.

My first book signing was in Lubbock, Texas. Two thousand people showed up. I was thrilled to see a lot of old friends and fans. Oftentimes the book signings felt like big reunions. The outpouring of support in Texas and Oklahoma was overwhelming. At a Barnes & Noble in Dallas, we sold more books than Sarah Palin and just missed breaking Ozzy Osbourne's record for books sold at the store.

I was touched by just how many people beyond die-hard football fans took an interest in *Swing Your Sword*. I think it's because there is something that everyone can relate to in the book. Everyone has goals. Everyone has struggles and tough choices to make. Everyone has been on some path and pursues it in their own way.

When *Swing Your Sword* made it to number five on the New York Times bestseller list, it was humbling. It felt a lot like winning a game, because, just like accomplishments on the field, you couldn't do it without the support of the team or the fans.

In the two seasons that I was out of coaching, I was visited by a lot of reporters who were curious to see what my life was like in Key West. After spending some time with them, I realized that there was this sense that I was a man without a country after we left Texas Tech—just this lost soul out on an island, both literally and figuratively.

They wanted to know what my typical day was like; how life had changed for me; how much I missed coaching and what it was like to live in Key West. Invariably, they had become fascinated about being around all of these interesting characters, like I did.

After my daily radio show with Jack Arute, my wife and I would go to a coffee shop in the late afternoon. We'd sit on the porch of The Coffee Plantation and people watch. One day, we see this guy riding up the street on a scooter. The closer he gets, we realize the guy is dressed like a truly authentic pirate. He even has a live parrot on his shoulder who is holding on for dear life. The pirate pulls up and parks at the convenience store across from us. We notice he doesn't have on a shiny pirate costume like some people might buy for Halloween. Instead, his outfit has holes in it and stains, like he wears it every day.

He looks like a real pirate would look. For all I know he is a real pirate. I mean right out of central casting. He has eighteenth-century clothing and looks all scruffy and sunburned. He has this weathered, leathery face, long beard—the whole deal. His only difference from an eighteenth-century pirate is the fact that he is riding a scooter.

I elbow my wife and say, "Listen, I'm gonna die if this guy gets off his scooter and he has a wooden leg." Well sure enough, he hops off the scooter and he's got this wooden peg extending out from the knee. It was like a two-by-four fastened to his knee, but more square. It's also got this hinge that it's attached to, so he can whip his leg forward so that the wooden portion hits the ground in front of him and he can pull himself forward over the top of it.

We were amazed. He hobbled into the grocery store with his parrot on his shoulder, came back out a few minutes later with some shopping bags, got back on his scooter, and rode off down the street.

As it turned out, he'd do the same thing at about the same time every day. I never met this particular individual, but at some point in the future, I hope to. I regret to this day that I never wandered over to meet him.

Key West, in its own unique way, was ideal for me, for us, especially after how things went down with Texas Tech.

What happened with Texas Tech, Craig James, and ESPN was unfortunate and unfair. What made it even more difficult was knowing how hard this was for my family. My youngest daughter, Kiersten, would cry several times a day, for weeks. She wouldn't leave our side and she listened intently to our every conversation. She knew her life was about to change dramatically and was trying to understand what it all meant. You had people at ESPN saying all of these horrible things about her father in the media—there was no way to not hear it. My wife Sharon's emotions would go up and down based on everything that was coming through, whether it was something she saw on TV, read on the Internet, or got in an e-mail. Worst of all, it was all maliciously false.

I had quite a bit of practice and experience ignoring things and blocking stuff out. My wife and children did not. For them, they were exposed to it in a magnified and unfair fashion.

Those days in the hotel at the Alamo Bowl were miserable. After I was fired, we decided to keep a previously arranged ski trip to Colorado. We knew we needed time away to sort things out and make some family decisions. It was very difficult for us there too. I know we were all wondering, "How's this gonna work out for us? And how do we defend ourselves?"

My main objective was to focus on doing my best every day and to stay positive in front of them, no matter what, even if I didn't feel very positive that particular day.

Getting fired, on top of the way things had been manipulated, was devastating. I was in the prime of my coaching career. We had just won twenty-nine games in three years. When I first got to

Tech, few people would've thought that kind of successful stretch was possible. We had a team on the rise. My last season (2009), we won nine games playing three different quarterbacks. I don't know of many teams that have had to play three different starting quarterbacks that even make it to a bowl game. We beat Oklahoma and Nebraska in the same year.

I just had this overwhelming sense that I had some unfinished business. Our program at Texas Tech had gotten better, and as a coach, I had gotten better too. Just as players develop, coaches develop. I know that as a head coach I had.

Moving to Key West proved to be a much wiser move than I anticipated. The people—like that pirate and many of the friends we made—make the place compelling. There was also a perspective on things that you can get from the dynamic of Key West. It's both relaxing and stimulating. Of course, I figured eventually we'd move when I got my next coaching job, but I knew there were no guarantees of that happening.

I heard, both directly and indirectly, that if I just dropped my lawsuits I'd be able to get another coaching job—but only if I dropped the lawsuits. Well, I knew it wasn't that simple. I could not just drop my lawsuits because then I would have been allowing people to presume that a bunch of false accusations were true, and that would come to the detriment of my family and the program that I helped build. I wasn't prepared to do that then, and I'm not now. On top of all that, Texas Tech to this day has not paid me for what they owe me for the 2009 season. They owe me more than $2 million for that season alone.

Texas Tech so far has been allowed to hide behind sovereign immunity for breach of contract with the state of Texas. This means that coaches and vendors at all state institutions are literally on day-to-day contracts, no matter what their contracts actually say. By definition, the government's role is to protect its citizens rather than to enact laws to cheat its citizens. Texas is the only state to do this with regard to contracts.

A number of publications and articles have come out in the

aftermath of my firing, detailing what I came up against. Nearly everyone who was interested now knows the truth of what actually happened at Texas Tech. The most revealing are in the perpetrators' own words through e-mails, legal documents, and depositions, some of which are included in the appendix of this book. Nearly all of the findings of independent media sources bear out my position as well.

Beyond that, there's also been the absurdity of Craig James running for senator. In addition to his previous actions and his spreading falsehoods about me, as well as his hiring of Spaeth Communications to work with Texas Tech and ESPN to smear me, James continued to spread falsehoods both in print and on national TV about me during his campaign. In the final month of his "campaign," James appeared on MSNBC where he initially denied having hired Spaeth Communications. Then, a few minutes later, he changed his story to concede that he did hire them, but then said he only hired them after I got fired. Well, check the dates on the e-mails between James and Spaeth where they're talking about working with ESPN's Joe Schad to smear me days before Tech fired me.

In the midst of that, the Dallas Morning News conducted a poll asking people whom they would vote for in a hypothetical senate race between James and me. I received more than 95 percent of the vote.

Those things notwithstanding, schools made it clear that they wouldn't hire me because of the lawsuits and the controversy created by other people. It did have a chilling effect. I know a significant number of schools that had job openings were intrigued by my record—both in terms of wins and losses, and for graduating players at an extremely high rate. But then I'd get wind of all of this bureaucracy and indecisiveness that would foul everything up.

Early on, I pursued things and tried to open the door. But you can drive yourself crazy dealing with that stuff. There was a Don Quixote quality to it. You come away realizing that those are the coaching jobs you don't want. Those programs are mired in bureaucracy. That's often the reason why those coaching jobs are open in the first place. Those are the places that can't get out of their own way.

I knew my record spoke for itself. My next coaching job needed to be the right fit, rather than me just trying to partner up with folks wired for a bunch of individual posturing.

In November, 2011, my agent told me that Bill Moos, the athletic director at Washington State, wanted to fly down to Key West to meet with me. I didn't know Bill personally, but I knew his body of work. I knew that, when he was the A.D. there, he'd done a great job helping build the Ducks athletic program to what it has become. I knew former Ducks coach Mike Bellotti, a friend of mine, liked working with him. I'd heard Bill had a really good way of elevating the energy around him and that he was a straight shooter and a program builder. I was intrigued.

I didn't know what to expect at the meeting, but I knew Bill wanted to talk about the possibility of me becoming the new head football coach. I had actually spoken at the WSU spring clinic in Spokane. I was aware of some difficult seasons the past few years, but I actually hadn't followed the Cougars that closely, so I read up on the team.

I had been up to Pullman to speak at a clinic when Mike Price was coaching there. I knew Coach Price and Coach Dennis Erickson pretty well. I'd studied their offenses quite a bit over the years. I knew how Washington State had quite a legacy of quarterbacks. But to be honest, I didn't know how extensive it really was. I'd also heard about their loyal and enthusiastic fan base. I'd always wondered how that big WSU flag always showed up on College GameDay every week.

We agreed to meet at the Marriott in Key West, which is at the top of the island. Our house is at the bottom of the island. So, I saddled up on my bike and peddled the three-mile ride over.

Bill immediately came across as this big guy who is very direct in his vision. He was very team-oriented. It wasn't one of these deals where we were sitting across a table just trying to impress one another. I could tell he and I have a lot in common, aside from the part about him having been a great college football player.

Bill had been a lineman at Washington State. He explained that he came back to his alma mater to go to the Rose Bowl, and how they were not that far off. He said he saw what Washington State could be and how they'd get there, and what my role would be in it. He was big on, "Here's what we want to do, and here's how we're gonna do it."

So many programs these days rely on search committees, and they're plagued with bureaucracy. I was sick and tired of dealing with bureaucracy. At Washington State, there would be none of it. Bill Moos was the search committee.

He said he would handle all of the administrative duties. I would handle the coaching. We'd work together on the fundraising. He used the word "sizzle" several times over the course of those three and a half hours, and he sounded very optimistic that we were about to create a lot of sizzle at Washington State.

I was impressed. Three weeks after Bill and I met in Key West, I was meeting with my new players at Washington State.

Whenever people asked me, "Why Washington State?" I'd always think, Well, that's a stupid question.

The reality is, despite being down the past few years, Washington State has had a culture of winning. It has already been proven that you can win big there. They'd been to a couple of Rose Bowls in the past fifteen years, and been there more recently than Arizona State has. Arizona has never played in a Rose Bowl. Programs often go through down periods. USC was dormant for about ten years before Pete Carroll showed up.

The timing was good to come into the Pac-12 because of some of the deals the conference had negotiated. The Pac-12 has also demonstrated great vision. With all of the conference realignment talk that had been swirling the past few years, the Pac-12 made sure it wasn't taking a back seat to anyone. This is a conference that is totally committed and where virtually every game you play will be on national TV.

I was also sold on the leadership and commitment to building at Washington State. Cranes are working seven days a week on a stadium expansion. After the 2012 season, they're going to break ground on an 89,000-square-foot football complex. The facilities are going to be among the best in the conference and the nation. Everyone is pulling in the same direction. This is the first school that I've ever seen where a building project of this magnitude is ahead of schedule and under budget. That speaks to how everyone here works together. It all starts with Dr. Elson Floyd, the school president. Dr. Floyd lets everybody do his job. Without his vision, Bill Moos doesn't get the freedom he has, and I don't get the freedom I have. The Floyds have really welcomed us. Not just me, but my family. Their wives, Carmento Floyd and Kendra Moos, have been instrumental in helping us settle in.

My first move after accepting the job was hiring Dave Emerick to be my chief of staff. I have known Dave since I was an assistant at Kentucky in the '90s. He was on my staff for a decade at Texas Tech. I trust him. Dave knew what I was looking for in my assistants. I wanted him to help me in putting together the staff and coordinate recruiting. He had been at the University of Arizona, and I was glad he decided to join me at Washington State. Antonio Huffman was another former Tech staffer who we brought up to Pullman as our director of football operations. He's really good with the players and helping them adjust to college life.

All of the offensive assistants I hired were guys that I had previously worked with. My offensive line coach, Clay McGuire, had played and coached for me at Texas Tech. My outside receivers coach, Dennis Simmons, had also been an assistant with the Red

Raiders. My inside receivers coach, Eric Morris, who had come to Pullman after two seasons as a graduate assistant at Houston, played for me at Tech. My running backs coach, Jim Mastro, who had been at UCLA, played and coached with me twenty years earlier at Cal Poly. Jim is one of the coaches who worked with Chris Ault at Nevada, where they developed the Pistol. I'd always planned on hiring him at Tech, but the timing never worked out.

After having been away from coaching for two years, I got to clean out the attic and focus on what counts. This allowed me to expand my thinking on some aspects of the game and be more specific on others. For example, with the Pistol idea, we have changed some alignments and made some subtle changes in some reads and blocking. There may be some subtle differences this time around.

My special teams coordinator and assistant head coach, Eric Russell, who I hired from Tennessee, is another guy I know really well. He had been my special teams coordinator at Tech and did a great job there. Better yet, by coming to Pullman, he was basically coming home.

When it came to bringing aboard coaches I hadn't worked with before, I looked for people who had a successful body of work, but who may not have had the best resources to do it with. I mean, how impressive is it really if you have great resources and only end up with average results? I wanted people who had a variety of obstacles they had to work through and overcome.

I considered a lot of guys to be my defensive coordinator. Mike Breske fit the profile best. He had a consistent body of work that had been successful wherever he'd coached. He always seemed to find a way to put pressure on people, which is something I looked for.

Breske had come up like me, starting out at smaller schools, and had developed nuances and a package that were unique to him. He had been with Joe Glenn at Division II Northern Colorado when they won a national championship. Breske also won a national championship at Montana. Then they went to coach at Wyoming where they were at the bottom of their league in resources, and yet Wyoming was still in the top three in defense most of the years Breske was there.

I also wanted a guy who had a strong relationship with Hawaii and the Island community. You're always looking for guys who have a big presence that people immediately respect. Joe Salave'a had played in the NFL for a decade as a nose tackle. He had coached with Emerick at Arizona and had an incredible amount of energy and passion. I always felt that his D-line played really hard and was happy when Joe decided to join us at Washington State.

Jeff Choate was another guy who had been a key part in a very successful program at Boise State. He'd been the Broncos special teams coordinator, where he was choreographing a lot of people at the same time. This is a great indicator of his ability to get people to respond and all be on the same page. He's also from this area, which was another big plus. I had found out Jeff was interested in joining our staff and wanted to coach on the defensive side of the ball, so he became our linebackers coach.

Paul Volero, who had worked at West Virginia and Central Michigan, was coaching down in Key West. I had the opportunity to see him work firsthand and was impressed with the way he communicated with people. He was another guy I was glad to get up here in Pullman. He coaches outside linebackers.

I really believe we have an ideal mix of personalities on this staff, and people with a wide range of knowledge and talents.

My family has really embraced the move to Pullman. They love it up here. The people have been fantastic. We are building something really exciting—literally, building it as when we went through our first spring practice. As we were on our practice fields, you couldn't help but notice those towering cranes overhauling Martin Stadium right next door.

I have great respect for the Cougars previous coach, Paul Wulff. He did some good things building the program. We inherited some really enthusiastic young players. I wish him the best. He and all

241

the previous coaches that have worked here are part of the legacy at Washington State that I am proud to be a part of.

I know people want to talk about bowl games, getting ranked in the Top 25, and going back to the Rose Bowl. I don't ever put any ceilings or limitations on anything. Here's what I can promise the Cougar fans: We're going to work hard, do our best as a team, and see how far our efforts can take us.

Appendix
Game Week

When I worked with Hal Mumme he was very spontaneous in his game-week preparation. He didn't watch as much film as we did at Texas Tech. He'd look at the opponent and get a sense of how to attack. We'd meet. Then he'd write the script. We'd have the game plan figured out by Monday and have it all installed by Tuesday.

With Bob Stoops, we had longer practices and more contact. Bob's very zeroed in on the fundamentals. Hal's bigger into scheme. Both Bob and Hal gave the players Sundays off and practiced on Mondays. In college football, the NCAA rules mandate that you give the players one day off every week. At Texas Tech, we'd give them off on Mondays and we practiced on Sundays.

On Sundays at OU, we'd come in as a staff and make corrections from the game film. We'd meet separately as an offense and a defense. We'd write down the corrections and start doing the preparation for the next opponent. We'd also prepare for our player meetings on Monday.

I preferred our game week preparation at Texas Tech because we'd do one task and then move on to the next one. It's less splintered that way. That's the NFL model, actually. In the NFL, they practice Monday and they're off Tuesday, since they play on Sunday. At Texas Tech we cleared Monday so we could gameplan, and it helped the players get caught up on their academics.

> *"I had heard about Mike and I reached out to him years ago. He invited me to come over from England in 2002. I spent 10 days at Tech. Then, Mike came over to visit England two years later. Our coaching staff went back over to Tech in 2005. We got into the real nitty-gritty of his offense so we could practice exactly how Mike does.*
>
> *"Everybody else around here [in the United Kingdom] does the I-formation and runs the football 40 times a game. We started chucking the ball a bunch and doing exactly what Mike runs. People over here thought it was a fad that would last one season. They'd say, 'How are you going to do that in the weather we have and bloody blah, blah, blah.' Seven years later, we're still running it. We've won three national titles. We've only lost two games in the regular season since. Now teams over here are trying to learn how we do things."*
> —Tony Athersmith, head coach, University of Birmingham Lions, United Kingdom

The story on us while I was at Tech, from what I understand, is that we had short practices and we didn't hit very much compared to other teams. That's not exactly the case, but it's fine by me. I've always felt—and I'm sure this is pretty accurate—that we had longer practices in the spring than most teams. We'd go two and a half hours in the spring. We weren't saving them for Saturday's game. We also didn't back off starters in the spring. If you're going to be a starter, it doesn't mean you don't need to develop your skills. We'd also work special teams hard. When it came to camp and the season, our practices were shorter than almost anybody else's I've heard of. We also did everything at a quick pace.

I'd want the players moving all the time at practice. When we're doing the "Routes-on-Air" drill or "Pass Skel," I had people running all over the place. We didn't just have one "Pass Skel," we'd have two going on at the same time. I wanted those third-teamers improving too. Why should they just stand around? You hear some people say, "Well, we don't have anyone to coach them." That's an excuse. Send your graduate assistant over there to coach them. It's more important than having him holding your notebook. This way you can help develop his coaching skills and get those third-teamers the reps they need to improve. Some of those guys will end up as first-teamers in a year or so if you get them better at catching, throwing, and defending.

I wanted as much full-speed action as possible. When it came to contact at a fall practice, it was full-speed, not full-contact. Hit but stay up, except for tackling or cutting drills. Overall, we probably had one less physical practice per week than most other teams. We also had longer meetings than a lot of other teams. Generally speaking, what I'd stick in their brains wouldn't tire their bodies, but too much talking can tire them as well, if you over do it. It's a fine line.

Years before the NCAA ever had the rule about alternating double practice sessions and single practice days in fall camp, it was part of our system. During my last couple of years at Texas Tech we didn't have any two-a-days. It's not because I have something against running the guys in hot weather. The only consideration for me was finding the most effective way to get things done. They lifted all summer to get their bodies stronger and able to move as fast as possible, so why would I try and zap it out of them in camp? That never made that much sense to me. I wanted them to be able to play through fatigue and pain, but I also needed them to retain their ability to play fast.

Something that seems to get overlooked a lot is how important it is to have good energy at practice. The coaches are responsible for that. They shouldn't be out there with slumped shoulders and their hands in their pockets. Attitude is contagious. It's the personalities of the coaches and the players interacting that helps keep things interesting, way more than changing up the practice schedule.

Our practice schedule at Tech was the same throughout the season. The periods on Tuesday were the same every single Tuesday. Wednesday was the same every week, etc. Our schedules were very regular, so everyone knew what was expected of them. It gave the guys one less thing to worry about, and it helped us monitor progress more easily. Going about it this way allowed us to have a consistent level of skill development.

When the energy is down across the board, the best thing you can do to raise morale and freshen up the team is to back off when you sense they're tired. We wouldn't send them home; instead, we'd keep the same drill periods, but shorten them.

I try to be as disciplined as possible when getting my teams ready during game week. Whether I'm playing at home or away, I want a high level of precision. I do things the same way each time, from week to week.

Day 1: Our game week starts when we get in on Sunday morning around 10 a.m. Hopefully, everyone—players, coaches, families—is feeling pretty good because we just whipped somebody the day before. I'll watch the previous game and then we meet as a staff and talk about how it went.

When we finish, I start watching the next opponent. I like to get as much of the film study done as I can on day 1, but there's no way to do it all that day—however many games your opponent has played, that's how many you have to watch.

Between the start of Sunday and the end of the day Monday, I'll watch every game the opposition has played in the current season, and maybe a few they played the previous year. I'll also watch a lot of cut-ups (a series of compiled plays of similar situations) taken from three to five games based on formation, down-and-distance, and run or pass. For example, we break them up into 1st and 2nd down passing plays out of two-by-two formation (with two receivers on each side of the formation); 1st and 2nd down pass plays out of three-by-one (three receivers on one side and one on the other); 1st and 2nd down pass plays out of pro set; there's a third-down tape; there's a red zone tape; there's a goal-line tape; there's a third-and-long; third-and-short; third-and-long out of trips (formation); third-and-short out of trips. And the list goes on. It's a lot to digest.

If the upcoming opponent is playing a team on the tape that doesn't have much in common with us, say, an option team, I'll go through it pretty fast. If they don't have much in common with us, it doesn't illustrate how our opponents will respond to what we do. But I won't dismiss it entirely. I want an overview and a working knowledge of the opponent and how they think.

After our staff meets, we have the team come in at 4 p.m. on Sunday. I'll address them. We'll talk about the previous game: what went well, what didn't go well. Then we split into position meetings and watch the film, making corrections. After that, we turn the players loose. I'll continue watching film while our staff gets together to chat about all of the various issues that come up after every game. Sometimes we have to talk about injuries, or who should start and who shouldn't.

"So now we have to move this guy over to play Y-receiver."

"OK, how are we gonna do that? Do we have to change something? This guy's not getting it done."

We're addressing a lot of things at once, but I do like putting the previous opponent behind us by the end of the day.

We'll practice at 8 p.m. Sunday night in helmets and shorts. Special teams gets the first half hour. Then we'll check plays based on what the next opponent tends to do. We'll draw those things up, write it on cards, and have the scout team line up in the opponent's defense. Then the QB will check to a play to address that defense. I want to see his response. He immediately has to analyze the defense he's going to see on Saturday. Then, he's going to call a play.

If we don't complete it or the receiver drops the ball, we'll run it again. I want their heads in it. They just played a game—hopefully, they're feeling good about beating someone—but I want focus. I do let them loosen up a little. During special teams, the O-line may be throwing passes to one another. But we've got about 35 plays, and if the ball isn't caught, the play isn't executed, or somebody runs the wrong way, we're gonna run it again.

That night, I'll go back in and jam through more film until about 1 a.m. before heading home.

Day 2: On Mondays, I do a press conference over the phone and another one live. Once that's out of the way, I go in and pour through the rest of the film. I expect to be there with the offensive coaches till about 2 a.m., but sometimes we can be finished by 11 p.m. We're very task-oriented, not time-oriented. You're done when you're done.

We analyze some statistical breakdowns, but I keep in mind that the statistical stuff is only important insofar as you can convey it to your players. I never liked the idea of a coach who stands up in front of the team and says, "OK, they're going to run the 'Iso' out of this formation 40 percent of the time. They're going to throw to the flat 20 percent. They're going to go deep 18 percent. Then, they like to throw an intermediate route . . ." How the hell is that helpful to your players? Anything that makes them hesitate and not react quickly is negative, not positive.

I don't mind the assistants watching some film together or having little sidebar discussions about what they're seeing. But the truth is, I really want each of them to watch the film independently because I want their unbiased opinions. I don't want five assistants to come into the room with the same idea because they arrived at it under the influence of the group. If they arrive at the same conclusions independently, great. As a group, it's too much like being married to your sister, the weak DNA doesn't get purged, the ideas are too inbred.

I want to hear everyone's own point of view when they come to the meeting, and everybody understands that just because they offer something up, it doesn't mean it's going to be accepted. Then we fill up the grease board with more plays then we can possibly run. We go back and forth trying to narrow the play choices down. That meeting lasts several hours because we're debating:

"Do we like this or do we like that?"

"Yeah, but if they do that, this would be good."

"OK, I like it. Do we want it on third down or from the open field?"

"Well, I like it from the open field. Hey, wouldn't it be better out of blue (formation)?"

It's this kind of debate and reasoning that goes into assembling the call sheet that we bring into the game.

When we have the plays we put them in various scripts, and I'll call them off the Call Sheet in any order I want. Some people go by a strict script with a distinct order to how they set up a game. I don't. I want flexibility. I can call a play twice or I can go away from the sheet. I can call plays depending on exactly where we are on the field, whether it's in the opponent's territory or in ours, and if the ball is in the middle of the field or on the far hash-mark.

I start with lists of plays, and they're somewhat in order of how I expect they'll roll out. Then I get in the game and call the plays and see how the other team is responding. Based on how they're defending things, I can select the plays and formations that

I think will be most effective.

Regardless of formation, you can basically run the ball, go vertical or run crossing patterns. You can run play-action, which is a combination of both.

We have our red zone package. In my view, the red zone is usually the plus-20 to the plus-5. It all depends on where the defense's philosophy changes to "red zone." Some don't change, but some, when they get pushed into the red zone, will come after you. Some start coming after you when you get to the plus-30. Or they may drop people into coverage. It's key to identify the point where they change their thinking and have plays that are good for a shorter field.

Teams tend to overcomplicate their goal-line package. It's really pretty simple. Regardless of formation, you can basically run, go vertical, or run crossers. Or you can run play-action, which is a combination of both.

We have screens, reverses, play-actions, nakeds, and any trick plays. The screens will be scattered around the different scripts. We have more screens than most teams. We also have plays for third-and-long situations and third-and-short situations (these are the ones that are specifically scripted for those cases, but we'll also call something else if the defense busted on it earlier).

That's the grocery list for the call sheet. The discussion goes on for hours. When we leave Monday night, we've got that list down to what we're going to put on the script for that week.

Day 3: Our offensive meeting on Tuesday starts at 10 or 11a.m. We print up the script before we meet with the entire staff later that morning, where we bat around some issues we need to address about the team we're facing. Then we have a team meeting where we talk about our upcoming opponent. I'll show highlights of players on our team who I thought had made a really great effort in the previous game. These aren't the flashy highlights. Instead, I show about six routine plays that led to good results because of the great effort we gave. The point here is that giving your best effort will pay big dividends to the team. Then we'll have a special teams meeting, followed by position meetings where we install our game-plan by position.

Tuesday is a heavy practice day. We start each practice with "Bull in the Ring." I heard Jimmy Johnson used to do it at the University of Miami. I don't know how he did it, or how often, but I love it. It's great for setting the tempo at the start of practice. I circle the whole team around and call out two guys who are similar in size. They line up in a stance a few yards apart, facing each other. Then, I just let them go at each other like they're shot out of a cannon. The loser is the guy who gets knocked back and can't maintain his positioning. When I call on someone to hit somebody, everybody had better be prepared. Plus, you have that crowd circled around. They're gonna let the combatants know what they think of the battle.

We call out three or four pairs of players at each practice. Sometimes it's O-lineman vs. D-lineman, or receiver vs. defensive back, or running back vs. linebacker. Or if two guys are battling for a position, I'll call them out and have them tee it up too. It's a psychological test. There are always a few emerging guys whose confidence may not have caught up to their physical ability, so I might stick them out there to see where they're at. There was one time when I put a guy out there and he got his ass kicked. It kinda broke his self-esteem and it took him some time to recover. This exercise tells you something about the players you're dealing with.

We do it on Tuesdays and Wednesdays, and without exception the team starts practice fired up.

The offense doesn't have any stretch period the way most other teams do. It saves us having to dedicate another 15 minutes of practice time. Animals don't stretch before they chase prey. We'll just start out one-quarter speed, then go to half speed, and then we're ready to go. Hal Mumme did it that way and I've never been a flexible guy anyway, so it didn't take much to convince me. We end up having fewer pulled muscles than most other teams, too.

After practice, the offensive staff watches the practice film together while we eat dinner. We get done around 9 p.m., and afterward—sometimes during— we'll call recruits.

Day 4: I get to the office around 10 a.m. on Wednesdays. That probably surprises a lot of people, because you hear so much about how this guy slept on an army cot in his office, or this other guy comes in at 3:57 a.m. every morning. Most of these people getting in before six in the morning end up taking off in the middle of the day. I want us to center our day on the activities, rather than have an empty block of time in the middle of the day when we could be at our most productive.

We don't have many staff meetings because everybody is already on the same page. I hate to meet just for the sake of meeting. Never confuse activity with results. However, when we do have staff meetings, we go as long as it takes to accomplish the task. We'll have the usual position meetings before we go out and have a heavy practice.

By heavy, I mean the practices last about an hour and 45 minutes. That probably sounds short to a lot of coaches, but that's how we do it.

One of the things we do that's a little different from some programs is that we keep stats of how we did in practice. It's a means of quality control. Attempts, completions, number of touches, or who did what in one-on-ones: the receiver had six shots and he caught three balls. Sometimes that means a ball was poorly thrown. Sometimes it means his route was bad. Sometimes it means the defender beat him. There were guys who played well in team drills but were lousy in one-on-ones. There may be a quarterback who is really effective throwing to the right, but not to the left. Well, is that him throwing or is that the people catching? We look for stuff we can adjust, address, and fix, and the stats help.

For example, we might have all of the corner routes broken

down to the right and to the left. We evaluate them to improve them or manipulate our offense so we're doing something more productive.

We're usually done for the day by 8 p.m.

Day 5: We start Thursdays with a staff meeting at 10 a.m. That's when the academics people come in to tell us how the players are doing, who might've missed a study hall, or who is doing a lot better in his classes. It's important for us to keep up on this. We'll call out the players who are doing well in school at the end of practice so their teammates can applaud them. We'll also get an update on injuries from our trainer. The coaches then set the travel squad roster for the upcoming game. For home games we travel 70 players, same as for road games. Then we set the itinerary for Friday and Saturday.

Thursday's practices probably lasts less than an hour for the varsity. We focus on our special teams first. Then we do a "team" period with plays from the script in an 11-on-11 setting. We end the practice and keep the players who won't play much on Saturday for Thursday Night Football. We'll have a live scrimmage for 35 plays or so. It's great work for them.

Their teammates often stay and watch and cheer. It used to be that we'd have guys whining, "Why do I have play Thursday Night Football?" I'd say to them, "What are you out here for? You're sitting on the bench. Those guys are all starting, and almost all of them played Thursday Night Football. How is it that you're too good to be out here?! You complain you don't get reps? We're giving you reps now." That'll change the wrong attitude in a hurry. We expect great effort out of these guys, and we usually get it. If they have the right attitude then they get fired up for it. They're jawing back and forth to one another. Some race in to see the film when it's over.

Day 6: I reinforce the key points on Friday. We may have some coaches out recruiting Thursday night and Friday, but I make sure there is a minimum of two coaches on offense and two on defense still with the team. We have a series of meetings and a few specific rituals that set the rhythm for the day and bring us all together.

We don't come into the office until about 2 p.m. or so. The players get their treatments from the training staff. There's a chapel service, which is voluntary. Then we have a mandatory special teams meeting for the entire team. When it's over, we go immediately to the offensive or defensive meetings. That involves a walk-through, which if we're home is on our field. If we're on the road, it's in a parking lot by our hotel. The schedule does not change much, if any, on the road.

It's probably really something to see our entire offense— starters, reserves, and staff—gathered in the parking lot outside the team hotel. We'll walk through our plays against various blitzes and defensive fronts for about 10-15 minutes. Unlike a lot of other teams, we never go to the stadium the day before an away game. We used to do it, but I quit it sometime during my first season at Tech. That stadium visit was a monumental waste of time. It was a logistical nuisance. And what did we learn from it? "Hey their field's the same dimension as ours."

In the parking lot, the players move through each rep at half speed, but the pacing between each rep is fast. Shortly after that, it's dinnertime. We eat buffet-style with prime rib, two kinds of chicken, and a legion of carb-heavy side dishes. Some teams have special seating arrangements. We don't. We want these guys to enjoy their time together. The time around the game will end up being an experience the players will always remember.

At 6 p.m. or so we take the team to the movies. The players are allowed to go to whatever movie they want, provided it won't run past the time we're leaving the Cineplex. After everyone gets out of their movie and makes their way back on the bus, I'll jot down some notes on the themes I want to remind the team about. These aren't necessarily unique to the particular game, they're more to reinforce the mindset our team will need to beat our opponents: Respect everyone but fear no one, make the routine plays, play the next play, have a great attitude on the sidelines, make sure we have great body language, play with low pad level, don't try to do too much, play with a clear mind.

Then I cover goals: Be a team, be the most excited to play, be the best at doing your job.

These are the intangible elements that I believe determine whether a team plays well or not, especially when you're playing on the road. Some of the elements, like being tough and aggressive, seem inherent to football. Others, like maintaining great body language, less so. Execution is a factor crucial to success in football and many elements can cloud how well a team executes. The same squad can look flawless one Saturday and like a train wreck the next. People may try to attribute that inconsistency to the emotional swells of 18- to 23-year-old men. I think that is an oversimplification, and buying fully into that idea is counterproductive as a coach.

As the bus fills up, I'll decide which 10 players or so I want to address the team. I don't give them any heads-up, but I make sure I'm picking players who won't be adversely affected by me calling on them to speak. I also try to choose players who might elicit the best response from the team, or those guys that by speaking to the team may perform better themselves.

Five minutes after the buses return to the hotel, we bring the team into one of the meeting rooms. I talk about the key issues, then I call on the first player I've chosen to speak to the team. Sometimes, like with one of my old linebackers, Bront Bird, they'll use some salty language and it'll be very intense. After that I'll have someone like Eric Morris, the Tech receiver we called "The Elf," stand up. The Elf was more upbeat, and more G-rated.

The team meeting lasts about 15 minutes. Then we send the offense into one room and the defense in another. We look back over Thursday's practice and sort out any other details that need to be covered. This goes about 30 minutes, then the players head out for a team snack in the meal room. After the snack, the players go to their rooms.

Day 7/Game Day: The times always vary depending on kickoff, but the next morning after wake-up and breakfast, we'll have a special teams meeting. When we're done with business we have one of our assistant coaches come up to the front of the room and give the guys a pep talk. We follow that up by playing some upbeat music. We shut off all the lights. You can feel the energy fill up the room. There's tension, enthusiasm, ambition, hunger, determination. It's a great vibe. Then we roll a few minutes of our best special teams highlights. That gets them even more fired up because we're showcasing effort. We're showcasing guys who are going all-out doing their jobs.

After special teams, we split up, offense in one room, defense in another. The offensive line coach runs our "blitz meeting," where he'll talk through a series of clips of the opponent's defenses, pointing out tendencies wherever possible. He'll show what he believes are the other team's main blitzes out of various situations, as well as what each of our O-linemen need to do to counter. We want this meeting to be short and to the point before we let the players go back to their rooms to watch other football games or listen to music.

We have our pregame meal about four hours before kickoff. The mood is usually very different than at any other time during the previous 24 hours. There's not much laughter or joking, and not a lot of talking. Eyes dart around as staffers and players try to get a read on the team. It's never easy to pick up on the team's mindset. Are they really focused or really tight? The only way you know for sure is after kickoff.

Once we finish eating we'll have a quick walk-through outside, and then one last team meeting before leaving the hotel.

I hit the same points I talked to them about the night before. Respect everyone, but fear no one. Do NOT talk to the other team. Make sure we're great on the sideline. Make sure we have great body language. Make the routine plays. Expect good things to happen. Be a team. Be the most excited to play. Be the best at doing your job.

We cut the lights. Music blares. This time, we show them the highlights from the previous week's game. If we played the day's opponent last year, we may show highlights of that game right before we board the busses to head to the stadium. The process is routine, but exciting. In the game we want to see good execution of the physical and mental skills that we worked on all week long.

Afterword

In 2005, I noticed Mike Leach on the cover of the *New York Times Magazine*. I had never heard of him. I read that article and I started trying to catch Texas Tech games on TV. I got into his whole philosophy of offense, and began reading more about him and talking to people who knew him. I worked with Mack Brown when he did an episode of *Friday Night Lights*. I talked to Mack about Leach for a while and he told me how innovative Mike was. Mack called him a real original thinker. That got me going even further. I was just enamored with Leach.

I remember reading a quote from him about how he wanted to challenge the way his opponents viewed time and space. I just loved that. It's such a unique perspective on competition. I've gotten to know so many football coaches through *Friday Night Lights* and most of them sort of sound the same. It might be slightly different sentences but the general idea is the same. Not Mike. He truly thinks outside the box.

I had this idea of a cameo for the show that he could do. It took a week or so before he got back to me. I was star-struck when I spoke to him, even though I tried hard not to be. I pitched him an idea. We got him to come down to the set for a few hours and he improvised the whole thing. The scene was him giving Kyle Chandler's character advice about how to pull out of a losing streak. Mike just went off for like a half-hour at a time. Everybody just sat there with their mouths open as he just rambled about competing, pirates, Geronimo, and all kinds of stuff. It was awesome.

In my business we meet a lot of unique dudes, you know, off-off people who go to the beat of their own drum, but it's very rare that you meet someone who is that eccentric and also knows how to get a football program up and running and can win games. At the end of the day, you've still gotta win games. Nobody cares how odd you are if you're losing. I knew there was a very competent and talented soul connected to this eccentricity.

I asked him to stay at my house when he was coming out here in 2010. We were in the pre-production stages of Battleship and really making decisions that were going to impact the direction of the movie. We were finishing the script and conceiving the look of the creatures in the film. I wanted Mike's opinion. He was incredibly clear in his thought process. He'd sit in on the meetings and raise unique questions that none of us had considered. We talked about the Civil War a lot and Blackbeard the Pirate and some of his battles. Mike would go off on these tangents but then he would always bring it right back to something that was relevant in a business that he didn't know much about. He makes a tremendous amount of sense when he talks to you. He knows exactly what he's doing all the time. I think he's brilliant.

While he was out in California, he also created an offense for my nine-year-old son's football team around our breakfast table in five minutes, and now we're unstoppable. He said young minds can't handle complex crossing patterns. If you run enough crossing patterns, there'll unquestionably be windows of opportunity. You just have to deliver in those windows.

We run nothing but crossing patterns. It is absolutely confounding to these defenses. It was awesome. We're beating teams with scores like 60–0.

Mike Leach is a Renaissance man through and through. He is thirsty for life. The commercials about the World's Most Interesting Man—that's Mike Leach. I love him so much. I aspire to live a full and rich life and he's doing it. He's as interested in literature as he is in football. He's just a very complicated, well-rounded individual, a real maverick and an inspiration.

We have a Wall of Legends up in our office and Mike's up there with Winston Churchill, Abraham Lincoln, Dean Martin. Just mavericks. We have a motto at our company: Who pushes you around? The answer is nobody. Nobody. Mike typifies that attitude.

Anybody can talk a good game. This business is littered with unfinished screenplays and films that almost got made but for whatever reason fell apart late in the fourth quarter. It's about finishing. Anybody can move to Hollywood and can proclaim himself a filmmaker or an actor or writer. What separates the small percentage of people that get it done is the ability to close. Mike Leach has that.

—**Peter Berg**

Notes

1. Email from Jim Sowell to Kent Hance regarding Mike Leach's contract negotiations.

From: Jim Sowell
To: Hance, Kent; Myers, Gerald
Sent: Tue Dec 30 22:08:25 2008
Subject: Re: Mike Leach

Kent, they have no leverage, don't give in. Also, I feel you should sign a contract that would not cost us too much to fire him. As I said earlier, I believe salaries have peaked so let's don't go too long term. He has to have a big buyout, he has shown no loyalty, he has tried to get another job every year for the past 4 years. What does he mean that a buyout would hinder him getting some things done at Tech? The only thing it would hinder is him accepting another job for the next couple of year. Buyouts are important, if we had lost Leach this year we couldn't have hired Briles if we wanted to because he had a $4 mil buyout. I love his comment about Crabtree, these agents will say anything to get a deal done, there is no chance Crabtree is staying plus Crabtree has 2 years of eligibility left and Leach has 2 years on his contract so that should be no impediment to his staying, which, of course, he has no intention of doing. Also, a buyout keeps you from getting blackmailed into giving Mike a raise when next year his 2 Jerry McGuire wannabes get him another phantom interview to put pressure on you to give Mike a raise. Briles tried to get a raise based on Scovell contacting his agent. Because Briles had only burned off one year of his $5 million buyout, Baylor knew they didn't have to do anything because no one was going to write them a $4 mil check in order to hire him. Don't let them convince you that a $2 mil completion bonus is the same as a buyout. Forfeiting a completion bonus does not compare to digging into your pocket to pay the buyout. His deal should be $2.4 per year for 5 years and if he leaves, he of course gets no completion bonus but also has a buyout of $1 mil for every year remaining on his contract. Otherwise it is a one way deal-he has you under contract but you don't have him under a contract that be can't walk away from any time. Finally, we can't afford what they are proposing and they have no other options. Tell them. Take it or leave it. I promise you our prospects for getting a better coach are much higher than Mike's prospects of getting a better job. Texas Tech has paid Mike more money than every football coach before him combined and I think we may have paid him more than every coach in every sport in our history combined. Somebody ought to add that up-what every coach in every sport in the history of Tech has made in total, other than Leach and his staff. That ought to put things in perspective. Bottom line, we can't afford what he is asking for. Every $100,000 we give him is $1.5 million in improvements we could have bonded.

2. Email from Jim Sowell to Kent Hance regarding Mike Leach's contract negotiations.

From: Jim Sowell
To: Hance, Kent
Sent: Fri Jan 09 23:31:56 2009
Subject: Re: Mike Leach Offer

Good. Ignore anything they do between now and Tuesday except acknowledging receipt of his fully executed contract as presented. I hope he doesn't sign, that gives us a full year to find another coach after we fire him after next season and payoff the remaining year on his contract. You may lose one or two recruits this year and Crabtree will use it as part of his excuse for going pro even though he is going pro regardless. I predict you get many frantic calls from the agents but in the end, you get a signed contract from leach at 4:55 on Tuesday. No matter which way this goes, you have done a good job and Leach has lost a lot of support during this process. By the way, did you see the 2 sentence story In today's paper that Gary Patterson signed an extension with TCU until 2014 today. No fanfare or drama.......kind of like his football program.......he has had four 11 win seasons in 6 years. He may have done the best job of any coach in the country the last 6 years. He probably makes half of what Leach does. Think what we could do with that 1 million a year in savings.

3. Email between Jerry Turner, John Scovell, and Larry Anders sent a day after Leach's contract was signed, regarding the completion bonus.

From: Turner, Jerry
Sent: Friday, February 20, 2009 11:48 AM
To: Scovell, John; Anders, Larry
Subject: Leach's 2006 Contract.

Contract obligates TTU to pay "completion bonuses" (800K in 2009 and 200K in 2010) only if he "is the Head Football Coach at University as of December 31, 2009" and 2010 respectively. We might have a lawsuit, but if we fired him on November 30, 2009, contract does not entitle him to receive the completion bonus.

Contract does not define "cause" (when discussion termination for cause) as including anything remotely resembling "insubordination." Rather, "cause" is defines in relation to NCAA violation or criminal indictment.

I'll forward a copy of contract when I get home. -JET

4. *See note 3.*

5. Email from Windy Sitton to Jerry Turner regarding Leach's dismissal.

From: Sitton, Windy
Sent: Wednesday, December 30, 2009 10:44 PM
To: Turner, Jerry
Subject: Leach

Hi Jerry, Hope all is well with all of your family. May God bless all of you abundantly in 2010.

Jerry, please know that I respect you as much as anyone I know and I greatly value you and your opinions when it comes to Texas Tech; but I want you to know that I am very upset with the end result of what happened today. How in the world can the Regents justify suspending, much less firing Mike Leach, over this issue. Maybe he made mistakes, but people do have a sense of justice. This action did not rise to the level of suspension much less firing him. Why can TT not relish in success? Mike Leach is not perfect by any means but he cares about his students, he wins games, he fills the seats, he has brought us from last to second in graduation rates. I do not understand why TT has never supported him. I guess we just want to go back to mediocrity. Jerry, I know his firing has been in the works since the Chancellor and the AD were out maneuvered by Leach. That is our problem. The problem rests with arrogance of the Chancellor and the ineptness of the AD. Everyone sees through this injustice to Mike Leach and Texas Tech. The Sitton family has given scholarships and have had multiple seats since 1976. We will not renew our options our 12 seats or for that matter our PSLs for basketball. This whole thing smells, and we do not want to be a part of this blight on Texas Tech.

Windy Sitton

6. From Craig James deposition, March 13, 2010.

Paul Dobrowski: Did you call Lincoln Riley at that time?
Craig James: Yes.
PD: What did you say?
CJ: Left a message for him to call me.
PD: What did you say on the message?
CJ: "Give me a call. I would like to talk to you."
PD: Why did you call him?
CJ: The same reason, to find out what Adam had done, what we could do to keep him on track here and not go into the tank.
PD: And did you leave a message to the effect that, "if you have the balls and I don't think you do, call me back?"
CJ: I may have. I may have.
PD: Well, when you say you may have, that indicates to me that that kind of rings a bell or sounds familiar.
CJ: I could have. I could have.
PD: Okay. As you sit here today, do you believe that you left that kind of a message?
CJ: I believe I could have, yes.

7. From Adam James' deposition, March 13, 2010. Mr. McLaughlin is a representative for James.

Adam James: I had it [a cellphone] with me. I had just came (*sic*) from class.
Ted Liggett: Okay. So—okay—we'll get back there. You were in the shed when you sent this; is that right?
AJ: Yes, sir.
TL: So it's 2009 at 3:54 p.m., right?
AJ: Yes, sir.
TL: And you said, "you're going to like this," that's how you start it. Why did you think your father was going to like the fact that you had had a

concussion and your coach thought it was impossible for you to have one?
Mr. McLaughlin: Objection. Form. Go ahead.
AJ: Well, we have the same sense of humor and personality, and I thought—
we thought it was funny. So I said "you're going to like this."
TL: Oh, so you thought it was funny?
AJ: At the time, yes, sir.

8. Reproduced from an article entitled "Statements contradict Adam James' version of events at Texas Tech" published January 2, 2010 by Kate Hairopoulos for the *Dallas Morning News*.

Statement from head football trainer Steve Pincock, dated Dec. 31:

"In regard to the Adam James situation, the first building was an athletic training storage garage, two of which were adjacent to the football field. Adam was placed in the sports medicine garage; there is no lock on this building. Normally, injured players are asked to perform exercises, however Adam could not participate in these drills, and was originally asked to walk around the field during practice. Adam showed up to practice in street clothes, no team gear, and dark sunglasses. Adam walked about 40 to 50 yards, very slowly and with a non-caring attitude. Coach Leach noticed Adam's poor effort and non-team attire, and asked that Adam be placed in a location where sunlight could not bother him as he was wearing sunglasses. Two trainers, including myself, monitored Adam at all times. I instructed Adam to stay in the garage and out of the sun, so the light would not worsen his condition. While in the garage, Adam was walking around, eating ice, sitting on the ground, and, at one point, sleeping; at no point was there any enforcement to make Adam stand up. Adam was checked by doctors every day."

"On the second occasion, practice was in the stadium, and Coach wanted Adam to be in a dark location to help his concussion and wanted him out of public view because of his poor attitude and bad work ethic. Zack Perry, our equipment manager, suggested using the visiting team media room. I walked Adam to the room, which was at least as big as a two-car garage. Inside the room there is an electrical closet. I looked in the closet and stated that there was 'no way that Adam would be placed in there'. I shut the door to the electrical closet, and it was never opened again. At no time during this practice was Adam ever placed in the electrical closet. The door to the media room was never locked, and trainers attending to Adam stated that he was sitting at times during the practice. Adam was never locked in any facility, and was never placed in an electrical closet or tight space, or instructed to do so."

"I received calls about both incidents from Charlotte Bingham, and was asked and answered many questions on the subject, and pictures were taken of both locations. Adam exhibited no symptoms of a concussion after the first day: no memory loss, no confusion, and no dizziness."

9. Email from Jerry Turner regarding Adam James matter.

From: Turner, Jerry
Sent: Monday, December 21, 2009 9: 11 AM
To: Anders, Larry; Hance, Kent; Bailey, Guy
Subject: Confidential

Let me call your attention to Sections 03.02.1(f), (I), and (n) and 03.02.3 of Regents Rules. Also, please refer to Articles IV and V of the attached contract, particularly the following from Article IV: "Coach shall assure the fair and responsible treatment of student athletes in relation to their health, welfare and discipline. Breach of such rules and standards, whether willful or through negligence, may be subject to disciplinary actions and penalties ranging from termination, public or private reprimand to monetary fines or adjustments in compensation or adjustments in the terms of this contract as determined by the President following consultation and review with the Director of Intercollegiate Athletics." JET

Jerry E. Turner
Partner
Andrews Kurth LLP

10. Email from Larry Anders regarding Adam James matter.

From: Anders, Larry
Sent: Sunday, December 27, 2009 10:07 PM
To: Hance, Kent
Subject: Leach Letter

Kent

I read the draft letter we discussed

I strongly urge you to not close this matter concerning Adam James with this approach As I mentioned earlier today I don't want to eliminate our ability to use this to our advantage should we determine to use it to terminate Leach I am sorry that he has put us all in this awful predicament Talk tomorrow

Larry

11. Email from Nancy Neal to Jerry Turner regarding Leach's contested

bonus and the Adam James matter.

From: Neal, Nancy
To: Turner, Jerry
Sent: Wed Dec 30 08:42:32 2009
Subject: solution

Any hope for outcome other than path we are on? Dr's letter really hurts us ... said it may have helped him to do what was ordered ... where did that come from? Is there any other hope to make this right?

I am pleading that the course we are on wait until Monday after game ... if we owe the $, let's not be so cheap that it isn't paid ... that being said, wait until Monday to act If still necessary. I understand we will be on a call later ... Nancy

   12. The following email exchange is in regard to the January 2, 2010 *Dallas Morning News* article by Kate Hairopoulos entitled "Statements contradict Adam James' version of events at Texas Tech" published. The statement by physician Michael Phy follows the exchange.

From: Spaeth, Merrie
Sent : Friday, January 01, 2010 7:57 PM
To: Post, Sally
Subject: FW: Latest story posted on DMN

Sally - I assume you and the Chancellor have seen these. We will not make any comment until we talk to you and you let me know what the university has done.

The doctor: other than the 'mild' - concussion. (There is no such thing.) it's not really in dispute. The issue isn't whether the other treatment harmed Adam ... But he needs to confirm the diagnosis, recant "mild" and talk about the need for rest etc.

The trainer: this is a rather dramatically different account than Adam's and from what we understand he provided to the university. How to handle?

The Chisum statement is really irrelevant ...

Merrie

Statement from Texas Tech team physician Michael Phy, dated Dec. 25:

   I saw Adam James as a patient on December 17th. At that visit I diagnosed him with a mild concussion. I made recommendations regarding level of activity and treatment. These were shared with Adam and the athletic training staff and are documented in Adam's medical record. I was not aware of any incident until I was contacted by (Tech representative) Charlotte Bingham. She provided details of a complaint, and I completed a short phone interview and answered questions for her. According to the information given to me, no additional risks or harm were imposed on Adam by what he was asked to do.

Sincerely,

Michael Phy

13. Email from Rebecca Shaw to Craig James regarding Spaeth press releases in Adam James matter.

From: Rebecca Shaw
Sent: Monday, December 28, 2009 11:30 PM
To: James, Craig
Subject: RE: ESPN 6:29 PM

Craig - Merrie's position - and I agree - is that the story has been put to bed tonight. Let's take a look at the coverage first thing in the morning and make a decision then if we want to forward the players' names and numbers exclusively to Joe, whether we want to include the AP reporter, or if we want to hold off a day to see if the university makes a statement. I'll be up early checking the coverage. Merrie's good with the statement that I drafted for you for ESPN. Would you like it circulated to Kevin and Jim or do you want to noodle on it awhile?

Rebecca Shaw
Executive Vice President
Spaeth Communications, Inc.

14. Emails from Marrie Spaeth, Brooke Robbins, and Rebecca Shaw regarding best practices for popularizing online video.

From: Merrie Spaeth
Sent: Thursday, December 31, 2009 3:12 PM
To: Brooke Robbins, Rebecca Shaw
Cc: Maggie Moran, Katie Hiatt, Emily Turner
Subject: Re: You Tube Concussions

Can you send me the link? And how can we link it to the awful comments in lubbock?

-------Original Message-------

From: Brooke Robbins
To: Rebecca Shaw

Cc: Merrie
Cc: Maggie Moran
Cc: Katie Hiatt
Cc: Emily Turner
Subject: Re: You Tube Concussions
Sent: Dec 31, 2009 2:37 PM

When I Created the You Tube account, I put in the following key words: concussion, James, Leach, Coach Leach, Mike Leach, Adam James, Craig James, sport concussions, Texas Tech sports ... And a few more.

When people google any of the words... Our you tube will EVENTUALLY come up. It takes a while for search engines to find these new things.

What could expedite the process is if a few of YOU have the time and desire to go onto some of the blogs and say things like ... "Hey I came across this new you tube ... Then paste in the link ... That really has great info on concussions ... "That's one grass roots way of generating hits ... We can also just keep hitting it ourselves. But remember ... Anyone can research ip addresses and it's all too easy to determine that all the hits are coming from just a few computers.

LOL ... LSL knows all about that'

Happy New Year!

Brooke

www.brookerobbins.net

On Dec 31, 2009, at 11 :25 AM, Rebecca Shaw wrote:

> Nice job. This has great information in it. Unfortunately, it's only
> had 2 hits. Does anyone have any ideas about how to get more
> visibility? Do we need to send it out on PR Newswire?
>
> Rebecca Shaw
> Executive Vice President
> Spaeth Communications, Inc.

15. Email from Merrie Spaeth regarding the use of pseudonyms when commenting on Mike Leach and Craig James in blogs.

From: Merrie Spaeth
Sent: Tuesday, December 29, 2009 2:53 PM
To: Brooke Robbins
Cc: Katie Hiatt, Rebecca Shaw, Brooke Robbins
Subject: RE: my thoughts

Brooke of course, if you felt you could log on with a pseudoname (*sic*) onto the blogs and share these thoughts, it would be wonderful....

------Original Message-----

From: Brooke Robbins
Sent: Tuesday, December 29, 2009 1:50 PM
To: Merrie Spaeth
Cc: Katie Hiatt; Rebecca Shaw; Brooke Robbins
Subject: Re: my thoughts

DAVID STANLEY brought down SMU ... not Craig James. Yes, James played at SMU during that time and may or may not have participated in the incentive payments.

FYI ... David Stanley had a drug problem and was blackmailing for more and more money. When they finally stopped and said, do what you have to do ... that's when David Stanley blew the whistle.

Let's get focus off James as a part of that old mess.

Brooke
www.brookerobbins.net

16. *See note 12.*

17. The following email is in regard to backlash against Texas Tech after Leach's initial suspension. The reference in the email to the "story below" refers to an article by Adam Zuvanich published in the *Lubbock Avalanche-Journal* on December 29, 2009, in which former Texas Tech players Daniel Loper, Cody Campbell, Graham Harrell, Eric Morris, and Glenn January (who is quoted as saying, "[Leach] doesn't deviate from the [NCAA] rule book at all and wouldn't do anything to put a player in harm") come to the support of Leach.

From: Kevin Brannon
Sent: Tuesday, December 29, 2009 8:32 AM
To: Rebecca Shaw; Katie Hiatt
Subject: FW: my thoughts

Merrie asked that I send this to both of you.

From: Kevin Brannon
Sent: Tuesday, December 29, 2009 7:53 AM
To: Merrie Spaeth
Subject: my thoughts

After an initial burst of postings by Leach haters, we're getting killed on the blogs. Here are two emails from friends whose judgment I trust:

#1 Actually, my initial reaction was that Leach is a psycho. But, the Facebook/Twitterverse hates Craig James (prima donna, tanked SMU by taking cash, cars, etc to play, etc). He now has 100% name ID in West Texas and they are not happy.

#2 I think it reaks (*sic*) of foul play. Political. Some didn't like the contract renegotiations, etc ... so now they are catering to the James family. I am not so young that I don't remember James bringing down SMU 25 years ago.

Combined with the story below, this underscores the need for those players (who are willing to support Adam) to be activated as soon as possible this morning.

18. Emails from Brooke Robbins and Merrie Spaeth regarding best practices for spreading information on concussions via YouTube in relation to the Adam James matter.

From: **Brooke Robbins**
Sent: Wednesday, December 30, 2009 2:13 PM
To: **Merrie Spaeth**
Cc: Rebecca Shaw; Katie Hiatt; Kevin Brannon
Subject: **Re: URGENT FW: Concussion**

Leach was just fired.

Does this impact the you tube piece?

Brooke

> On Dec 30, 2009, at 8:24 AM, **Merrie Spaeth** wrote:
>
> Brooke - we have the go ahead. I envision this as the simplest of interview(s) with you and doctors, etc., posted on YouTube. We need to get something up today. I envision all of these would go something like this:
>
> "I'm Brooke Robbins, an independent journalist. We've all heard the news about Texas Tech Coach Mike Leach and the player who had a concussion. The Coach is saying it was "only" a "mild" concussion. Over the past year or so, there have been a number of high profile stories about player concussions. We're going to ask some leading doctors, sports medicine experts and trainers – what's the proper treatment for a concussion? Can you "fake" a concussion, the way coach Leach charges, just how serious is a concussion? If you have a child who plays football, or you're just a concerned parent or citizen, let's look into this together ... "

And then ask anyone you can get your hands on this morning:
- should concussions be taken seriously?
- what are the signs of a concussion?
- can you "fake" a concussion? (and how could a coach on the field just tell by looking at a player ...)
- what's the proper treatment? (e.g. rest, etc ...)

... and I know there have been some high profile examples ... Liz says that an NFL player committed suicide this year because of a series of concussions left him damaged ...

19. Email from Craig James To Kent Hance regarding the Adam James matter.

From: Craig James
Sent: Saturday, December 26, 2009 2:15 PM
To: Kent Hance
Subject: Adam James

Kent,

I hope you had a Merry Christmas.

After considering our conversation Thursday, I want to add a few thoughts. We called you last Saturday night extremely concerned for our son's safety and wellbeing. We are looking to Texas Tech for protection of our son and your student athletes. We know there is an established process to investigate serious charges and that the university is committed to approach each situation with a fair and thorough investigation.

Mike Leach's actions with Adam were inhumane and dangerous, designed to inflict punishment and create great mental anguish. Action must be taken to not only insure the safety of Adam but to protect his · teammates from this and other forms of abuse coach Leach inflicts on hi players.

Bottom line: Tech is absolutely exposed as a university with each hour that passes. The team, the staff, and increasingly others at the school know that a substantial charge has been made, and we understand it has been verified by your own investigative team. We urgently solicit an update about the process underway, the time frame for proceeding and what the University intends to do to make our son, and the other young men on the team, safe and protected from further harmful acts.

Kent, I ask you and the board members this: Have each of you seen the shed and electrical closet Adam was confined to? I'd recommend each of you visit the

272

Places ... walk in them and turn the lights off. NOW, imagine standing there for three hours in the cold without being allowed to sit down or lean against the wall. This story will become public at some point and you can count on the fact that some television cameras will show this picture. This is certainly not the image of the university we support. Further, this entire matter happened because Adam sustained a concussion during practice.

Again, Marilyn and I appreciate your openness to our concerns as parents. Craig.

20. Emails from Brooke Robbins and Merrie Spaeth regarding best practices for spreading information on concussions via YouTube in relation to the Adam James matter.

From: Maggie Moran
Sent: Friday, January 01, 2010 1:07 PM
To: Merrie Spaeth
CC: Rebecca Shaw; Katie Hiatt
Subject: Re: Concussion You Tube Video

So posting the video with our account didn't make a difference at that point. We were already out there.

On Jan 1, 2010, at 12:44 PM, "Merrie Spaeth" wrote:

Did no one think that this connects our name with this? Brooke is right – can we link the doctors to this?

----Original Message-----
From: Brooke Robbins
Sent: Friday, January 01, 2010 12:11 PM
To: Merrie Spaeth
Cc: Brooke Robbins; Rebecca Shaw; Maggie Moran; Katie Hiatt
Subject: Re: Concussion You Tube video

I am adding all related videos as "subscriptions" to our concussion video. That should help.

Also, I noticed the Adam James video posted by "Spaethcomm8181" has generated over 120,000 hits! Great job! How did they get so many hits? Can we load the concussion piece to the "spaethcomm8181" account and ride that wave?

Brooke

On Dec 31, 2009, at 11:35 PM, merrie@spaethcom.com wrote:

Thank you. HOW can we get more blog exposure?

-----Original Message-----
From: Brooke Robbins
To: Merrie
To: Rebecca Shaw
To: Maggie Moran
To: Katie Hiatt
ReplyTo: Brooke Robbins
Subject : Concussion You Tube video
Sent: Dec 31, 2009 8:21 PM

Our You Tube Video has been online for just over 12 hours, and we've had 66 hits ... Not bad for a holiday week.

I uploaded more descriptive words that will help it come up in more people's searches surrounding this topic. But it does take time.

To mention again, I uploaded the video to You Tube in the fastest format available ... a format that enables the video to be viewed on mobile phones. The quality is not as good this way on computers, but people on mobile phones can watch it.

21. *See note 7.*